"The world is going to hell in a handbasket. What can we do about it? We say—read one book, see one movie . . . Call your friends, your enemies and your family. Get your hands on a copy of this movie and a copy of this book."
Counterpunch

"Bakan's analysis is strong on pinpointing problems with current business."
Harvard Business Review

"All senior business executives should find the time to read this well-researched and well-written book . . . *The Corporation* will force you to reflect on what really matters, both in one's life and in one's company."
The Globe and Mail

"His prose is soothing, free of scholarly clottedness and leftist stridency. The reader is impressed—thrilled even—to watch him coolly denude the corporate person until it stands naked and vulnerable . . ."
Vancouver Sun

THE CORPORATION

THE PATHOLOGICAL PURSUIT OF PROFIT AND POWER

Joel Bakan

CONSTABLE • LONDON

CONSTABLE

First published in the USA by Free Press,
a division of Simon & Schuster Inc, 2004

Published in the UK by Constable,
an imprint of Constable & Robinson Ltd, 2004

This edition published in 2005 by Constable
an imprint of Constable & Robinson Ltd

9 10

Copyright © Joel Bakan 2004, 2005

The moral right of the author has been asserted.

A CIP catalogue record for this book
is available from the British Library.

ISBN 978-1-84529-174-7

Printed and bound in Great Britain by Clays Ltd, St Ives plc

Papers used by Constable are from well-managed forests
and other responsible sources

MIX
Paper from
responsible sources
FSC® C104740

Constable
An imprint of
Little, Brown Book Group
Carmelite House
50 Victoria Embankment
London EC4Y 0DZ

An Hachette UK Company
www.hachette.co.uk

www.littlebrown.com

For Marlee

Contents

THE CORPORATION

Introduction

As images of disgraced and handcuffed corporate executives parade across our television screens, pundits, politicians, and business leaders are quick to assure us that greedy and corrupt individuals, not the system as a whole, are to blame for Wall Street's woes. "Have we just been talking about some bad apples?" Sam Donaldson recently asked former New York Stock Exchange chief Richard Grasso on ABC's *This Week*, "or is there something in the system that is broken?" "Well, Sam," Grasso explained, "we've had some massive failures, and we've got to root out the bad people, the bad practices; and certainly, whether the number is one or fifteen, that's in comparison to more than ten thousand publicly traded corporations—but one, Sam, just one WorldCom or one Enron, is one too many." Despite such assurances, citizens today—and many business leaders too—are concerned that the faults within the corporate system run much deeper than a few tremors on Wall Street would indicate. These larger concerns are the focus of this book.

A key premise is that the corporation is an *institution*—a unique structure and set of imperatives that direct the actions of people within it. It is also a *legal* institution, one whose existence and capacity to operate depend upon the law. The corporation's legally defined mandate is to pursue, relentlessly and without exception, its own self-interest, regardless of the often harmful consequences it might cause to others. As a result, I argue, the corporation is a pathological institution, a dangerous possessor of the great power it wields over people and societies. That raises a number of questions, which I address in subsequent chapters. How did the corporation become what it is today (Chapter 1)? What is the nature, and what are the implications, of its pathological character (Chapters 2 and 3) and of its power over society (Chapters 4 and 5)? And what should and can be done to mitigate its potential to cause harm (Chapter 6)? These are the central questions that inform the book. By revealing the institutional imperatives common to all corporations and their implications for society, I hope to provide a crucial and missing link in people's attempts to understand and do something about some of the most pressing issues of our time.

Peter Drucker, perhaps the world's leading management thinker, was one of the first to analyze the corporation as an institution in his groundbreaking 1946 work, *Concept of the Corporation.* It was Drucker who thought it significant that all corporations have the same institutional order and purpose. For most of us, however, the daily details of corporate life tend to obscure the bigger picture. Like Pfizer CEO Hank McKinnell, we have "great difficulty thinking of corporations as an institution." We understand them, instead, mainly in terms of how they differ from one another—transnational versus local, high-tech versus smokestack, progressive versus traditional, cool versus stodgy, blue-chip versus risky, brand name versus no-name, good versus bad—and miss the fact that all corporations, at least all publicly traded ones, share a common institutional structure; that it makes sense to talk about *the corporation,* as well as *corporations.* As veteran Harvard Business School scholar Joe Badaracco remarked when asked the simple question "What is a corporation?": "It's funny that I've taught in a business school for as long as I have without ever having been asked so pointedly to say what I think a corporation is."[1]

The purpose of this book is to explore what the corporation, as an institution, truly is. Institutions are, of course, composed of people, and much of what follows is based upon original interviews with players from the corporate world, pundits who analyze it, and critics who highlight its dangers and propose solutions.[2] As for the style and tone of the book, I have sought to avoid unduly academic and technical jargon. My objective has been to make it accessible to the lay reader and the professional, without compromising its grounding in rigorous research and in my knowledge and insight as a legal scholar. Throughout the book I use the word "corporation" to describe the large Anglo-American publicly traded business corporation, as opposed to small incorporated businesses, or small and large not-for-profit or privately owned ones. As for the focus on the Anglo-American corporation, the world's largest and most powerful corporations are based in the United States, and economic globalization has extended their influence beyond national borders. Elements of the Anglo-American model also increasingly shape its counterparts in other countries, especially in European nations and Japan.[3] For these reasons, the analyses and arguments presented in this book have important implications for the rest of the world.

The Corporation's Rise to Dominance

Over the last 150 years the corporation has risen from relative obscurity to become the world's dominant economic institution. Today, corporations govern our lives. They determine what we eat, what we watch, what we wear, where we work, and what we do. We are inescapably surrounded by their culture, iconography, and ideology. And, like the church and the monarchy in other times, they posture as infallible and omnipotent, glorifying themselves in imposing buildings and elaborate displays. Increasingly, corporations dictate the decisions of their supposed overseers in government and control domains of society once firmly embedded within the public sphere. The corporation's dramatic rise to dominance is one of the remarkable events of modern history, not least because of the institution's inauspicious beginnings.

Long before Enron's scandalous collapse, the corporation, a fledgling institution, was engulfed in corruption and fraud. Throughout the late seventeenth and early eighteenth centuries, stockbrokers, known as "jobbers," prowled the infamous coffee shops of London's Exchange Alley, a maze of lanes between Lombard Street, Cornhill, and Birchin Lane, in search of credulous investors to whom they could sell shares in bogus companies. Such companies flourished briefly, nourished by speculation, and then quickly collapsed. Ninety-three of them traded between 1690 and 1695. By 1698, only twenty were left. In 1696 the commissioners of trade for England reported that the corporate form had been "wholly perverted" by the sale of company stock "to ignorant men, drawn in by the reputation, falsely raised and artfully spread, concerning the thriving state of [the] stock."[1] Though the commissioners were appalled, they likely were not surprised.

Businessmen and politicians had been suspicious of the corporation from the time it first emerged in the late sixteenth century. Unlike the prevailing partnership form, in which relatively small groups of men, bonded together by personal loyalties and mutual trust, pooled their resources to set up businesses they ran as well as owned, the corporation separated ownership from management—one group of people, directors and managers, ran the firm, while another group, shareholders, owned it. That unique design was believed by many to be a recipe for corruption and scandal. Adam Smith warned in *The Wealth of Nations* that because managers could not be trusted to steward "other people's money," "negligence and profusion" would inevitably result when businesses organized as corporations. Indeed, by the time he wrote those words in 1776, the corporation had been banned in England for more than fifty years. In 1720, the English Parliament, fed up with the epidemic of corporate high jinks plaguing Exchange Alley, had outlawed the corporation (though with some exceptions). It was the notorious collapse of the South Sea Company that had prompted it to act.

Formed in 1710 to carry on exclusive trade, including trade in slaves, with the Spanish colonies of South America, the South Sea

Company was a scam from the very start. Its directors, some of the leading lights of political society, knew little about South America, had only the scantiest connection to the continent (apparently, one of them had a cousin who lived in Buenos Aires), and must have known that the King of Spain would refuse to grant them the necessary rights to trade in his South American colonies. As one director conceded, "unless the Spaniards are to be divested of common sense . . . abandoning their own commerce, throwing away the only valuable stake they have left in the world, and, in short, bent on their own ruin," they would never part with the exclusive power to trade in their own colonies. Yet the directors of the South Sea Company promised potential investors "fabulous profits" and mountains of gold and silver in exchange for common British exports, such as Cheshire cheese, sealing wax, and pickles.[2]

Investors flocked to buy the company's stock, which rose dramatically, by sixfold in one year, and then quickly plummeted as shareholders, realizing that the company was worthless, panicked and sold. In 1720—the year a major plague hit Europe, public anxiety about which "was heightened," according to one historian, "by a superstitious fear that it had been sent as a judgment on human materialism"[3]—the South Sea Company collapsed. Fortunes were lost, lives were ruined, one of the company's directors, John Blunt, was shot by an angry shareholder, mobs crowded Westminster, and the king hastened back to London from his country retreat to deal with the crisis.[4] The directors of the South Sea Company were called before Parliament, where they were fined, and some of them jailed, for "notorious fraud and breach of trust."[5] Though one parliamentarian demanded they be sewn up in sacks, along with snakes and monies, and then drowned, they were, for the most part, spared harsh punishment.[6] As for the corporation itself, in 1720 Parliament passed the Bubble Act, which made it a criminal offense to create a company "presuming to be a corporate body," and to issue "transferable stocks without legal authority."

Today, in the wake of corporate scandals similar to and every bit as nefarious as the South Sea bubble, it is unthinkable that a government would ban the corporate form. Even modest reforms—such as, for example, a law requiring companies to list employee stock options as expenses in their financial reports, which might avoid the kind of misleadingly rosy financial statements that have fueled recent scandals[7]—seem unlikely from a U.S. federal government that has failed to match its strong words at the time of the scandals with equally strong actions. Though the Sarbanes-Oxley Act, signed into law in 2002 to redress some of the more blatant problems of corporate governance and accounting, provides welcome remedies, at least on paper,[8] the federal government's general response to corporate scandals has been sluggish and timid at best. What is revealed by comparing that response to the English Parliament's swift and draconian measures of 1720 is the fact that, over the last three hundred years, corporations have amassed such great power as to weaken government's ability to control them. A fledgling institution that could be banned with the stroke of a legislative pen in 1720, the corporation now dominates society and government.

How did it become so powerful?

The genius of the corporation as a business form, and the reason for its remarkable rise over the last three centuries, was—and is—its capacity to combine the capital, and thus the economic power, of unlimited numbers of people. Joint-stock companies emerged in the sixteenth century, by which time it was clear that partnerships, limited to drawing capital from the relatively few people who could practicably run a business together, were inadequate for financing the new, though still rare, large-scale enterprises of nascent industrialization. In 1564 the Company of the Mines Royal was created as a joint-stock company, financed by twenty-four shares sold for £1,200 each; in 1565, the Company of Mineral and Battery Works raised its capital by making calls on thirty-six shares it had previously issued. The New River Company was formed as a joint-stock company in 1606 to transport fresh water to London, as were a number of other utilities.[9] Fifteen joint-stock companies were operating in England in 1688, though none with more than a few hundred members. Corporations began to proliferate during the final decade of the seventeenth century, and the total amount of investment in joint-stock companies doubled as the business form became a popular vehicle for financing colonial enterprises. The partnership still remained the dominant form for organizing businesses, however, though the corporation would steadily gain on it and then overtake it.

In 1712, Thomas Newcomen invented a steam-driven machine to pump water out of a coal mine and unwittingly started the industrial revolution. Over the next century, steam power fueled the development of large-scale industry in England and the United States, expanding the scope of operations in mines, textiles (and the associated trades of bleaching, calico printing, dyeing, and calendaring), mills, breweries, and distilleries.[10] Corporations multiplied as these new larger-scale undertakings demanded significantly more capital investment than partnerships could raise. In postrevolutionary America, between 1781 and 1790, the number of corporations grew tenfold, from 33 to 328.[11]

In England too, with the Bubble Act's repeal in 1825 and incorporation once again legally permitted, the number of corporations grew dramatically, and shady dealing and bubbles were once again rife in the business world. Joint-stock companies quickly became "the fashion of the age," as the novelist Sir Walter Scott observed at the time, and as such were fitting subjects for satire. Scott wryly pointed out that, as a shareholder in a corporation, an investor could make money by spending it (indeed, he likened the corporation to a machine that could fuel its operations with its own waste):

Such a person [an investor] buys his bread from his own Baking Company, his milk and cheese from his own Dairy Company . . . drinks an additional bottle of wine for the benefit of the General Wine Importation Company, of which he is himself a member. Every act, which would otherwise be one of mere extravagance, is, to such a person . . . reconciled to prudence. Even if the price of the article consumed be extravagant, and the quality indifferent, the person, who is in a manner his own customer, is only imposed upon for his own benefit. Nay, if the Joint-stock Company of Undertakers shall unite with the medical faculty . . . under the firm of Death and the Doctor, the shareholder might contrive to secure his heirs a handsome slice of his own death-bed and funeral expenses.[12]

At the moment Scott was satirizing it, however, the corporation was poised to begin its ascent to dominance over the economy and society. And it would do so with the help of a new kind of steam-driven engine: the steam locomotive.[13]

America's nineteenth-century railroad barons, men lionized by some and vilified by others, were the true creators of the modern corporate era. Because railways were mammoth undertakings requiring huge amounts of capital investment—to lay track, manufacture rolling stock, and operate and maintain systems—the industry quickly came to rely on the corporate form for financing its operations. In the United States, railway construction boomed during the 1850s and then exploded again after the Civil War, with more than one hundred thousand miles of track laid between 1865 and 1885. As the industry grew, so did the number of corporations.[14] The same was true in England, where, between 1825 and 1849, the amount of capital raised by railways, mainly through joint-stock companies, increased from £200,000 to £230 million, more than one thousand-fold.[15]

"One of the most important by-products of the introduction and extension of the railway system," observed M. C. Reed in *Railways and the Growth of the Capital Market*, was the part it played in "assisting the development of a national market for company securities."[16] Railways, in both the United States and England, demanded more capital investment than could be provided by the relatively small coterie of wealthy men who invested in corporations at the start of the nineteenth century. By the middle of the century, with railway stocks flooding markets in both countries, middle-class people began, for the first time, to invest in corporate shares. As *The Economist* pronounced at the time, "everyone was in the stocks now . . . needy clerks, poor tradesman's apprentices, discarded service men and bankrupts—all have entered the ranks of the great monied interest."[17]

One barrier remained to broader public participation in stock markets, however: no matter how much, or how little, a person had invested in a company, he or she was *personally* liable, without limit, for the company's debts. Investors' homes, savings, and other personal assets would be exposed to claims by creditors if a company failed, meaning that a person risked financial ruin simply by owning shares in a company. Stockholding could not become a truly attractive option for the general public until that risk was removed, which it soon was. By the middle of the nineteenth century, business leaders and politicians broadly advocated changing the law to limit the liability of shareholders to the amounts they had invested in a company. If a person bought $100 worth of shares, they reasoned, he or she should be immune to liability for anything beyond that, regardless of what happened to the company. Supporters of "limited liability," as the concept came to be known, defended it as being necessary to attract middle-class investors into the stock market. "Limited liability would allow those of moderate means to take shares in investments with their richer neighbors," reported the Select Committee on Partnerships (England) in 1851, and that, in turn, would mean "their self-respect [would be] upheld, their intelligence encouraged and an additional motive given to preserve order and respect for the laws of property."[18]

Ending class conflict by co-opting workers into the capitalist system, a goal the committee's latter comment subtly alludes to, was offered as a political justification for limited liability, alongside the economic one of expanding the pool of potential investors. An 1853 article in the *Edinburgh Journal,* stated:

> The workman does not understand the position of the capitalist. The remedy is, to put him in the way by practical experience. . . . Working-men, once enabled to act together as the owners of a joint capital, will soon find their whole view of the relations between capital and labour undergo a radical alteration. They will learn what anxiety and toil it costs even to hold a small concern together in tolerable order . . . the middle and operative classes would derive great material and social good by the exercise of the joint-stock principle.[19]

Limited liability had its detractors, however. On both sides of the Atlantic, critics opposed it mainly on moral grounds. Because it allowed investors to escape unscathed from their companies' failures, the critics believed it would undermine personal moral responsibility, a value that had governed the commercial world for centuries. With limited liability in place, investors could be recklessly unconcerned about their companies' fortunes, as Mr. Goldbury, a fictitious company promoter, explained in song in Gilbert and Sullivan's sharp satire of the corporation, *Utopia Ltd:*

> Though a Rothschild you may be, in your own capacity,
> As a Company you've come to utter sorrow,

But the liquidators say, "Never mind—you needn't pay,"
So you start another Company Tomorrow!

People worried that limited liability would, as one parliamentarian speaking against its introduction in Englan said, attack "The first and most natural principle of commercial legislation . . . that every man was bound to pay the debts he had contracted, so long as he was able to do so" and that it would "enable persons to embark in trade with a limited chance of loss, but with an unlimited chance of gain" and thus encourage "a system of vicious and improvident speculation."[20]

Despite such objections, limited liability was entrenched in corporate law, in England in 1856 and in the United States over the latter half of the nineteenth century (though at different times in different states). With the risks of investment in stocks now removed, at least in terms of how much money investors might be forced to lose, the way was cleared for broad popular participation in stock markets and for investors to diversify their holdings. Still, publicly traded corporations were relatively rare in the United States up until the end of the nineteenth century. Beyond the railway industry, leading companies tended to be family-owned, and if shares existed at all they were traded on a direct person-to-person basis, not in stock markets. By the early years of the twentieth century, however, large publicly traded corporations had become fixtures on the economic landscape.[21]

Over two short decades, beginning in the 1890s, the corporation underwent a revolutionary transformation. It all started when New Jersey and Delaware ("the first state to be known as the home of corporations," according to its current secretary of state for corporations[22]), sought to attract valuable incorporation business to their jurisdictions by jettisoning unpopular restrictions from their corporate laws. Among other things, they

- Repealed the rules that required businesses to incorporate only for narrowly defined purposes, to exist only for limited durations, and to operate only in particular locations

- Substantially loosened controls on mergers and acquisitions; and

- Abolished the rule that one company could not own stock in another

Other states, not wanting to lose out in the competition for incorporation business, soon followed with similar revisions to their laws. The changes prompted a flurry of incorporations as businesses sought the new freedoms and powers incorporation would grant them. Soon, however, with most meaningful constraints on mergers and acquisitions gone, a large number of small and medium-size corporations were quickly absorbed into a small number of very large ones—1,800 corporations were consolidated into 157 between 1898 and 1904.[23] In less than a decade the U.S. economy had been transformed from one in which individually owned enterprises competed freely among themselves into one dominated by a relatively few huge corporations, each owned by many shareholders. The era of corporate capitalism had begun.

"Every tie in the road is the grave of a small stockholder," stated Newton Booth, a noted antimonopolist and railroad reformer, in 1873, when he was governor of California. Booth's message was clear: in large corporations stockholders had little, if any, power and control. By the early twentieth century, corporations were typically combinations of thousands, even hundreds of thousands, of broadly dispersed, anonymous shareholders. Unable to influence managerial decisions as individuals because their power was too diluted, they were also too broadly dispersed to act collectively. Their consequent loss of power in and control of large corporations turned out to be managers' gains. In 1913, a congressional committee set up to investigate the "money trust," led by Congressman Arsène Pujo, reported:

> None of the witnesses called was able to name an instance in the history of the country in which the stockholders had succeeded in overthrowing an existing management in any large corporation, nor does it appear that stockholders have ever even succeeded in so far as to secure the investigation of an existing management of a corporation to ascertain whether it has been well or honestly managed.... [In] all great corporations with numerous and widely scattered stockholders ... the management is virtually self-perpetuating and is able through the power of patronage, the indifference of stockholders and other influences to control a majority of stock.[24]

Shareholders had, for all practical purposes, disappeared from the corporations they owned.

With shareholders, real people, effectively gone from corporations, the law had to find someone else, some other person, to assume the legal rights and duties firms needed to operate in the economy. That "person" turned out to be the corporation itself. As early as 1793, one corporate scholar outlined the logic of corporate personhood when he defined the corporation as

> a collection of many individuals united into one body, under a special denomination, having perpetual succession under an artificial form, and vested, by the policy of law, with the capacity of acting, in several respects, as an individual, particularly of taking and granting property, of contracting obligations, and of suing and being sued, of enjoying privileges and immunities in common.[25]

In partnerships, another scholar noted in 1825, "the law looks to the individuals"; in corporations, on the other hand, "it sees only the creature of the charter, the body corporate, and knows not the individuals."[26]

By the end of the nineteenth century, through a bizarre legal alchemy, courts had fully transformed the corporation into a "person," with its own identity, separate from the flesh-and-blood people who were its owners and managers and empowered, like a real person, to conduct business in its own name, acquire assets, employ workers, pay taxes, and go to court to assert its rights and defend its actions. The corporate person had taken the place, at least in law, of the real people who owned corporations. Now viewed as an entity, "not imaginary or fictitious, but real, not artificial but natural," as it was described by one law professor in 1911, the corporation had been reconceived as a free and independent being.[27] Gone was the centuries-old "grant theory," which had conceived of corporations as instruments of government policy and as dependent upon government bodies to create them and enable them to function. Along with the grant theory had also gone all rationales for encumbering corporations with burdensome restrictions. The logic was that, conceived as natural entities analogous to human beings, corporations should be created as free individuals, a logic that informed the initiatives in New Jersey and Delaware, as well as the Supreme Court's decision in 1886 that, because they were "persons," corporations should be protected by the Fourteenth Amendment's rights to "due process of law" and "equal protection of the laws," rights originally entrenched in the Constitution to protect freed slaves.[28]

As the corporation's size and power grew, so did the need to assuage people's fears of it. The corporation suffered its first full-blown legitimacy crisis in the wake of the early-twentieth-century merger movement, when, for the first time, many Americans realized that corporations, now huge behemoths, threatened to overwhelm their social institutions and governments. Corporations were now widely viewed as soulless leviathans—uncaring, impersonal, and amoral. Suddenly, they were vulnerable to popular discontent and organized dissent (especially from a growing labor movement), as calls for more government regulation and even their dismantling were increasingly common. Business leaders and public relations experts soon realized that the institution's new powers and privileges demanded new public relations strategies.

In 1908, AT&T, one of America's largest corporations at the time and the parent company of the Bell System, which had a monopoly on telephone services in the United States, launched an advertising campaign, the first of its kind, that aimed to persuade a skeptical public to like and accept the company. In much the same way that law had transformed the corporation into a "person" to compensate for the disappearance of the real people within it, AT&T's campaign imbued the company with human values in an effort to overcome people's suspicions of it as a soulless and inhuman entity. "Bigness," worried one vice president at AT&T, tended to squeeze out of the corporation "the human understanding, the human sympathy, the human contacts, and the natural human relationships." It had convinced "the general public [that] a corporation is a thing." Another AT&T official believed it was necessary "to make the people understand and love the company. Not merely to be consciously dependent upon it—not merely regard it as a necessity—not merely to take it for granted—but to love it—to hold real affection for it." From 1908 into the late 1930s, AT&T trumpeted itself as a "friend and neighbor" and sought to give itself a human face by featuring real people from the company in its advertising campaigns. Employees, particularly telephone operators and linemen, appeared regularly in the company's advertisements, as did shareholders. One magazine advertisement entitled "Our Shareholders," depicts a woman, presumably a widow, examining her AT&T share certificates as her two young children look on; another pronounces AT&T "a new democracy of public service ownership" that is "owned directly by the people—controlled not by one, but controlled by all."[29]

Other major corporations soon followed AT&T's lead. General Motors, for example, ran advertisements that, in the words of the agency responsible for them, aimed "to personalize the institution by calling it a *family*." "The word 'corporation' is cold, impersonal and subject to misunderstanding and distrust," noted Alfred Swayne, the GM executive in charge of institutional advertising at the time, but "'Family' is personal, human, friendly. This is our picture of General Motors—a big congenial household."[30]

By the end of World War I, some of America's leading corporations, among them General Electric, Eastman Kodak, National Cash Register, Standard Oil, U.S. Rubber, and the Goodyear Tire & Rubber Company, were busily crafting images of themselves as benevolent and socially responsible. "New Capitalism," the term used to describe the trend, softened corporations' images with promises of good corporate citizenship and practices of better wages and working conditions. As citizens demanded that governments rein in corporate power and while labor militancy was rife, with returning World War I veterans, having risked their lives as soldiers, insisting upon better treatment as workers, proponents of the New Capitalism sought to demonstrate that corporations could be good without the coercive push of governments and unions.[31]

A leader of the movement, Paul W. Litchfield, who presided over Goodyear Tire for thirty-two years through the middle part of the twentieth century, believed capitalism would not survive unless equality and cooperation between workers and capitalists replaced division and conflict. Though branded a socialist and a Marxist by some of his business peers at the time, Litchfield forged ahead with programs designed to promote the health, welfare, and education of his workers and their families, and to give his workers a greater voice in company affairs. One of his proudest achievements was a workers' Senate and House of Representatives, modeled after the national one, that had jurisdiction over employment issues, including wages. Litchfield defended his benevolent policies as necessary for Goodyear's success. "Goodyear has all about her the human quality," he said, "and it has been to this human quality fully as much as to her business methods, that Goodyear owes her meteoric rise in the ranks of American Industry."[32]

Corporate social responsibility blossomed again during the 1930s as corporations suffered from adverse public opinion. Many people believed at the time that corporate greed and mismanagement had caused the Great Depression. They shared Justice Louis Brandeis's view, stated in a 1933 Supreme Court judgment, that corporations were "Frankenstein monsters" capable of doing evil.[33] In response, business leaders embraced corporate social responsibility. It was the best strategy, they believed, to restore people's faith in corporations and reverse their growing fascination with big government. Gerard Swope, then president of General Electric, voiced a popular sentiment among big-business leaders when, in 1934, he said that "organized industry should take the lead, recognizing its responsibility to its employees, to the public, and to its shareholders *rather than that democratic society should act through its government*" (italics added).[34]

Adolf Berle and Gardiner Means had endorsed a similar idea two years earlier in their classic work *The Modern Corporation and Private Property*. The corporation, they argued, was "potentially (if not yet actually) the dominant institution of the modern world"; its managers had become "princes of industry," their companies akin to feudal fiefdoms. Because they had amassed such power over society, corporations and the men who managed them were now obliged to serve the interests of society as a whole, much as governments were, not just those of their shareholders. "[T]he 'control' of the great corporations should develop into a purely neutral technocracy," they wrote, "balancing a variety of claims by various groups in the community and assigning to each a portion of the income stream on the basis of public policy rather than private cupidity." Corporations would likely have to embrace this new approach, Berle and Means warned, "if the corporate system [was] to survive." Professor Edwin Dodd, another eminent scholar of the corporation at the time, was more skeptical about corporations becoming socially responsible, but he believed they risked losing their legitimacy, and thus their power, if they did not at least appear to do so. "Modern large-scale industry has given to the managers of our principal corporations enormous power," Dodd wrote in 1932 in the *Harvard Law Review*. "Desire to retain their present powers accordingly encourages [them] to adopt and disseminate the view that they are guardians of all the interests which the corporation affects and not merely servants of its absentee owners."[35]

Despite corporate leaders' claims that they were capable of regulating themselves, in 1934 President Franklin D. Roosevelt created the New Deal, a package of regulatory reforms designed to restore economic health by, among other things, curbing the powers and freedoms of corporations. As the first systematic attempt to regulate corporations and the foundation of the modern regulatory state, the New Deal was reviled by many business leaders at the time and even prompted a small group of them to plot a coup to overthrow Roosevelt's administration. Though the plot (which is more fully discussed in Chapter 4, as is the New Deal itself) failed, it was significant for reflecting the depth of hostility many business leaders felt for Roosevelt. The spirit of the New Deal, along with many of its regulatory regimes, nonetheless prevailed. For fifty years following its creation, through World War II, the postwar era, and the 1960s and 1970s, the growing power of corporations was offset, at least in part, by continued expansion of government regulation, trade unions, and social programs. Then, much as steam engines and railways had combined with new laws and ideologies to create the corporate behemoth one hundred years earlier, a new convergence of technology, law, and ideology—economic globalization—reversed the trend toward greater regulatory control of corporations and vaulted the corporation to unprecedented power and influence.

In 1973, the economy was shaken by a surge in oil prices due to the formation of the Organization of the Petroleum Exporting Countries (OPEC), which operated in cartel-like fashion to control the world's oil supply. High unemployment, runaway inflation, and deep recession soon followed. Prevailing economic policies, which, true to their New Deal lineage, had favored regulation and other modes of government intervention, came under sustained attack for their inability to deal with the crisis. Governments throughout the West began to embrace neoliberalism, which, like its laissez-faire predecessor, celebrated economic freedom for individuals and corporations and prescribed a limited role for government in the economy. When Margaret Thatcher became prime minister of Britain in 1979, and then Ronald Reagan president of the United States in 1980, it was clear that the economic era inspired by New Deal ideas and policies had come to an end. Over the next two decades, governments pursued neoliberalism's core policies of deregulation, privatization, spending cuts, and inflation reduction with increasing vigor. By the early 1990s, neoliberalism had become an economic orthodoxy.

In the meantime, technological innovations in transportation and communications had profoundly enhanced corporations' mobility and portability. Fast and large jet planes and new container-shipping techniques (which allowed for sea shipping to be smoothly integrated with rail and truck networks) drove down the costs and increased the speed and efficiency of transportation. Communications were similarly improved with innovations to long-distance phone networks, telex and fax technology, and, more recently, the creation of the Internet. Corporations, no longer tethered to their home jurisdictions, could now scour the earth for locations to produce goods and services at substantially lower costs. They could buy labor in poor countries, where it was cheap and where environmental standards were weak, and sell their products in wealthy countries, where people had disposable income and were prepared to pay decent prices for them. Costly tariffs had gradually come down since 1948, when the General Agreement on Tariffs and Trade (GATT) was introduced, enabling corporations to take advantage of their newfound mobility without suffering punishing financial penalties.

By leveraging their freedom from the bonds of location, corporations could now dictate the economic policies of governments. As Clive Allen, a vice president at Nortel Networks, a leading Canadian high-tech company, explained, companies "owe no allegiance to Canada. . . . Just because we [Nortel Networks] were born there doesn't mean we'll remain there. . . . The place has to remain attractive for us to be interested in staying there."[36] To remain attractive, whether to keep investment within their jurisdictions or to lure new investment to them, governments would now have to compete among themselves to persuade corporations that they provided the most business-friendly policies. A resulting "battle to the bottom" would see them ratchet down regulatory regimes—particularly those that protected workers and the environment—reduce taxes, and roll back social programs, often with reckless disregard for the consequences.[37]

With the creation of the World Trade Organization (WTO) in 1993, the deregulatory logic of economic globalization was deepened. Given a mandate to enforce existing GATT standards, and also to create new ones that would bar regulatory measures that might restrict the flow of international trade, the WTO was poised to become a significant fetter on the economic sovereignty of nations. By the time tens of thousands of people spilled into the streets of Seattle in 1999 to protest against a meeting of WTO officials and member-state representatives, the organization had evolved into a powerful, secretive, and corporate-influenced overseer of government's mandate to protect citizens and the environment from corporate harms.[38]

When Enron collapsed and accounting firm Arthur Andersen's role in its misdeeds was revealed, people called for better regulatory oversight of the accounting industry. What few knew at the time, however, was that the U.S. government, through its membership in the WTO, had already relinquished some of its authority to fix the problem. Driven by a stated belief that "regulations can be an unnecessary, and usually unintended, barrier to trade in services"[39] and in response to intense lobbying from industry groups and firms, the WTO in the late 1990s had established a set of "disciplines" designed to ensure that member states do not regulate accounting in ways that are "more trade restrictive than . . . necessary to fulfill a legitimate objective."[40] In 1998, member states, including the United States, agreed to abide by these new rules, which do not formally come into full effect until 2005, and thus subjected themselves to standards imposed by, and soon to be adjudicated by, an outside and undemocratic body.[41]

When the disciplines were first being considered, U.S. representatives inquired of WTO officials whether a law that prohibited accounting firms from working both as consultants and as auditors for the same company—a law that might help avoid another Enron/Andersen debacle, and that has recently been enacted as part of the Sarbanes-Oxley Act of 2002[42]—would contravene them. A final answer to the question must await a WTO ruling once the disciplines are officially operative, which likely will take the form of a tribunal's decision in a member-state's complaint against the Act. But, in the meantime, the fact that the question even had to be asked demonstrates the discipline's potential impact on government's authority to regulate the accounting industry and hence "the people's" democratic sovereignty over it.[43]

Regulation of accounting is not unique as an area in which the WTO has the authority to restrict governments' policy choices. On numerous occasions the organization has required nations, under threat of punishing penalties, to change or repeal laws designed to protect environmental, consumer, or other public interests.[44] In one case, for example, a U.S. law that banned shrimp imports from producers that refused to use gear that protected sea turtles from being accidentally caught was deemed to violate WTO standards;[45] in another case, an EU measure that banned production and imports of beef from cows treated with synthetic hormones was similarly treated. The full extent of the WTO's impact cannot be gauged from its formal decisions alone, however. As is true of any set of legal standards, WTO rules exert their strongest influence through informal channels. Governments might self-censor their behavior to ensure that they comply with the rules—as the State of Maryland did when it scuttled a proposed law that would have barred it from buying products from companies doing business in Nigeria (while that country was under the rule of a cruel dictatorship) after warnings from the U.S. State Department that such a law could expose the United States to a WTO challenge. Governments can also use WTO standards to pressure other governments to change their policies, threatening to initiate a WTO complaint if they refuse to do so—as the United States and Canada did to get the European Union to back off proposed regulations that would have banned the import of fur from animals caught in leg-hold traps and of cosmetics that had been tested on animals.[47]

That the WTO's policies and decisions tend to champion corporations' interests is hardly surprising, given the privileged place and considerable influence industry groups enjoy within the organization. The trade and commerce ministers who represent the member states are usually "closely aligned with the commercial and financial interests of those in the advanced industrial countries," as Nobel laureate economist Joseph Stiglitz notes, and thus easy targets for corporations to influence.[48] Corporations and industry groups also enjoy close relationships with the organization's bureaucrats and officials. "We want neither to be the secret girlfriend of the WTO nor should [our group] have to enter the World Trade Organization through the servant's entrance" is how one member of the International Chamber of Commerce, an influential group at the WTO, describes the special relationship between his organization—and, one can infer, industry groups in general—and the WTO.[49]

Over its relatively short life, the WTO has become a significant fetter on nations' abilities to protect their citizens from corporate misdeeds. More generally, economic globalization, of which the WTO is just one element, has substantially enhanced corporations' abilities to evade the authority of governments. "Corporations have become sufficiently powerful to pose a threat to governments," says William Niskanen, chairman of the Cato Institute, and that is "particularly the case with respect to multinational corporations, who will have much less dependence upon the positions of particular governments, much less loyalty in that sense." As Ira Jackson, former director of the Center for Business and Government at Harvard's Kennedy School of Government, observes, corporations and their leaders have "displaced politics and politicians as . . . the new high priests and reigning oligarchs of our system." And, according to Samir Gibara, former CEO of Goodyear Tire, governments have "become powerless [in relation to corporations] compared to what they were before."[50]

Corporations now *govern* society, perhaps more than governments themselves do; yet ironically, it is their very power, much of which they have gained through economic globalization, that makes them vulnerable. As is true of any ruling institution, the corporation now attracts mistrust, fear, and demands for accountability from an increasingly anxious public. Today's corporate leaders understand, as did their predecessors, that work is needed to regain and maintain the public's trust. And they, like their predecessors, are seeking to soften the corporation's image by presenting it as human, benevolent, and socially responsible. "It's absolutely fundamental that a corporation today has as much of a human and personal characteristic as anything else," says public relations czar Chris Komisarjevsky, CEO of Burson-Marsteller. "The smart corporations understand that people make comparisons in human terms . . . because that's the way people think, we think in terms that often are very, very personal. . . . If you walked down the street with a microphone and a camera and you stopped [people] on the street . . . they will describe [corporations] in very human terms."

Today, corporations use "branding" to create unique and attractive personalities for themselves. Branding goes beyond strategies designed merely to associate corporations with actual human beings—such as AT&T's early campaigns that featured workers and shareholders or the more recent use of celebrity endorsements (such as Nike's Michael Jordan advertisements) and corporate mascots (such as Ronald McDonald, Tony the Tiger, the Michelin Man, and Mickey Mouse). Corporations' brand identities are "personification[s]" of "who they are and where they've come from," says Clay Timon, chairman of Landor Associates, the world's largest and oldest branding firm. "Family magic" for Disney, "invent" for Hewlett-Packard, "sunshine foods" for Dole are a few examples of what Timon calls "brand drivers." "Corporations, as brands . . . have . . . soul[s]," says Timon, which is what enables them to create "intellectual and emotional bond[s]" with the groups they depend upon, such as consumers, employees, shareholders, and regulators.[51]

Timon points to Landor's brand drivers for British Petroleum—"progressive, performance, green, innovative"—as evidence of how corporate environmental and social responsibility are emerging today as key branding themes. However, he says, even companies that do not explicitly brand themselves as such must now embrace corporate social responsibility. "Out of necessity," says Timon, "companies, whether they want it or not, have had to take on a social responsibility." And that is partly a result of their new status as dominant institutions. They must now show that they deserve to be free of governmental constraints and, indeed, to participate in governing society. "Corporations need to become more trustworthy," says Sam Gibara, a successor to social responsibility pioneer P. W. Litchfield. "There has been a transfer of authority from the government . . . to the corporation, and the corporation needs to assume that responsibility . . . and needs to really behave as a corporate citizen of the world; needs to respect the communities in which it operates, and needs to assume the self-discipline that, in the past, governments required from it."

Beginning in the mid-1990s, mass demonstrations against corporate power and abuse rocked North American and European cities. The protestors, part of a broader "civil society" movement, which also included nongovernmental organizations, community coalitions, and labor unions, targeted corporate harms to workers, consumers, communities, and the environment. Their concerns were different from those of post-Enron worriers, for whom shareholders' vulnerability to corrupt managers was paramount. But the two groups had something in common: they both believed the corporation had become a dangerous mix of power and unaccountability. Corporate social responsibility is offered today as an answer to such concerns. Now more than just a marketing strategy, though it is certainly that, it presents corporations as responsible and accountable to society and thus purports to lend legitimacy to their new role as society's rulers.[52]

Business as Usual

Business leaders today say their companies care about more than profit and loss, that they feel responsible to society as a whole, not just to their shareholders. Corporate social responsibility is their new creed, a self-conscious corrective to earlier greed-inspired visions of the corporation. Despite this shift, the corporation itself has not changed. It remains, as it was at the time of its origins as a modern business institution in the middle of the nineteenth century, a legally designated "person" designed to valorize self-interest and invalidate moral concern. Most people would find its "personality" abhorrent, even psychopathic, in a human being, yet curiously we accept it in society's most powerful institution. The troubles on Wall Street today, beginning with Enron's spectacular crash, can be blamed in part on the corporation's flawed institutional character, but the company was not unique for having that character. Indeed, all publicly traded corporations have it, even the most respected and socially responsible among them, such as Pfizer Inc.

In 1849, Charles Pfizer and his cousin Charles Erhart established a small chemical firm in Williamsburg, then a rural section of Brooklyn accessible from Manhattan only by boat. Over the last century and a half the firm, Pfizer Inc., has prospered and become the world's largest pharmaceutical company. Williamsburg, now linked to Manhattan by bridges and tunnels, also prospered, then declined, and now, at least in part because of Pfizer, it has enjoyed something of a revival.

On a recent summer afternoon, Tom Kline, a senior vice president at Pfizer, took a documentary film crew on a walkabout tour of the inner-city neighborhood that now surrounds his company's original plant in Williamsburg. A tall white man in late middle age, dressed in neat blue slacks and a matching wrinkle-free short-sleeved shirt, Kline looked conspicuous in this predominantly low-income neighborhood, but he clearly felt at home here. (During the tour he greeted strangers on the street as if they were old friends, promising one woman that "working with you and Pfizer and our other partnerships, we'll make this a better place" and saying "Love you" to another person after a brief conversation.) The tour commenced at the Flushing Avenue subway station, whose stairwell entrance lies just across the street from the entrance to Pfizer's plant. Kline explained how he had almost been mugged on the subway station's platform one evening in the early 1980s as he waited for a train to take him home from the plant, where he then worked as plant manager. He had fled from the would-be muggers, made it safely to the far side of the tracks, and hid there terrified but oddly inspired by his plight to do something about the spiral of crime and drugs that was ruining the neighborhood. He had decided, at that perilous moment, to scuttle Pfizer's recently devised plan to close the plant and instead work "to make a change to make this community better."[1]

Today the plant is still open, and thanks to Kline and Pfizer, the subway station is safer. Kline showed the film crew a yellow box attached to the wall of a designated waiting area on the subway platform. The box is connected to a sophisticated security system, financed and maintained by Pfizer, which allows threatened subway patrons to summon help from Pfizer security guards at the nearby plant. Down the block from the station, at Pfizer's original corporate headquarters, there is a children's school, developed by Kline, and partly funded by the company. Though the school is officially part of the New York City public school system, principal Sonia Gerrardo explained that the "children really have an ongoing relationship with the company" through Pfizer mentors and volunteers. There is also a middle-income housing development in the neighborhood, spearheaded by the company's Redevelopment Program and administered jointly with the city.[2]

Kline believes that "if we really want to improve the conditions of American cities, we business people . . . have to take responsibility," and his actions show that these are not empty words. As Hank McKinnell, chairman and CEO of Pfizer, said, Kline is "the driving force behind the rejuvenation of a very devastated inner city area."[3]

McKinnell, however, wants Pfizer to do more than just save cities. "Pfizer can be the company which does more good for more people than any other company on the planet," he said. Every year his company donates hundreds of millions of dollars' worth of products and cash around the globe, making it, it claims, "one of America's most generous companies." McKinnell is especially proud of the company's work to end trachoma, an infection that blinds eight to ten million people every year. Pfizer produces Zithromax, a drug that prevents trachoma with just a single dose per year, and donates it to African countries. McKinnell claims that the drug has cut the infection rate in Africa in half and could eliminate the disease altogether by the year 2020. "We at Pfizer never stop looking for innovative solutions to society's problems," the company proclaims on its Web site. "Whether it's donating medicine to people in need or lending employees to local schools [or] rebuilding our first neighborhood . . . we are dedicated to our company purpose: helping people around the world live healthier, more productive lives."[4]

Corporations have always been philanthropic. They have donated to charities, sponsored Little League teams, and helped to build theaters. Traditionally, such generosity was quietly practiced and peripheral to their main goal of making money. Now, however, large corporations such as Pfizer have put corporate good deeds at the core of their business plans. A sense of responsibility to society, not just to a company's shareholders, has come to define the very nature of the corporation, what it is supposed to be and what it must and cannot do. Corporations are now often expected to deliver the good, not just the goods; to pursue values, not just value; and to help make the world a better place.

During the 1980s, testosterone-fueled corporate slashers such as Sunbeam's "Chainsaw" Al Dunlap, who once posed on a magazine cover wielding a machine gun to symbolize his take-no-prisoners approach to management, were cheered as heroes and fearless knights of the bottom line. These men now seem like barbarians, uncouth and uncool, as ridiculous as their red suspenders. Today's leading CEOs cultivate compassion and seem genuinely concerned about how their corporations' actions affect social and environmental interests, not just their stockholders'; they say they are obliged to meet social and environmental bottom lines, not just the financial one. As Goodyear Tire's Samir Gibara explained, today "the corporation is much broader than just its shareholders. . . . The corporation has many more constituencies and needs to address all these needs." Its obligations are no longer limited to making money for investors but, according to William Ford, Jr., chairman of the Ford Motor Company and great-grandson of corporate social responsibility pioneer Henry Ford, "corporations could be and should be a major force for resolving environmental and social concerns in the twenty-first century."[5]

Former Harvard business scholar Ira Jackson believes that such attitudes herald the start of an entirely new stage of capitalism, what he calls "capitalism with a conscience." There is much evidence to support his view. Corporations now boast about social and environmental initiatives on their Web sites and in their annual reports. Entire departments and executive positions are devoted to these initiatives. The business press runs numerous features on social responsibility and ranks corporations on how good they are at it. Business schools launch new courses on social responsibility, and universities create centers devoted to its study (at the University of Nottingham, tobacco giant ABT donated $7 million to create an International Centre for Corporate Social Responsibility). Social responsibility is on the agenda wherever business leaders meet—at the World Economic Forum in Davos, Switzerland, WTO ministerial meetings, industry conferences, and international trade and investment summits—and corporations compete against one another for ever higher moral ground.[6]

Pious social responsibility themes now vie with sex for top billing in corporate advertising, whether on television or in the pages of glossy magazines and newspapers. A recent television advertisement by Shell is typical. It shows self-styled "romantic" environmentalist Frances Abbots-Guardiola flying around beautiful mountains and lakes in a helicopter and talking to aboriginal people in grass-roofed huts. She eyes skeptically a convoy of heavy dump trucks lumbering across the pristine landscape. "This woman is trying to protect a fragile environment from being destroyed by oil and gas," a lyrical Scottish-accented narrator tells us (she must be one of those anticorporate Greenpeace types, we think). "Despite that, she's not at war with the oil company. She *is* the oil company"—a Shell geologist, we learn.

The message is clear, as is that of legions of similar advertisements: corporations care about the environment and communities, not just the soulless pursuit of profit; they are part of the solution to world ills, not the cause; they are allies of governments and non-governmental organizations, not enemies.

Just a few years ago, says Jackson, "you'd have been laughed out of the office, if not escorted out by an armed guard" for suggesting to a CEO that his corporation should abide by the UN Universal Declaration of Human Rights. Yet recently in New York, a hundred CEOs from the world's largest corporations met with their counterparts from NGOs such as Greenpeace and Amnesty International, along with national ambassadors, to sign a promise to adhere to the general principles of the Universal Declaration of Human Rights. This is just one example, says Jackson, of the new corporate order of conscience. He, along with many other business pundits, applauds big-business leaders who embrace the values of corporate social responsibility and predicts failure for those who do not.[7]

Even President Bush now says that corporate responsibility is a fundamental business value, indeed a patriotic duty. "America is ushering in a responsibility era, a culture regaining a sense of personal responsibility," he told a group of top business leaders in a speech addressing Enron's collapse, "and this new culture must include a renewed sense of corporate responsibility. . . . Business relationships, like all human relationships, are built on a foundation of integrity and trust."

Not everyone, however, is convinced of corporate social responsibility's virtue. Milton Friedman, for one, a Nobel laureate and one of the world's most eminent economists, believes the new moralism in business is in fact immoral.

When Friedman granted me an interview, his secretary warned that he would get up and walk out of the room if he found my questions dull. So I was apprehensive as I waited for him in the lobby of his building. This must be how Dorothy felt, I thought, just before Toto pulled back the curtain to reveal the real Wizard of Oz. Friedman is an intellectual giant, revered and feared, deified and vilified, larger than life. So I felt some relief when he entered the room smiling, a charming little man who, like the wizard himself, barely broke five feet. Friedman surveyed the lobby, now a chaotic makeshift television studio (the interview was for a government-funded TV documentary). Lights and cameras cluttered the room, tangles of wire covered the floor. Two crew members stood ready, cotton balls in hand, to remove the shine on the great man's nose. Bemused, Friedman curmudgeonized, "ABC came in here the other day with two guys and one camera. Here we see government fat and waste at its worst."

Friedman thinks that corporations are good for society (and that too much government is bad). He recoils, however, at the idea that corporations should try to *do* good for society. "A corporation is the property of its stockholders," he told me. "Its interests are the interests of its stockholders. Now, beyond that should it spend the stockholders' money for purposes which it regards as socially responsible but which it cannot connect to its bottom line? The answer I would say is no." There is but one "social responsibility" for corporate executives, Friedman believes: they must make as much money as possible for their shareholders. This is a moral imperative. Executives who choose social and environmental goals over profits—who try to act morally—are, in fact, immoral.

There is, however, one instance when corporate social responsibility can be tolerated, according to Friedman—when it is insincere. The executive who treats social and environmental values as means to maximize shareholders' wealth—not as ends in themselves—commits no wrong. It's like "putting a good-looking girl in front of an automobile to sell an automobile," he told me. "That's not in order to promote pulchritude. That's in order to sell cars." Good intentions, like good-looking girls, can sell goods. It's true, Friedman acknowledges, that this purely strategic view of social responsibility reduces lofty ideals to "hypocritical window dressing." But hypocrisy is virtuous when it serves the bottom line. Moral virtue is immoral when it does not.[8]

Though Friedman's views are rejected by many sophisticated

businesspeople, who think his brand of cynicism is old-fashioned, mean-spirited, and out of touch with reality, his suspicion of corporate social responsibility attracts some weighty support. William Niskanen, a former Ford economist and now chairman of the Cato Institute, said he "would not invest in a firm that pioneered in corporate social responsibility." "I think Ford Motor Company still makes fine cars and trucks," he continued, "but I think the [socially responsible] actions by the new Mr. Ford are likely to undermine the value of the corporation to the owners."[9] Peter Drucker, the guru of all business gurus, who believes that Friedman is "probably our greatest living economist," echoes his view that corporate social responsibility is a dangerous distortion of business principles. "If you find an executive who wants to take on social responsibilities," Drucker said, "fire him. Fast." Harvard Business School professor Debora Spar insisted that corporations "are not institutions that are set up to be moral entities. . . . They are institutions which have really only one mission, and that is to increase shareholder value." And Noam Chomsky—Friedman's intellectual and ideological nemesis—shares his view that corporations must "be concerned only for their stockholders and . . . not the community or the workforce or whatever."[10]

Corporations are created by law and imbued with purpose by law. Law dictates what their directors and managers can do, what they cannot do, and what they must do. And, at least in the United States and other industrialized countries, the corporation, as created by law, most closely resembles Milton Friedman's ideal model of the institution: it compels executives to prioritize the interests of their companies and shareholders above all others and forbids them from being socially responsible—at least genuinely so.

In 1916, Henry Ford learned this legal lesson the hard way and unwittingly helped entrench the law's intolerance of corporate social responsibility.

Ford believed that his Ford Motor Company could be more than just a profit machine. He paid his workers substantially more than the going rate at the time and rewarded customers with yearly price cuts on his Model T cars (their original price of more than $900 was slashed to $440 by 1916). "I do not believe that we should make such awful profits on our cars," he is reported to have said. "A reasonable profit is right, but not too much."[11]

John and Horace Dodge had helped Ford establish his company in 1906 with a $10,500 investment. They were major shareholders, and John Dodge became a director of the company. The brothers had also pledged that their Chicago machine shop would make parts exclusively for Ford, having turned down overtures from the more established Oldsmobile company. By 1916, however, the Dodge brothers had larger ambitions. John Dodge quit the Ford board and devised a plan with his brother to build their own car company. They hoped to finance the venture with the quarterly dividends from their Ford shares but were stopped by Ford's decision to cancel the dividend and divert the money to customers in the form of further price reductions on Model T automobiles. The Dodge brothers took Ford to court. Profits belong to shareholders, they argued, and Ford had no right to give their money away to customers, however good his intentions. The judge agreed. He reinstated the dividend and rebuked Ford—who had said in open court that "business is a service, not a bonanza" and that corporations should be run only "incidentally to make money"—for forgetting that "a business corporation is organized and carried on primarily for the profit of the stockholders"; it could not be run "for the merely incidental benefit of shareholders and for the primary purpose of benefiting others."[12]

Dodge v. Ford still stands for the legal principle that managers and directors have a legal duty to put shareholders' interests above all others and no legal authority to serve any other interests—what has come to be known as "the best interests of the corporation" principle. That principle provided a legal fix to a flaw in the corporate form that had famously worried Adam Smith 140 years before *Dodge v. Ford* was decided. Smith, in his 1776 classic, *The Wealth of Nations,* said he was troubled by the fact that corporations' owners, their share-holders, did not run their own businesses but delegated that task to professional managers. The latter could not be trusted to apply the same "anxious vigilance" to manage "other people's money" as they would their own, he wrote, and "negligence and profusion therefore must prevail, more or less, in the management of such a company."

The "best interests of the corporation" principle, now a fixture in the corporate laws of most countries, addresses Smith's concern by compelling corporate decision makers always to act in the best inter-ests of the corporation, and hence its owners. The law forbids any other motivation for their actions, whether to assist workers, improve the environment, or help consumers save money. They can do these things with their own money, as private citizens. As corporate offi-cials, however, stewards of other people's money, they have no legal authority to pursue such goals as ends in themselves—only as means to serve the corporation's own interests, which generally means to maximize the wealth of its shareholders.[13]

Corporate social responsibility is thus illegal—at least when it is genuine.

Corporate lawyer Robert Hinkley quit his job at international legal powerhouse Skadden, Arps when he realized, after twenty-three years in practice, "that the law, in its current form, actually inhibits execu-tives and corporations from being socially responsible." As he puts it:

[T]he corporate design contained in hundreds of corporate laws throughout the world is nearly identical . . . the people who run cor-porations have a legal duty to shareholders, and that duty is to make money. Failing this duty can leave directors and officers open to being sued by shareholders. [The law] dedicates the corporation to the pursuit of its own self-interest (and equates corporate self-interest with shareholder self-interest). No mention is made of responsibility to the public interest. . . . Corporate law thus casts ethical and social concerns as irrelevant, or as stumbling blocks to the corporation's fundamental mandate.[14]

Does this mean that the big corporations that now embrace social responsibility—Pfizer, Ford, Goodyear, BP, to name just a few—are outlaws? Not exactly. Recall Milton Friedman's belief that social responsibility can be tolerated when in the service of corporate self-interest. On this point, the law again agrees with him.

Hutton v. West Cork Railway Company, a case from nineteenth-century England, established the relevant principle. One company, Bandon, had bought another, West Cork Railway. When West Cork announced a bonus of several thousand pounds to its soon-to-be redundant directors, Bandon's shareholders took the railway to court. The money from which the bonus would be drawn now belonged to them, they argued, and it could not be used to benefit others, i.e., the West Cork directors. Lord Bowen, one of the judges who heard the case, agreed with their claim, but he also insisted that corporate generosity was, in some cases, permissible under the law. "Take this sort of instance," he wrote. "A railway company, or the directors of the company, might send down all the porters at a railway station to have tea in the country at the expense of the company. Why should they not?" After all, Lord Bowen observed, the company might itself derive considerable benefit from such generosity in light of the fact that "a company which always treated its employés with Draconian severity, and never allowed them a single inch more than the strict letter of the bond, would soon find itself deserted." Hence, Lord Bowen concluded,

The law does not say that there are to be no cakes and ale, but there are to be no cakes and ale except such as are required for the benefit of the company . . . charity has no business to sit at boards of direc-

tors *qua* charity. There is, however, a kind of charitable dealing
which is for the interest of those who practise it, and to that extent
and in that garb (I admit not a very philanthropic garb) charity may
sit at the board, but for no other purpose.[15]

Today, the law remains the same: charitable dealing must be in the
interest of those who practice it—the corporation and its shareholders. "While allowing directors to give consideration to the interests of
others," states the American Bar Association, "[the law] compel[s]
them to find some reasonable relationship to the long-term interests
of shareholders when so doing."[16] The rule is now thoroughly
entrenched within the corporation's culture, so it is a rare case when
shareholders must resort to the courts to enforce it, as the Dodge
brothers had to do in 1916. As Burson-Marsteller head Chris
Komisarjevsky put it, "The expectations of investors, whether they're
institutional or individual, will always make sure that the driving force
is to make sure that we produce the profits, we produce the returns
and therefore give back to the investors. So there's rarely going to be
a situation where philanthropy or corporate giving will undermine
the corporate performance from a financial perspective."[17]

The rule that corporations exist solely to maximize returns to
their shareholders is "the law of the land," to quote business journalist
Marjorie Kelly, "universally accepted as a kind of divine, unchallenge-
able truth."[18] And, today, even the most inspired leaders of the corporate social responsibility movement obey it.

On April 22, 1999, Earth Day, at the UN Building in New York City, Sir
John Browne, head of BP, the world's second largest oil company and
the largest single supplier of oil and gas in the United States, received an
award. After just four years at the helm, Browne had restored the once
great company to its former glory. The queen of England had knighted
him for his efforts, business chiefs had lionized him, and Wall Street

had responded to his success with record prices for BP shares. But Browne was not being honored for this spectacular corporate turn-around. Surprisingly, Browne, leader of an industry vilified by environmentalists, was at the United Nations to collect an award for environmental leadership— *"astonishing"* leadership, according to Denis Hayes, whose coalition of environmental groups, Earth Day Network, had joined with the United Nations to bestow this honor.[19]

In 1998, Browne acknowledged that greenhouse-gas emissions might cause global warming, a heretical admission for an oil industry executive. He then endorsed the Kyoto Protocol on reducing greenhouse-gas emissions, pulled out of the oil-led Global Climate Coalition, which had spent tens of millions of dollars lobbying against the protocol, and promised that his own company would exceed, not just meet, the Kyoto targets. By 1999, Browne had "left the church of the oil industry," as he puts it (paraphrasing a fellow oilman's accusation), to become the world's first "green" oil titan.[20]

Browne, who is slight in stature and always impeccably groomed, is no macho oilman. He regularly attends the opera and ballet, collects pre-Columbian art, and is a top Cambridge University physics graduate. He speaks with a quiet but authoritative voice and delivers eloquent and inspirational speeches, like the one he gave at the United Nations upon receiving his award. "We meet at an historic moment, on the edge of a new century," he began his speech.

There is a sense of trepidation about the new century and, of course, many of the fears are raised by the unresolved challenges to the natural environment. . . . I know there is a view that business is simply the cause of many of the environmental problems, but I hope we're moving beyond that argument. . . . We have to help people transcend the harsh trade off which says—you can have economic growth and pollution . . . or you can have a clean environment but no growth. That's an unacceptable trade off.[21]

When he made this speech in 1999, many industry insiders still considered Browne an eccentric, a maverick. Just a year later he was "Mr. Oil and Gas in the World Today," according to Calgary oilman Jim Gray, who chaired the World Petroleum Conference 2000 and invited Browne to be its keynote speaker. In that short time Browne's green agenda had become the industry's agenda, embraced by Shell Oil and other big players. "Ethical issues are starting to become big issues in terms of social responsibility," Jim Gray explained. "Sir John Browne has said if you're not with it in these areas, you're a dinosaur, you're living yesterday. Well, we're living tomorrow."[22]

"Can business be about more than profits?" asks a Browne-inspired BP ad. "We think so." Sir John Browne's deep convictions, along with the company's green brand image, imply a promise that the company's environmental values are more than just talk. They are at least on a par with profits, positioned alongside them on a "multiple bottom" (a favorite metaphor of Browne's) rather than subordinate to the single bottom line of financial performance. Browne's vision implies that corporations, and those who run them, can genuinely care about values other than profit. Yet that is exactly what the law forbids, at least when such caring might diminish profitability. The real question, then, is whether a business can be about *less* than profits? Can BP be not just Beyond Petroleum—the clever wordplay used in its ad campaigns—but also Beyond Profit? Can it sacrifice its own interests and those of its shareholders to realize environmental and social goals?

Not surprisingly, Milton Friedman said "no" when I asked him how far John Browne could go with his green convictions. "You take that case insofar as he wants to pursue those environmental interests," he said. "He can do it with his own money. If he pursues those environmental interests in such a way as to run the corporation less effectively for its stockholders, then I think he's being immoral. He's an employee of the stockholders, however elevated his position may appear to be. As such, he has a very strong moral responsibility to them."[23]

Norma Kassi hopes Friedman is wrong. She wants Browne to do the right thing for the environment, even if that is not the best thing for his company. And, for her, the question of what Browne should or might do is more than academic—it is a matter of survival.

Norma Kassi recently traveled to London, England, from Old Crow, a remote Yukon village sixty miles north of the Arctic Circle, to attend BP's annual general meeting. She went there for one purpose: to try to stop the company from "coming to the Arctic to destroy us." Kassi is a member of the Gwich'in Nation, an Arctic aboriginal people whose seventeen villages, built thousands of years ago, straddle the U.S.-Canadian border. She believes that drilling on the Arctic Slope's coastal plain will wipe out the Porcupine caribou herd and, along with it, her people's twenty-thousand-year-old way of life.[24]

Huge oil and natural gas reserves may sit just below the coastal plain, and huge profits could await the companies granted the right to explore and drill there. BP is a likely candidate for that privilege if the U.S. government ends its moratorium on drilling in the area.[25] The company is already the major player in the region, with a large presence at nearby Prudhoe Bay, one of the world's biggest oil-drilling sites (astronauts report being able to see it from space at night, when it is lit up). The coastal plain also provides calving grounds for the Porcupine caribou herd. Each spring the herd treks four hundred miles across mountains, rivers, and tundra, past Gwich'in villages strategically located along the caribou's trail, so that the pregnant cows can give birth to their young on the coastal plain. The Gwich'in rely on the Porcupine herd for their survival, as they have for thousands of years. And it's not just food and clothing, but also their cultural and spiritual lives, that depend upon the herd's yearly migration.

Kassi recalls how her family would pack up its dogsled each spring and head to the tundra to wait for the caribou. They would live in a tent atop the packed ice, with a spruce-bough floor and a wood-burning stove to keep them warm, and her mother would keep watch for the caribou from a hole in the tent door. "Sometimes she'd go outside and she'd ask the ravens, 'Where are the caribou?' " recalls Kassi. "I'd watch her and I'd watch her face. And I'd know when the caribou were coming close." Kassi's grandfather and the other hunters would travel to the back of the herd to hunt the older bulls, leaving alone the pregnant cows at the front. When the hunters returned to camp, sometimes three or four days later, the Gwich'in would feast, and they would watch, reverentially, as the caribou passed by on their way to the coastal plain. "It's a very sacred time, it's a quiet time," says Kassi. "You have to give thanks to the caribou. And we give special thanks to the cows. We pray for them, especially the women, we can connect with them, we can feel what they feel as women and as mothers."[26]

The Gwich'in say that drilling on the coastal plain will destroy the Porcupine herd, and their way of life along with it.

BP has played down their concerns. "Exploration and production, done to the highest standards, has minimal environmental impact and takes place in harmony with healthy wildlife populations," says John Gore, one of the company's top officials.[27] And contrary to the caribou being harmed by development, they could thrive on it, according to the company's Web site: "The number of caribou in the Central Arctic herd spending a portion of the year in the Prudhoe Bay area has increased more than six-fold since development began in the mid-'70s."[28] Many scientists, however, agree with the Gwich'in that coastal plain development would very likely result in drastic and irreversible consequences for the Gwich'in and the Porcupine caribou. The caribou would be forced into the adjacent mountains, they say, where newborn calves would be killed by predators and starvation. The herd would thus be greatly diminished (a conclusion scientists have reached despite the more positive fate of the Central Arctic herd, which they say is irrelevant to assessing drilling's impact on the Porcupine herd). So hundreds of scientists have joined environmentalists, some U.S. politicians, the Canadian government, and the Gwich'in to call for application of the precautionary principle—an international legal principle that enjoins activities that could irreversibly harm people or the environment, even if there is no definitive proof the harm will occur—to forbid exploration and drilling on the coastal plain.[29]

Sir John Browne is one of the leading advocates of the precautionary principle in the world today. When other oil industry leaders rejected the Kyoto Protocol, citing absence of proof that greenhouse-gas emissions cause global warming, Browne invoked the precautionary principle to defend it. Despite the lack of proof, he said, "it would be dangerous to ignore the mounting evidence and concern [over global warming and greenhouse gases] . . . there is a need to take precautionary action now," which is what he did by endorsing the protocol and committing his company to respect its standards.[30] Yet Browne seems unwilling to take precautionary action on the coastal plain. He has rejected calls to refrain from drilling, despite the strong scientific evidence that disaster could strike the Gwich'in and the caribou if drilling proceeds.[31]

John Browne may be a maverick. He may even be one of the most outspoken advocates of social responsibility in big business today. But he's neither a radical nor an outlaw. He well understands the corporate canon that social and environmental values are not ends in themselves but strategic resources to enhance business performance. "This is not a sudden discovery of moral virtue or a sense of guilt about past errors," he says of his green agenda. "It is about long-term self-interest—enlightened, I hope, but self-interest nonetheless." BP's social responsibility, he says, is "good business"; "driven by practical commercial reality" and "hard-headed business logic." The company's good deeds are "in our direct business interest," "not acts of charity but of what could be called enlightened self-interest," "coldly realistic." "The fundamental test for any company," says Browne, "is performance. That is the imperative."[32]

By implication, social responsibility is not appropriate when it could undermine a company's performance. That is why BP *must* drill on the coastal plain if that is the most beneficial—i.e., profitable—long-term course for the company, when all factors are considered. Concerns about destroying a caribou herd, the Arctic environment, or an entire aboriginal people have no place—at least not as ends in themselves—in the corporation's decision-making lexicon. The costs to the company of not drilling could be huge. The benefits—customer goodwill or positive publicity—would likely be relatively small by comparison. So if the coastal plain is opened to drilling, BP will surely be there, as long as drilling is profitable. Browne really has no choice in the matter. Regardless of how deep and sincere his personal commitment to the environment is, as a CEO Browne must put his company and its shareholders' interests above all others.

Unlike a refusal to drill on the coastal plain, BP's green initiatives to date have been relatively inexpensive, designed to enhance performance and yield short- and long-term benefits that outweigh their costs. BP met its commitment to implement the Kyoto Protocol's standards, for example, at no net cost to itself.[33] Other BP programs, such as solar-powered gas stations, school programs, and urban clean air initiatives have similarly helped the company bolster its green image at little cost. The benefits to BP of these initiatives are obvious. As Browne says, they create a corporate image that serves as a source of competitive advantage over other companies, giving consumers of oil and gas a greener alternative. "Performance is enhanced," he says, "when a company is aligned with the interests and wishes of its consumers. . . . The reputation of a company in the widest sense has a direct impact on its commercial fortunes."[34]

There is, however, another, longer-term benefit that BP seeks to gain from its green image. Plenty of oil and gas remains in the ground, and Browne knows that there is still much money to be made by getting it out. Yet consumers could be driven away from oil and gas by environmental concerns and toward alternative forms of energy. Browne says that he believes "it is possible to explore for, produce, refine, distribute and use hydrocarbons in ways which don't damage the environment," that "you can have a powerful car, which is great to drive" and still not damage the environment. He wants consumers to believe that too. Despite the company's claim to be "beyond petroleum" and its involvement with solar energy and other alternatives, the primary goal behind Browne's green agenda, it would appear, is to maintain consumer demand for petrochemicals:

> The days when our business had a captive market for oil are probably ending. There are new sources of supply in almost every part of the energy market. Even in transportation it is likely that advances in the technology of fuel cells will soon give us cars with different engines. So we have to compete to ensure that oil remains a fuel of choice.[35]

More generally, for Browne and all other big business leaders, social and environmental goals are, and must be, strategies to advance the interests of their companies and shareholders; they can never legitimately be pursued as ends in themselves. That may seem an unduly narrow view, especially when one considers the concrete social and environmental benefits corporate initiatives could foster, but no one among leaders of publicly traded companies is prepared, or legally authorized, to take corporate social responsibility any further.

Hank McKinnell, the CEO of Pfizer, who says he wants his company to do more good for more people than any other company in the world, concedes that corporate self-interest is, and must be, the primary motivation behind his company's good deeds. "There's a very direct benefit [to Pfizer]," McKinnell says of the company's security system at the Flushing Avenue subway station. "In order to attract the best colleagues, we need to be a safe place to work, a good place to work, people need to be able to use the subways in order to get to work. So if we have a subway station that people are fearful of passing through, clearly that's a disincentive to be able to hire the best employees." The Pfizer-sponsored school in the neighborhood, and a host of other education projects Pfizer has initiated and supported, are also linked to "the success of our own enterprise," McKinnell says. "Unless we have a large pool of candidates who are trained in our business and the sciences and mathematics, we won't succeed in our business."[36]

McKinnell similarly justifies Pfizer's free drug programs as beneficial to the company. He emphasized that they cost the company little—"the marginal cost of our drugs is very low, so if we give away a drug to somebody who wouldn't otherwise buy it, the profit impact of that action on us is just about zero." Yet the benefits to Pfizer are substantial. The programs generate goodwill among doctors, the primary dispensers of Pfizer products; they help them "realize that we're there working with them to help solve their problems." They also help Pfizer with its employees, as morale, productivity, and the attraction and retention of good workers all depend upon employees' feeling good about their company. McKinnell says, "It's important to the people who work here that we be seen as accomplishing both high profits and growth but at the same time contributing to society's well-being. . . . It makes our colleagues extremely proud that we are able to provide a necessary drug to somebody who otherwise wouldn't have access."[37]

Finally, Pfizer can write off the free drugs as charitable donations and thus save itself money at tax time. It is hard to get precise numbers on how much Pfizer saves, and Hank McKinnell was not about to disclose them. But the Nobel Prize–winning organization Doctors Without Borders estimates that U.S. taxpayers spend four times as much money to donate fluconazole to South Africa through tax benefits to drug companies as they would to send the drugs to South Africans through aid programs (assuming companies sold the drugs to governments at reduced prices).[38]

"Our primary mission," says McKinnell, "is to sustain the enterprise, and that, of course, requires profit." The free drug programs do not impede that mission, they help it—a classic case of doing well by doing good. "I have the ability to do both well for shareholders and to do a lot of good in many, many parts of the world," McKinnell claims. "We can meet the needs of both our shareholders and the world's poor." But if Pfizer's *primary* mission is to sustain the enterprise—to promote its own interests—how far can McKinnell really go toward meeting the needs of the world's poor? Not very far, since, following his own logic, which is also the corporation's, only those free drug programs that benefit the company will be pursued, and those that no longer benefit the company will be discontinued.[39]

That is why when Doctors Without Borders set up its trachoma treatment program in the African country of Mali, it said "No, thank you" to Pfizer's offer of free Zithromax. Instead it imported, and paid for, a generic version of the drug. Thus, the organization's Rachel Cohen explained, "If Pfizer decides one day to just leave the country or do away with its program or cut back for some reason . . . we can ensure that that drug remains available for the people that need it in the country." Other free drug programs are also vulnerable to the risk of abandonment by pharmaceutical corporations. "If shareholders' priorities change, if the media spotlight no longer shines on AIDS in Africa," points out Cohen, "what are these people going to do if Pfizer just simply takes away, for example, its Diflucan or fluconazole donation program?"[40]

Unreliability of support is not the only, or even the greatest, limita-

tion on drug companies' ability to help the world's poor. More fundamental are the demands of the corporate form itself—Pfizer and its
shareholders make more money from drugs that treat baldness and
impotence than they would from drugs to treat diseases, such as malaria
and tuberculosis, that are leading causes of death in the developing
world. Pfizer and other pharmaceutical companies likely have the know-
how and the physical capacity to place more emphasis on developing
and making drugs to fight these killer diseases. Though such drugs
would do immense good for the world and could save millions of lives
every year, the costs to any company that developed them would almost
certainly outweigh the benefits. That's because, says Cohen, the 80 percent of the world's population that lives in developing countries represents only 20 percent of the global market for drugs. (The entire African
continent represents only 1.3 percent of the world market.) Conversely,
the 20 percent of the world's population who live in North America,
Europe, and Japan constitute 80 percent of the drug market.
Predictably, of the 1,400 new drugs developed between 1975 and 1999,
only 13 were designed to treat or prevent tropical diseases and 3 to treat
tuberculosis. In the year 2000, no drugs were being developed to treat
tuberculosis, compared to 8 for impotence or erectile dysfunction and 7
for baldness. Developing drugs to deal with personality disorders in family pets seems to have a higher priority than controlling diseases that kill
millions of human beings each year.[41]

Whatever the rhetoric about social responsibility and stakeholders, whatever the good sentiments and intentions of people like Hank
McKinnell who run drug companies, whatever good works programs
the companies have in place, and however many people could be
saved from horrible deaths, for-profit corporations make drugs for
profit. That's the bottom line.

Thus, there may have been a lesson in Tom Kline's attempt, ultimately unsuccessful, to demonstrate how Pfizer's security system at
the Flushing Avenue subway station works. When he pushed the but-

ton on the yellow call box and said "Hello, hello, Tom Kline speaking," there was no response. The same thing happened when he tried another box a few steps down the platform. Eventually he gave up and wondered out loud what had happened to the Pfizer security guard who was supposed to be on duty.

Corporate social responsibility is like the call boxes. It holds out promises of help, reassures people, and sometimes works. We should not, however, expect very much from it. A corporation can do good only to help itself do well, a profound limit on just how much good it can do. That is the reality faced by Norma Kassi and her Gwich'in Nation, who legitimately fear devastating consequences if drilling proceeds on the coastal plain, and by millions of people who die each year from diseases that remain untreatable because development of the necessary drugs is unprofitable. The benevolent rhetoric and deeds of socially responsible corporations create attractive corporate images, and likely do some good in the world. They do not, however, change the corporation's fundamental institutional nature: its unblinking commitment to its own self-interest.

The people who run corporations are, for the most part, good people, moral people. They are mothers and fathers, lovers and friends, and upstanding citizens in their communities, and they often have good and sometimes even idealistic intentions. Many of them want to make the world a better place and believe their jobs provide them the opportunity to do so. Despite their personal qualities and ambitions, however, their duty as corporate executives is clear: they must always put their corporation's best interests first and not act out of concern for anyone or anything else (unless the expression of such concern can somehow be justified as advancing the corporation's own interests). The money they manage and invest is not theirs. They can no sooner use it to heal the sick, save the environment, or feed the poor than they can to buy themselves villas in Tuscany.

Danny Schechter, an award-winning journalist who has worked for some large corporations, such as ABC and CNN, makes the point this way: "Corporations are made up of people, and people make decisions, and not all the people who work in corporations are bad people or are people who have a desire to exploit. . . . On the other hand, there's a logic to business—there's a logic to these corporations. Which means that certain values get emphasized while others get de-emphasized. And the ones that get emphasized are what's going to bring up the bottom line."[43]

The consequence of this dynamic, as moral philosopher Alisdair MacIntyre has observed, is that, for corporate executives, "moral concerns are at best marginal, engaging [them] *qua* citizen or *qua* consumer rather than *qua* executive." Few businesspeople would dispute that their decisions must be designed primarily to serve their company's and its owners' interests. As former Goodyear Tire CEO Sam Gibara said, "If you really did what you wanted to do that suits your personal thoughts and your personal priorities, you'd act differently. But as a CEO you cannot do that."[44]

Anita Roddick, however, believes it is exactly this kind of moral bifurcation between the worlds of business and life that has corrupted businesspeople and the corporations they run. As founder and head of the Body Shop, she was proud of the fact that she had avoided it— hence the title of her book, *Business as Unusual: The Triumph of Anita Roddick.* More recently, however, Roddick has sounded less triumphant. "The last three years have been the most painful time in my life," she said. "[I]t's been the loss of intimacy, it has been a loss of being heard. . . . It is an absolute lesson in humility."[45]

From humble beginnings as a soap maker in her kitchen to head of the Body Shop and one of the world's most successful businesswomen, Roddick always refused to separate her personal values from her business. That's what made her business unusual. "I just want an extension of my home, I want to be able to bring my heart to the workplace," she says. "I've always reflected the company as to my behaviour, it's always been my alter ego." The Body Shop became a platform for Roddick's progressive worldview. "The whole purpose of business if you're accumulating profits is to give it away, give the bloody stuff away," she says. "Do the best you can in the community. Just be a beacon in the community." Program after program was put into place, supporting cause after cause—human rights, the environment, social justice, women's rights.[46]

In 1982, an initial public offering of shares in the Body Shop was floated on the London Stock Exchange. Roddick needed the money to grow, and going public was the best way to raise it. By the mid-1990s, however, the Body Shop, under pressure from investors, had to overhaul its management and adopt a new business plan. Patrick Gournay was brought in to head the company, and it was reorganized in ways designed to promote performance and efficiency. Roddick dutifully reported at the time that the changes would leave the company's progressive values and actions untouched—"they are now well embedded and institutionalized in everything we do," she said[47]—but now looks back on the initial stock floatation (which inevitably invited investor scrutiny) as a "pact with the Devil." "You go onto the stock market," she says, "and the imperative is to grow—and by a small group of people's standards, financial investors who are gamblers . . . like in a casino."[48]

Things came to a head when, in the wake of Seattle's protest against the World Trade Organization, Roddick, who remained cochair of the company, wanted the Body Shop to take a stance against the WTO. Here was an opportunity for her to do what she had always done: use her business as a platform for her values. But the company refused. "I wanted every shop to challenge the WTO," she said. "And they won't do that." Roddick then realized that her once maverick, eccentric, unusual Body Shop had become all too usual. She hoped to regain control of the company, she said—"We will go private again, I'm sure"—as she believes that is the only way she, and corporate social responsibility, can once again triumph.[49]

Soon after Roddick spoke with us, the Body Shop was put up for sale, a move made necessary by plummeting profits and declining share prices. Though she hoped that any potential buyer would share her social values, the company made it clear that Roddick and her husband, Gordon, who together own 24 percent of the company (cofounder Ian McGlinn owns a similar share), were open to all offers. As a company spokesperson said, "They are very aware of their legal, moral and financial responsibilities to all shareholders equally." A Mexican company, Group Omnilife, was poised to buy the company for £290 million, a deal that would have made the Roddicks £43 million, but failed to secure the necessary financing. The company was taken off the sales block after that deal fell through and reorganized to improve performance. The Roddicks stepped down from their cochair positions, and Anita's role in the company was diminished to consultant, on a two-year, 55-to-80-day-per-year contract. And, as new executive chairman Adrian Bellamy commented, most likely to assure investors that Roddick's corporate sensibility was no longer as much a factor at the Body Shop: "We believe in social responsibility but we are very hard-nosed about profit. We know that success is measured by the bottom line."[50]

Roddick's story illustrates how an executive's moral concerns and altruistic desires must ultimately succumb to her corporation's overriding goals. That is not the worst of it, however. Corporations and the culture they create do more than just stifle good deeds—they nurture, and often demand, bad ones.

Marc Barry knows this all too well, but he is not bothered by it.

Marc Barry, a competitive intelligence expert ("Essentially I'm a spy," he says), likes to think of himself as a good date. "I like to be able to go out and have a nice dinner with someone," he says. "There's so much trickery and deception in my job that I don't really want it in my private life." At work, Barry says, he is a predator engaged in morally dubious tasks. Corporations hire him to get information from other corporations: trade secrets, marketing plans, or whatever else might be useful to them. In his work, he lies, deceives, exploits, and cheats. He has set up a phony recruiting firm, he says, complete with pictures of his phony family on the desk, and called executives from a competitor's firm to offer them better jobs. "When the executive shows up," he boasts, "he doesn't realize . . . I'm actually debriefing him on behalf of a competitor . . . it's all just a big elaborate ruse to glean competitive information from him." Barry has also posed as a venture capitalist to a young inventor to steal, on behalf of a large multinational corporation client, the inventor's technique for transmitting video over a wireless phone. For Barry, a regular day at the office is filled with venal actions and moral turpitude.[51]

Yet Barry believes he is a decent person because he can draw the line at his personal life. "I don't want that in my personal life," he says. "I'm looking for something a little bit purer." His work's absence of moral concern does not affect his personal life (though he admits that "there are some women walking the world that will tell you that I haven't quite made that distinction yet"), and his life's moral concerns do not affect his work. "I can go and pick the pocket of some executive at a trade show in Miami," he says, "so badly that I know his company's going to be out of business in six months, and I can go home and sleep like a baby, and it's no big deal, you know, because it's business." "The way you live with yourself," he says, "[is] to have a very compartmentalized life."[52]

Barry also takes comfort from the fact that he is no more morally wanting than the top executives and CEOs who hire him (he says he's worked for more than a quarter of the Fortune 500 companies). "If you're a CEO," says Barry, "do you think your shareholders really care whether you're Billy Buttercup or not? Do you think that they really would prefer you to be a nice guy over having money in their pocket? I don't think so. I think people want money. That's the bottom line." Greed and moral indifference define the corporate world's culture, which is why, he says, his business is booming. As pressure builds on CEOs to increase shareholder value, corporations are doing anything and everything they can to be competitive, he says. "Anybody who knows me knows that I have no problem using trickery or deception to glean intelligence information," he says. And "there's a big 'nudge-nudge, wink-wink'" going on when CEOs who hire him ask him to follow ethical rules. "I have a nickname, as being 'the kite,' " he says. "You can fly the kite out there, to collect whatever information you want, and if the storm comes on the horizon in the form of, say, a lawsuit or some sort of criminal justice prosecution or something, then you can just cut the string and walk away."[53]

Barry's morally compartmentalized life is exactly what Anita Roddick tried, unsuccessfully, to avoid at the Body Shop. She and Barry likely would not be friends or dinner companions. The two do have one thing in common, however—a view of the corporate world as amoral. Barry accepts it, Roddick regrets it, but both believe it to be true. Roddick blames the "religion of maximizing profits" for business's amorality, for forcing otherwise decent people to do indecent things: "Because it has to maximize its profits . . . everything is legitimate in the pursuit of that goal, everything. . . . So using child labor or sweatshop labor or despoiling the environment . . . is legitimate in the maximizing of profit. It's legitimate to fire fifteen thousand people to maximize profits, keep the communities just in such pain."

The managers who do these things are not monsters, Roddick says. They may be kind and caring people, loving parents and friends. Yet, as philosopher Alisdair MacIntyre observed—and Barry lives—they compartmentalize their lives. They are allowed, often compelled, by the corporation's culture to disassociate themselves from their own values—the corporation, according to Roddick, "stops people from having a sense of empathy with the human condition"; it "separate[s] us from who we are. . . ." "The language of business is not the language of the soul or the language of humanity," she says. "It's a language of indifference; it's a language of separation, of secrecy, of hierarchy." It "is fashioning a schizophrenia in many of us."[54]

Psychology, as Roddick's last comment suggests, may provide a better account of business executives' dual moral lives than either law or economics. That is why we asked Dr. Robert Hare, a psychologist and internationally renowned expert on psychopathy, for his views on the subject. He told us that many of the attitudes people adopt and the actions they execute when acting as corporate operatives can be characterized as psychopathic. You try "to destroy your competitors, or you want to beat them one way or another," said Hare, echoing Roddick and Barry, "and you're not particularly concerned with what happens to the general public as long as they're buying your product." Yet, despite the fact that executives must often manipulate and harm others in pursuit of their corporation's objectives, Hare insists they are not psychopaths. That is because they *can* function normally outside the corporation—"they go home, they have a warm and loving relationship with their families, and they love their children, they love their wife, and in fact their friends are friends rather than things to be used." Businesspeople should therefore take some comfort from their ability to compartmentalize the contradictory moral demands of their corporate and noncorporate lives, for it is precisely this "schizophrenia," as Roddick calls it, that saves them from becoming psychopaths.[55]

The corporation itself may not so easily escape the psychopath diagnosis, however. Unlike the human beings who inhabit it, the corporation is *singularly* self-interested and unable to feel genuine concern for others in any context. Not surprisingly, then, when we asked Dr. Hare to apply his diagnostic checklist of psychopathic traits (italicized below) to the corporation's institutional character, he found there was a close match. The corporation is *irresponsible,* Dr. Hare said, because "in an attempt to satisfy the corporate goal, everybody else is put at risk." Corporations try to *"manipulate* everything, including public opinion," and they are *grandiose,* always insisting "that we're number one, we're the best." A *lack of empathy* and *asocial tendencies* are also key characteristics of the corporation, says Hare—"their behavior indicates they don't really concern themselves with their victims"; and corporations often *refuse to accept responsibility for their own actions* and are *unable to feel remorse:* "if [corporations] get caught [breaking the law], they pay big fines and they . . . continue doing what they did before anyway. And in fact in many cases the fines and the penalties paid by the organization are trivial compared to the profits that they rake in."[56]

Finally, according to Dr. Hare, corporations relate to others *superficially*—"their whole goal is to present themselves to the public in a way that is appealing to the public [but] in fact may not be representative of what th[e] organization is really like." Human psychopaths are notorious for their ability to use charm as a mask to hide their dangerously self-obsessed personalities. For corporations, social responsibility may play the same role. Through it they can present themselves as compassionate and concerned about others when, in fact, they lack the ability to care about anyone or anything but themselves.[57]

Take the large and well-known energy company that once was a paragon of social responsibility and corporate philanthropy. Each year the company produced a Corporate Responsibility Annual Report; the most recent one, unfortunately its last, vowed to cut greenhouse-gas emissions and support multilateral agreements to help stop climate change. The company pledged further to put human rights, the environment, health and safety issues, biodiversity, indigenous rights, and transparency at the core of its business operations, and it created a well-staffed corporate social responsibility task force to monitor and implement its social responsibility programs. The company boasted of its development of alternative energy sources and the fact it had helped start the Business Council for Sustainable Energy. It apologized for a 29,000-barrel oil spill in South America, promised it would never happen again, and reported that it had formed partnerships with environmental NGOs to help monitor its operations. It described the generous support it had provided communities in the cities where it operated, funding arts organizations, museums, educational institutions, environmental groups, and various causes throughout the world. The company, which was consistently ranked as one of the best places to work in America, strongly promoted diversity in the workplace. "We believe," said the report, "that corporate leadership should set the example for community service."[58]

Unfortunately, this paragon of corporate social responsibility, Enron, was unable to continue its good works after it collapsed under the weight of its executives' greed, hubris, and criminality. Enron's story shows just how wide a gap can exist between a company's cleverly crafted do-gooder image and its actual operations and suggests, at a minimum, that skepticism about corporate social responsibility is well warranted.

There is, however, a larger lesson to be drawn from Enron's demise than the importance of being skeptical about corporate social responsibility. Though the company is now notorious for its arrogance and ethically challenged executives, the underlying reasons for its collapse can be traced to characteristics common to all corporations: obsession with profits and share prices, greed, lack of concern for others, and a penchant for breaking legal rules. These traits are, in turn, rooted in an institutional culture, the corporation's, that valorizes self-interest and invalidates moral concern. No doubt Enron took such characteristics to their limits—indeed, to the point of self-destruction—and the company is now notorious for that. It was not, however, unusual for the fact it had those characteristics in the first place. Rather, Enron's collapse is best understood as showing what can happen when the characteristics we normally accept and take for granted in a corporation are pushed to the extreme. It was not, in other words, a "very isolated incident," as Pfizer's Hank McKinnell described it and as many commentators seem to believe, but rather a symptom of the corporation's flawed institutional character.[59]

3

The Externalizing Machine

As a psychopathic creature, the corporation can neither recognize nor act upon moral reasons to refrain from harming others. Nothing in its legal makeup limits what it can do to others in pursuit of its selfish ends, and it is compelled to cause harm when the benefits of doing so outweigh the costs. Only pragmatic concern for its own interests and the laws of the land constrain the corporation's predatory instincts, and often that is not enough to stop it from destroying lives, damaging communities, and endangering the planet as a whole. Enron's implosion, and the corporate scandals that followed, were, ironically, violations of corporations' own self-interest, as it was shareholders, the very people—indeed, the only people—corporations are legally obliged to serve, who were chief among its victims. Far less exceptional in the world of the corporation are the routine and regular harms caused to *others*—workers, consumers, communities, the environment—by corporations' psychopathic tendencies. These tend to be viewed as inevitable and acceptable consequences of corporate activity—"externalities" in the coolly technical jargon of economics.

"An externality," says economist Milton Friedman, "is the effect of a transaction . . . on a third party who has not consented to or played any role in the carrying out of that transaction." All the bad things that happen to people and the environment as a result of corporations' relentless and legally compelled pursuit of self-interest are thus neatly categorized by economists as externalities—literally, other people's problems.[1] Friedman cites as a mundane example the case of a person whose shirt is dirtied by the smoke emissions from a power plant. That person pays a price—the cost of cleaning the dirty shirt and the inconvenience of wearing it—that flows directly from the power plant's operations. The corporation that owns the power plant, in turn, gains benefits by saving money through not building higher smokestacks, installing better filters, finding a less populated location in which to operate, or taking other costly measures that might avoid dirtying people's shirts.[2]

Beyond the dirty shirt example, however, corporate externalities have "enormous effects on the world at large," as Friedman points out.[3] Though they can be positive—jobs are created and useful products developed by corporations in pursuit of their self-interest—it is no exaggeration to say that the corporation's built-in compulsion to externalize its costs is at the root of many of the world's social and environmental ills. That makes the corporation a profoundly dangerous institution, as Patricia Anderson painfully learned.

In the dark early hours of Christmas Day 1993, Patricia Anderson was driving home from midnight mass, her four children in the backseat of her 1979 Chevrolet Malibu car, the youngest six years old and the eldest fifteen. She stopped at a red light, and as she waited for it to change, a car slammed into the back of her car, causing it to burst into flames. Anderson and her children suffered horrible and disfiguring second- and third-degree burns (the driver of the other car, who was drunk at the time, got away with minor injuries). Three of the children were burned over 60 percent of their bodies, and one of them had to have her hand amputated. Anderson, though thankful no one was killed—"I just thank God that me and my kids survived," she said—sued General Motors, blaming the company for the explosion and fire. The fuel tank on her Malibu, her lawyers argued, had been insufficiently protected from the impact of the collision.[4]

After a lengthy trial the jury found that GM had dangerously positioned the fuel tank to save costs, and Los Angeles Superior Court Judge Ernest G. Williams later upheld its verdict (though he reduced the damages). "The court finds that clear and convincing evidence demonstrated that defendants' fuel tank was placed behind the axle on automobiles of the make and model here in order to maximize profits—to the disregard of public safety," he wrote, which put GM in breach of applicable laws. The fuel tank on Ms. Anderson's 1979 Malibu was eleven inches from the rear bumper. The fuel tank on the previous year's Malibu, a larger vehicle, had been twenty inches from the rear bumper. A 1969 directive at the company had recommended fuel tanks be at least seventeen inches from the rear bumper. Also, on the 1979 model there was no metal brace to separate the fuel tank from the rear of the car, a standard feature on the previous year's model.[5]

The evidence in the trial showed that General Motors had been aware of the possibility of fuel-fed fires when it had designed the Malibu and some of its other models as well. Six fuel-fed fire suits had been filed against the company in the late 1960s, twenty-five more in the early 1970s, and in May 1972, a GM analyst predicted that there would be another sixty by the mid-1970s. On June 6, 1973, around the time GM began planning the new smaller Malibu that Patricia Anderson was driving, GM management asked an engineer from the company's Advance Design department, Edward C. Ivey, to analyze fuel-fed fires in GM vehicles. He submitted his report, "Value Analysis of Auto Fuel Fed Fire Related Fatalities," shortly thereafter.[6]

In the report, Ivey multiplied the five hundred fuel-fed fire fatalities that occurred each year in GM vehicles by $200,000, his estimate of the cost to GM in legal damages for each potential fatality, and then divided that figure by 41 million, the number of GM vehicles operating on U.S. highways at the time. He concluded that each fuel-fed fatality cost GM $2.40 per automobile. The calculation appeared like this in the memorandum:

$$\frac{500 \text{ fatalities} \times \$200,000/\text{fatality}}{41,000,000 \text{ automobiles}} = \$2.40/\text{automobile}$$

The cost to General Motors of ensuring that fuel tanks did not explode in crashes, estimated by the company to be $8.59 per automobile, meant the company could save $6.19 ($8.59 minus $2.40) per automobile if it allowed people to die in fuel-fed fires rather than alter the design of vehicles to avoid such fires.[7]

The jury, as the judge indicated, found General Motors' behavior to be morally reprehensible and against applicable laws because it had put profits above public safety. It awarded Armstrong and her children (and a friend who had also been riding in the car) compensatory damages totaling $107 million and punitive damages of $4.8 billion, an unprecedented amount in a product-liability case. The total amount of the award was reduced to $1.2 billion in a later settlement, and General Motors filed an appeal of the lower court's decision in the California Court of Appeals.[8] In support of that appeal, the U.S. Chamber of Commerce, a representative and leading voice of big business, weighed in with a brief that reflected the general acceptance of cost-benefit analysis in corporate decision making. The jury's decision, according to the Chamber, was an "illegitimate result," one that is "deeply troubling" for its message "that manufacturers should not engage in cost-benefit analyses when they design products" and for its implication that cost-benefit analysis is "'despicable' in itself."

Cost-benefit analysis, the Chamber said, is a "hallmark of corporate good behavior"; "the logic underlying it is unimpeachable."[9]

The Chamber of Commerce is right that cost-benefit analyses are at the heart of corporate decision making. "The manufacturer [in a case like *Anderson v. General Motors*] may defend its decision by showing that the net increase in safety would be outweighed by the increase in cost and/or loss of utility of the alternative design,"[10] as one legal scholar has stated. The corporation's institutional makeup, its compulsion to serve its own financial interests above everything else, requires executives to make only those decisions that create greater benefits than costs for their corporations. Executives have no authority to consider what harmful effects a decision might have on other people, such as Patricia Anderson and her children, or upon the natural environment, unless those effects might have negative consequences for the corporation itself. "Once the executive is at work," according to philosopher Alisdair MacIntyre, "the aims of the . . . corporation must be taken as a given . . . tasks characteristically appear to him as merely technical. He has to calculate the most efficient, the most economical way of mobilizing the existing resources to produce the benefits . . . at the lowest costs. The weighing of costs against benefits is not just his business, it is business."[11]

Though Edward Ivey acknowledged in his report that "a human fatality is really beyond value, subjectively," that "it is really impossible to put a value on human life," he knew it was equally impossible for him *not* to put a value on a human life for the purpose of his analysis. As an analyst who had been asked to provide useful information for a corporate decision about the costs and benefits associated with placement of fuel tanks, his task was to value human life in "an objective matter," as he put it in the report, and that meant assessing its dollar value.[12]

The jury in Patricia Anderson's case, on the other hand, refused to operate by the corporation's institutional presumptions. It chose, instead, to judge General Motors from the standpoint of human moral decency. That was its mistake, according to the Chamber of Commerce in its submission to the California appeals court. Jurors, it says, are "not well-positioned to make accurate risk-utility assessments in cases involving complex engineering issues"; they are "sometimes led astray by the fact that they see before them the injured plaintiff"; they "tend to balk at any attempt to put a dollar value on human life"; they are too easily led by skillful plaintiff's lawyers to feel the "traditional public sense of the sanctity of life" and to view "risk-utility balancing as unspeakable callousness." The jurors in the case, in other words, mistakenly valued life for its own sake—for reasons of family, love, friendship, joy, and all the other intangibles that make life worthwhile. They were, the Chamber of Commerce implies, all too human in judging General Motors as inhuman and for refusing to turn life into a numbers game.[13]

General Motors is not unique, however. In all corporate decision making, life's intangible richness and fragility are made invisible by the abstract calculations of cost-benefit analyses, something Charles Kernaghan learned firsthand on a visit to a garbage dump in the Dominican Republic.

Following garbage trucks to dumps and then sifting through what they leave behind, is helpful, Kernaghan has found, for discovering the locations of factories in the new global economy, and for finding out what goes on inside of them. The factories, which Kernaghan monitors as director of the National Labor Committee, an organization with a mandate to stop American corporations from using sweatshop labor, are located in impoverished countries where labor is cheap and easy to exploit. Thanks to the greater flexibility corporations now have with liberalized international trade laws and new communications and transportation technologies, such factories do the bulk of light manufacturing for the industrialized West.[14] Their locations are a secret, closely guarded by the predominantly U.S. and European corporations that use them. "They hide these factories and sweatshops all over the world," says Kernaghan, and refuse requests for the factories' names and addresses "because they know it's easier to exploit teenagers behind locked metal gates, with armed guards, behind barbed wire."[15]

Kernaghan struck gold on one of his garbage dump forays when, in the Dominican Republic, he found copies of Nike's internal pricing documents in a box that had been left by one of the garbage trucks. The documents contained calculations every bit as chilling as those in Edward Ivey's report. Their purpose was to maximize the amount of profit that could be wrung out of the girls and young women who sew garments for Nike in developing-world sweatshops. Production of a shirt, to take one example, was broken down into twenty-two separate operations: five steps to cut the material, eleven steps to sew the garment, six steps to attach labels, hang tags, and put the shirt in a plastic bag, ready to be shipped. A time was allotted for each task, with units of ten thousandths of a second used for the breakdown. With all the units added together, the calculations demanded that each shirt take a maximum of 6.6 minutes to make—which translates into 8 cents' worth of labor for a shirt Nike sells in the United States for $22.99.[16]

"The science of exploitation" is how Kernaghan describes the pricing documents. Their cold calculations, he says, mask the suffering and misery of the work they demand. The typical factory Kernaghan visits in a country such as Honduras or Nicaragua, China or Bangladesh, is surrounded by barbed wire. Behind its locked doors, mainly young women workers are supervised by guards who beat and humiliate them on the slightest pretext and who fire them if a forced pregnancy test comes back positive. Each worker repeats the same action—sewing on a belt loop, stitching a sleeve—maybe two thousand times a day. They work under painfully bright lights, for twelve-to fourteen-hour shifts, in overheated factories, with too few bath-room breaks and restricted access to water (to reduce the need for more bathroom breaks), which is often foul and unfit for human consumption in any event. "They don't want you to have feelings, they don't want you to dream," says Kernaghan of the factories' owners. The young women "work to about twenty-five, at which point they're fired because they're used up. They're worn out. Their lives are already over. And the company has replaced them with another crop of young girls."[17]

Despite everything he has seen on his developing-world beat—and some of it is almost surreal, like the school bus marked "Southampton School District" that he saw on a Honduras highway taking kids to work at a factory to stitch garments for The Gap—Kernaghan still recalls that his most disconcerting moment was at the corner of Fifty-first Street and Madison Avenue in Manhattan in the mid-1990s. There the labor activist was huddled behind a building, hiding out with a frightened sixteen-year-old girl, a diminutive sweat-shop worker from Honduras named Wendy Díaz. Their eyes were trained on the doorway of the cardinal of St. Patrick's Cathedral's house across the street. The two were "frightened to death," says Kernaghan, of what was about to happen.[18]

Kernaghan and Díaz had first met at a food stand on the Pan-American Highway in Honduras, about one hundred yards from the factory where Díaz worked. Díaz and a group of young workers, aggrieved by the horrible working conditions at the factory, had contacted Kernaghan and asked to meet with him. Kernaghan agreed to meet the women at the food stand. Close to fifty of them showed up for the meeting. They found a spot behind a wooden fence where no one would see them—or so they thought. "All of a sudden, we're about to start the meeting," says Kernaghan, "when in walk three guys, very tough-looking guys." The women jumped to their feet, told Kernaghan the men were spies, and quickly began to disperse.

As they left, however, some of the women surreptitiously passed to Kernaghan, under a table, their pay stubs from the factory, which they had concealed in their hands. "I took my hand out after everyone had left," he recalls, "and in the palm of my hand was the face of Kathie Lee Gifford," imprinted on the pay stub to identify the label the women were working for. Now, for the first time, Kernaghan knew who reaped the benefit of the work done by Wendy Díaz and her coworkers at the Global Fashions factory. It was Wal-Mart, the megaretailer that sold Kathie Lee Gifford's line of clothing. So Kernaghan contacted Wal-Mart and Gifford and badgered them into meeting with him. The cardinal's home at St. Patrick's Cathedral was chosen as a neutral site for the meeting, which is what brought Kernaghan and Díaz to the corner of Fifty-first Street and Madison Avenue.[19]

The two arrived early, but they panicked before Gifford showed up, overcome by the prospect of an acrimonious encounter with a big celebrity. So they ran across the street to hide. When Gifford showed up for the meeting, flanked by an entourage of men in dark suits, they watched as she approached the entrance to the cardinal's residence. Eventually, they summoned enough courage to leave their hideout and join the meeting. Once there, Díaz told her story to Gifford: how she had worked, from the time she was thirteen years old, stitching together apparel for American companies in Honduran sweatshops—the thirteen-hour workdays, the pitiful wages, the humiliation and physical beatings by guards, how she would go to bed hungry each night after running home through dark streets with her friends, whistling and singing, in the hope rapists would leave them alone. "It was the most amazing thing I'd seen," says Kernaghan. "This powerful celebrity leans over and says, 'Wendy, please believe me, I didn't know these conditions existed. And now that I do, I'm going to work with you, I'm going to work with these other people and it'll never happen again.' "[20]

An agreement was drafted and signed with Kathie Lee Gifford that night, says Kernaghan. In it Gifford promised to stop using sweatshops, to pay decent wages to her workers, and to allow independent inspectors into her factories to ensure compliance with human rights and labor laws.

Yet Kernaghan is certain that Wal-Mart still uses sweatshop labor in developing countries, despite its initiation of third-party monitoring of its suppliers. He points out that Wal-Mart has roughly 4,400 supplier factories in China and that a large proportion of these are almost surely sweatshops. His claim is supported by a *Business Week* investigation that found that as late as 1999, Kathie Lee handbags were being made in a Chinese factory where employees worked fourteen-hour days, seven days a week, thirty days a month, for an average wage of 3 cents an hour, and were beaten, fined, and fired if they complained about it.[21] It is therefore not surprising that when Kernaghan signed the agreement with Gifford he was skeptical about whether it would result in significant change. He surmises that the corporate reaction to such a document would have been "What are you nuts? We're going to pay a living wage? That's not how the system works."[22]

Nor could it be how the system works. The corporation, like the psychopathic personality it resembles, is programmed to exploit others for profit. That is its only legitimate mandate. From that perspective, Wendy Díaz, and the millions of other workers across the globe who are driven by poverty and starvation to work in dreadful conditions for shocking wages, are not human *beings* so much as human *resources*. To the morally blind corporation, they are tools to generate as much profit as possible. And "the tool can be treated just like a piece of metal—you use it if you want, you throw it away if you don't want it," says Noam Chomsky. "If you can get human beings to become tools like that, it's more efficient by some measure of efficiency . . . a measure which is based on dehumanization. You have to dehumanize it. That's part of the system."[23]

That does not mean the people who run corporations are inhuman. Indeed, "these people would make great neighbors . . . when you meet with them in person they're quite decent," Kernaghan says of the corporate executives he has met on his beat. They must, however, serve the corporation's dehumanizing mandate. "The structure," says Kernaghan, "the whole system, just drags everybody with it." At the heart of that structure is a simple dynamic: a corporation "tends to be more profitable to the extent it can make other people pay the bills for its impact on society," as businessman Robert Monks describes it. "There's a terrible word that economists use for this called 'externalities.' "[24]

"The corporation," says Monks, "is an externalizing machine, in the same way that a shark is a killing machine. . . . There isn't any question of malevolence or of will; the enterprise has within it, and the shark has within it, those characteristics that enable it to do that for which it was designed." As a result, says Monks, the corporation is "potentially very, very damaging to society." Monks is not among the usual suspects of activists, radicals, and intellectuals who criticize the corporation. He is, to the contrary, one of America's most important and influential businessmen, a business insider who is as inside as an insider can be. Monks has helped reform and run numerous Fortune 500 companies and banks, served as adviser to Republican administrations, and ran twice as a Republican candidate for a Senate seat in Maine (both times unsuccessfully). He founded and heads an international investment firm. From his vantage point within the corporate world, Monks worries about what he sees in the modern business corporation.[25]

Monks recalls the moment he first realized what was wrong with the corporation. Lodged in a motel room in a small town where he had stopped for the night during an early-1970s election campaign, he awoke with a start in the middle of the night, his eyes aflame with irritation. When he got up to look out the window, he was shocked by what he saw—mounds of white foam floating down the river on whose banks the motel was perched. Monks went back to sleep and the next morning asked a clerk what had happened during the night. "Well, look," the clerk told him, "every night the paper company sends the stuff down the river. . . . Don't you understand, that's how we get rid of the effluent from the paper mills." Monks knew a lot of people in the town—the mayor, the people who worked in the mills, the mill owners. "And," he says, "I knew that there wasn't a person in there who wanted to have the river polluted, not a person. And yet here we're living in a world where it's happening every night."[26]

Monks realized at that moment, he says, that the corporation, an institution to which he had devoted his life, was in fact a "doom machine." "The difficulty with the corporate entity," he now believes, "is that it has a dynamic that doesn't take into account the concerns of flesh-and-blood human people who form the world in which it exists"; that "in our search for wealth and for prosperity, we created a thing that's going to destroy us."[27]

Ray Anderson, another highly successful businessman, agrees with Monks. He describes the corporation as a "present day instrument of destruction" because of its compulsion to "externalize any cost that its unwary or uncaring public will allow it to externalize." Like Monks, Anderson, founder and chairman of Interface, Inc., the world's largest commercial carpet manufacturer, had a late-career epiphany about the institution to which he had devoted his life. Until that moment, he says, he never "gave a thought to what we were taking from the earth or doing to the earth in the making of our products." Today, he believes, "the notion that we can take and take and take and take, waste and waste, and waste and waste, without consequences is driving the biosphere to destruction."[28]

Anderson remembers the moment when his beliefs about the corporation shifted. It was the summer of 1994. Environmentalism had become a mainstream worry, and Interface, Inc.'s customers had begun to inquire about what the company was doing for the environment. "We didn't have answers," recalls Anderson, "the real answer was 'Not very much.'" At the time Anderson was not bothered by his lack of answers, but others in his company were. In response to their concerns, he created a task force to investigate the company's worldwide environmental position, and he agreed to give a speech describing his own personal environmental vision.[29]

The difficulty, Anderson quickly realized, was that "I didn't have an environmental vision. . . . I began to sweat," he recalls. "Oh my, what to say?" Desperate for material and inspiration, he began to read a book about ecology. There he came across the phrase "the death of birth," a description of species extinction. "It was a point of a spear into my chest," he now recalls, "and I read on, and the spear went deeper, and it became an epiphanal experience, a total change of mind-set for myself and a change of paradigm." "We're all sinners, we're all sinners," says Anderson today of his position as a corporate chief. "Someday people like me will end up in jail." But he now rejects as dangerously misguided the beliefs he once shared with the large majority of business leaders—"that nature is unlimited, the earth . . . a limitless source for raw material, a limitless sink into which we can send our poisons and waste"; "that the relevant timeframe is my lifetime, maybe my working life, but certainly not more than my lifetime"; and that the market's invisible hand will take care of everything. The market alone cannot provide sufficient constraints on corporations' penchant to cause harm, Anderson now believes, because it is "blind to . . . externalities, those costs that can be externalized and foisted off on somebody else."[30]

All businesspeople understand that corporations are designed to externalize their costs. What makes Monks and Anderson unique is that they fear the consequences of this design, rather than celebrating its virtue. The corporation, as they say, is deliberately programmed, indeed legally compelled, to externalize costs without regard for the harm it may cause to people, communities, and the natural environment. Every cost it can unload onto someone else is a benefit to itself, a direct route to profit. Patricia Anderson's family's burns—externalities; Wendy Díaz's exploitation and misery—externalities. These and a thousand other points of corporate darkness, from Bhopal and the *Exxon Valdez* to epidemic levels of worker injury and death and chronic destruction of the environment, are the price we all pay for the corporation's flawed character.[31]

The 1911 Triangle Shirtwaist Factory disaster stands as a notorious example of a company's callous disregard for its employees. The owners of the factory in lower Manhattan's garment district had kept their employees, mostly young immigrant women, locked in to prevent them from leaving their workstations and thus slowing production. When fire broke out at the factory, the workers had no way to get out. Some of them jumped out of windows to their deaths. Others stayed and were burnt alive. Altogether 146 of them died. Just two years earlier, sixty thousand New York City garment workers, led by the recently formed International Ladies' Garment Workers' Union, had taken to the streets to protest sweatshop conditions, low wages, and unsafe workplaces in what came to be known as "The Great Revolt." In the wake of the Triangle Shirtwaist Factory blaze, half a million people protested in the streets of New York. The union continued to press for legal protections of workers, though it was not until 1938 that sweatshops, child labor, and industrial homework were finally banned by President Franklin Roosevelt's administration's Fair Labor Standards Act.

The Fair Labor Standards Act, still in force today, is typical of the system of regulatory laws designed to solve, or at least mitigate, the problem of corporate externalities. Whether regarding workers' rights, environmental standards, or measures aimed at protecting consumers from unfair prices or unsafe products, the regulatory system imposes legal limits on the predilection of corporations to exploit people and the environment and punishes those corporations that fail to respect them. In theory, corporations, and the executives who run them, are thus deterred from engaging in socially irresponsible behavior. Like many other good theories, however, this one often has little to do with reality.

The Fair Labor Standards Act, to take just one example, is regularly and routinely violated by garment industry operators. Recently, in a scene eerily reminiscent of the Shirtwaist Factory fire, workers sat ready to jump out of the windows of a ten-story building that housed eight sweatshops in Manhattan's Garment District. Fire had broken out in a basement storage closet, and smoke was billowing through the building, terrifying workers on the floors above. The fire exits were either locked shut or blocked by stored supplies. The sprinkler systems in the building had been turned off, and there were no exit signs or fire extinguishers. Bienvenido Hernandez, a leather worker on the building's tenth floor, ran to the window when he saw the smoke and tried to escape by descending a cloth rope hanging out of it. He lost his grip in the freezing air of a cold January day and plummeted down, snapping his spine when he landed on a nearby rooftop. He died soon after.[32]

Despite the Fair Labor Standards Act's clear injunctions against them, sweatshops exist in North America, and every one of them is a fire disaster waiting to happen.[33] "Sweatshops were wiped out of the United States in 1938," says Charles Kernaghan, but "they are back now, with a vengeance. Sixty-five percent of all apparel operations in New York City are sweatshops. Fifty thousand workers. Forty-five hundred factories out of seven thousand. And we're talking about workers getting a dollar or two an hour."[34] Los Angeles is no better. The southern end of the city houses America's, and perhaps the world's, largest concentration of garment sweatshops, staffed by some one hundred and sixty thousand workers, many of them illegal, and thus powerless, immigrants. There, a U.S. Department of Labor survey found, "the overall level of compliance with the minimum wage, overtime and child labor requirements of the Fair Labor Standards Act is 33 percent"—in other words, 67 percent of the garment industry workplaces did not comply with the law.[35]

Such systemic unlawfulness is not unique to the garment industry, however. Corporate illegalities are rife throughout the economy. Many major corporations engage in unlawful behavior, and some are habitual offenders with records that would be the envy of even the most prolific human criminals.[36] Take, for example, General Electric, the world's largest corporation and one of the most highly respected. What follows is a record, compiled by *Multinational Monitor,* of some of the company's major legal breaches between 1990 and 2001:[37]

March 23, 1990: Shepherdsville, Kentucky: GE and others ordered to clean up PCB contamination of soil and water.

March 27, 1990: Wilmington, North Carolina: GE fined $20,000 for discrimination against employees who reported safety violations.

May 11, 1990: Fort Edward/Hudson Falls, New York: GE ordered to clean up PCB contamination of Hudson River.

July 27, 1990: Philadelphia, Pennsylvania: GE fined $30 million for defrauding government in defense contracts.

October 11, 1990: Waterford, New York: GE fined $176,000 for pollution at Silicone Products plant.

May 20, 1991: Washington, D.C.: GE ordered to pay $1 million in damages over improperly tested aircraft parts for air force and navy.

February 27, 1992: Allentown, Pennsylvania: GE ordered to

pay $80 million in damages for design flaws in nuclear plants.

March 4, 1992: Orange County, California: GE fined $11,000 for violating worker safety rules on handling PCBs.

March 13, 1992: Wilmington, North Carolina: GE fined $20,000 for safety violations at nuclear fuel plant.

May 22, 1992: Illinois: GE ordered to pay $65 million in damages for design flaws in nuclear plants.

July 22, 1992: Washington, D.C.: GE fined $70 million for money laundering and fraud related to the illegal sale of fighter jets to Israel.

September 13, 1992: Chicago, Illinois: GE ordered to pay $1.8 million in damages for airplane crash.

October 12, 1992: Nashville, Tennessee: GE ordered to pay $165,000 in damages for deceptive advertising of lightbulbs.

October 27, 1992: Washington, D.C.: GE ordered to pay $576,215 in damages for overcharging on defense contracts.

May 12, 1992: Washington, D.C.: GE ordered to pay $13.4 million in damages to whistleblower on illegal sale of fighter jets to Israel.

March 2, 1993: Riverside, California: GE and others ordered to pay $96 million in damages for contamination from dumping of industrial chemicals.

March 11, 1993: Grove City, Pennsylvania: GE and others ordered to clean up mining site.

July 18, 1993: Hudson Falls, New York: GE ordered to clean up PCB contamination of Hudson River.

September 16, 1993: New York: GE ordered to compensate commercial fisherman $7 million for PCB contamination of the Hudson River.

October 11, 1993: San Francisco, California: GE ordered to offer $3.25 million in rebates to consumers after deceptive lightbulb advertising.

February 2, 1994: Perry, Ohio: GE settles with utility companies on defective Perry Nuclear Plant.

March 14, 1994: Fort Edward, New York: GE ordered to clean up contamination of sediment in the Hudson River.

September 14, 1994: Washington, D.C.: GE fined $20 million for overcharges on defense contracts.

September 2, 1995: Waterford, New York: GE fined $1.5 million for air pollution and contamination of Hudson River.

September 15, 1995: Brandon, Florida: GE fined $137,000 for groundwater contamination.

September 9, 1996: Waterford, New York: GE fined $60,000 for Clean Air Act violations.

October 7, 1996: Hendersonville, North Carolina: GE ordered to clean up contaminated soil and groundwater.

October 8, 1996: Cook County, Illinois: GE ordered to pay $15 million as settlement for airline crash in Sioux City, Iowa.

February 22, 1997: Somersworth, New Hampshire: GE and others ordered to clean up contamination of groundwater and public water supply.

February 1998: Waterford, New York: GE fined $234,000 for pollution violations.

April 20, 1998: Waterford, New York: GE fined $204,000 for pollution violations.

October 1998: United Kingdom: GE ordered to pay £2 billion for asbestos cleanup and related pollution claims.

October 26, 1998: Puerto Rico: GE and others ordered to clean up contamination of drinking water supply.

November 5, 1998: South Whitehall, Pennsylvania: GE and others ordered to clean up contamination.

January 24, 1999: Chicago, Illinois: GE ordered to reimburse consumers $147 million for unfair debt collection practices.

August 19, 1999: Piscataway, New Jersey: GE and others ordered to clean up contaminated groundwater.

September 2, 1999: Malvern, Pennsylvania: GE and others ordered to clean up groundwater contamination.

September 17, 1999: Moreau, New York: GE ordered to build drinking water system after PCB contamination of water supply.

October 9, 1999: Pittsfield, Massachusetts: GE ordered to clean up PCB pollution in Housatonic River.

October 18, 2000: New York, New York: GE and others ordered to clean up contamination of soil.

January 2001: New York: GE and others ordered to refund $4 million in overcharges on mortgage insurance.

February 4, 2001: New York State: State Supreme Court rules that GE deceptively misled consumers into purchasing new dishwashers after recall even though it sent commercial customers a replacement part.

The corporation's unique structure is largely to blame for the fact that illegalities are endemic in the corporate world. By design, the corporate form generally protects the human beings who own and run corporations from legal liability, leaving the corporation, a "person" with a psychopathic contempt for legal constraints, the main target of criminal prosecution. Shareholders cannot be held liable for the crimes committed by corporations because of limited liability, the sole purpose of which is to shield them from legal responsibility for corporations' actions. Directors are traditionally protected by the fact that they have no direct involvement with decisions that may lead to a corporation's committing a crime. Executives are protected by the law's unwillingness to find them liable for their companies' illegal actions unless they can be proven to have been "directing minds" behind those actions. Such proof is difficult if not impossible to produce in most cases, because corporate decisions normally result from numerous and diffuse individuals' inputs, and because courts tend to attribute conduct to the corporate "person" rather than to the actual people who run the corporations.

The corporation itself is thus the most viable target for prosecution in most cases, and, because it has "no soul to be damned and no body to be kicked," as Edward Thurlow, lord chancellor of England, observed in the eighteenth century, punishing the corporation often has little impact. Like the psychopath it resembles, the corporation feels no moral obligation to obey the law. "Only people have moral obligations," as Frank Easterbrook, a judge and legal commentator, and law professor Daniel Fishel observe in an article they coauthored. "Corporations can no more be said to have moral obligations than does a building, an organization chart, or a contract."[38]

For a corporation, compliance with law, like everything else, is a matter of costs and benefits. "Again and again in America we have the problem that whether [corporations] obey the law or not is a matter of whether it's cost effective," says Robert Monks. "If the chance of getting caught and the penalty are less than it costs to comply, our people think of it as being just a business decision." Executives, when deciding whether to comply with or break a law, "behave rationally and . . . make cost effective decisions," says Monks, which means they ask, "What's the penalty, what's the probability of being caught, how much does that add up to, and how much does it cost to comply and which is bigger?"[39]

Law professor Bruce Welling states the logic this way:

> The practical business view is that a fine is an additional cost of doing business. A prohibited activity is not inhibited by the threat of a fine so long as the anticipated profits from the activity outweigh the amount of the fine multiplied by the probability of being apprehended and convicted. Considering the amount of the average fine, deterrence is improbable in most cases. The argument is even more obvious regarding prevention of recidivism. The corporation, once convicted and fined, will simply have learned how to cover its tracks better.[40]

The irony in all of this is that the corporation's mandate to pursue its own self-interest, itself a product of the law, actually propels corporations to break the law. No corporation is exempt from this built-in logic, not even those that claim they are socially responsible, as a second look at British Petroleum reveals.

On August 16, 2002, Don Shugak, a British Petroleum technician, was making his rounds at the company's Prudhoe Bay oil field in Alaska, checking wells for leaks and other problems. One of his assignments was to reactivate a well that had been shut down for repairs. BP engineers knew that the well still had problems and would operate at unusually high pressures once reactivated, but they gave

Shugak the green light anyway. Shugak opened the valve to reactivate the well and then left the site. Several hours later he returned to bleed off pressure from the wellhead, a routine procedure. Though he remembers opening the well-house door on his return visit, his recollection of what happened after that is vague. It was hard to breathe, he recalls; his ears were ringing and his legs were paralyzed. He clung to the side of his truck, which was parked nearby, and made his way to the other side of it to shield himself from the heat of the massive explosion that had just occurred. "I started crawling two and three inches at a time with my elbows," he recalls. "I tried rolling because my elbows were so tired, but my legs kept getting tangled up." Fortunately, a coworker had heard the explosion and seen the now-forty-foot flames from a distance. He rushed to the scene and called for help. "I didn't even feel like I was hurt," said Shugak, "I didn't feel anything. I just knew nothing was working the way it was supposed to. Everybody was talking in hushed tones."[41]

Shugak woke up in a Seattle hospital burn unit two weeks later with burns covering 15 percent of his body, a broken leg, and badly damaged knees and vertebrae. He was lucky to have survived.[42]

Many of Shugak's coworkers blame the accident on BP's persistent failure to comply with maintenance and safety regulations, about which they had complained well before the accident happened. In a 1999 letter to BP's chief executive John Browne, operators alleged that the company was not "in compliance with statutory and regulatory requirements."[43] They cited a leaky valve as a factor in a 1998 spill of 1,200 gallons of oil and thousands of cubic feet of gas. The incident was ranked by the company at the most serious level, in terms of potential employee deaths and environmental damage—"All we needed was a spark and that plant would have burned to the ground," one operator said at the time.[44] A report following the incident called for a proactive maintenance program to check all similar valves and replace them if necessary, echoing a recommendation made five years earlier by the state regulatory agency responsible for oversight of the valves.[45] Neither recommendation was implemented, according to BP operators, and the valves continued to be prone to leaks. Even three years later, in spring 2001, state inspectors found that one third (nine of thirty) of the pads at one of BP's drilling platforms were defective and did not comply with regulatory standards.[46]

On July 16, 2001, a month before Shugak's accident, a group of BP operators had contacted BP's probation officer, Mary Barnes, and alleged that the company was in breach of a 1999 probation order. The order had been issued by an Alaskan court, which had convicted BP of "one felony count of knowingly failing to immediately report the release into the environment of a hazardous substance." BP had wrongfully acquiesced, over a two-year period, to illegal discharges of hazardous substances by one of its contractors. The company was fined the maximum penalty of $500,000 and placed on "organizational probation." The probation conditions included an undertaking by the company to comply with "best environmental practices in order to effectively protect workers, the public and the environment, and to comply with all statutory and regulatory requirements."[47] In their letter to the company's probation officer, the BP operators alleged that "BP operations are . . . undeniably not in compliance with Government regulations," citing numerous examples of regulatory breaches, many relating to the safety valves.

For BP, however, it appears that regulatory standards are just another factor to be considered in its cost-benefit analyses. Like other large oil companies, BP allocates operating budgets to oil fields on a "cost per barrel" basis. As the production in a field declines, so too does that field's operating budget. From the perspective of profitability, that makes eminent sense, as companies want to maintain their profit levels even as fields become less productive. From a safety and maintenance perspective, however, according to BP operator William Burkett in testimony before a Senate committee on Alaskan oil,

This creates a situation that quickly impacts manager's ability to maintain the equipment in the field. The primary reason for that is, the equipment used to produce oil prior to decline is, for the most part, still in operation. In fact, often more equipment is added and more wells drilled as the field matures to slow the production decline. So, what happens is there is as much or more equipment in service with an increasing need for maintenance as it ages, while the budget to operate and maintain the equipment decreases with the production decline.

In 1988, production at the Prudhoe fields began to decline, and the dangerous logic of "cost per barrel" analysis went into play. "London knew what to do to keep the dollars coming," says Burkett. "Cut. Cut the budget, cut the employee numbers, cut wages, cut spare parts, cut maintenance, cut supervision—just CUT!" In 1992, BP began a downsizing program that would eventually leave the company with one-third fewer employees at its Prudhoe operations, the reason, says Burkett, that there are now too few technicians to monitor and maintain the aging infrastructure and ensure that it complies with regulatory standards.[48]

In the wake of Don Shugak's accident, the Alaska Oil and Gas Conservation Commission, the regulatory agency responsible for overseeing BP's operations, heard testimony on whether new regulations were needed to protect workers and the environment from poorly maintained wells. Not surprisingly, BP opposed the introduction of new regulations. But even if new regulations were enacted, would they make a difference? Burkett thinks not. "All the regulations in the world do little good if there is no enforcement," he says. Enforcement remains a serious problem in Alaska's oil fields, as a recent article in *The Wall Street Journal* observed:

Alaska's legislature . . . eager to please the industry, has gutted the state agencies responsible for regulating oil-field safety. . . . The paucity of resources makes it hard for Alaska's oil-safety inspectors to do their job. Stretched by the state's vast terrain and its 3,500 wells, the five inspectors say they schedule their field tests with the oil companies to ensure that inspectors don't travel hundreds of miles only to discover that necessary personnel or equipment aren't around. Lost is the element of surprise that regulators in some other major oil-producing states swear by as the crucial component in keeping oil companies honest. . . . Instead, Alaska's safety regulators operate on trust.[49]

Throughout the economy today, the regulatory system often fails because of lax regulations and ineffective enforcement. Until that changes, we shall continue to suffer unnecessary disasters and harm to people, communities, and the environment. That is the price we all pay for the proclivity of corporations to profit by harming others.

Democracy Ltd.

As institutional psychopaths, corporations are wont to remove obstacles that get into their way. Regulations that limit their freedom to exploit people and the natural environment are such obstacles, and corporations have fought, with considerable success over the last twenty years, to remove them. Through lobbying, political contributions, and sophisticated public relations campaigns, they and their leaders have turned the political system and much public opinion against regulation. The law's ability to protect people and the environment from corporate harm has suffered as a result. Business opposition to regulation did not begin in the current era, however. It can be traced back to the origins of the regulatory state itself. Surely, the most bizarre moment in its history was when a group of leading bankers and corporate executives conspired to overthrow President Franklin D. Roosevelt, who they believed had gone too far with his regulatory ambitions, and replace him with a fascist dictator. The story reads like a pulp fiction thriller, but it really happened.

Shortly after becoming president of the United States in the spring of 1933, Franklin D. Roosevelt created the New Deal, a sweeping and unprecedented set of regulatory laws and agencies that aimed to strengthen government's control of big corporations and banks. The New Deal reflected Roosevelt's conviction that the Great Depression would end only once the market's invisible hand was replaced by the very visible, and benevolent, hand of government. In that spirit, Roosevelt signed into law, among other things, new rights and protections for workers, debt relief for farmers, and fairness and transparency guarantees for investors. He later described his creation as follows:

> The word "Deal" implied that the Government itself was going to use affirmative action to bring about its avowed objectives rather than stand by and hope that general economic laws would attain them. The word "New" implied that a new order of things designed to benefit the great mass of our farmers, workers and business men would replace the old order of special privilege in a nation which was completely and thoroughly disgusted with the existing dispensation . . . we were not to be content with merely hoping for . . . [constitutional] ideals. We were to use the instrumentalities and powers of Government actively to fight for them . . . because the American system visualized protection of the individual against the misuse of private economic power, the New Deal would insist on curbing such power.[1]

Inevitably the New Deal did just that—it curbed corporations' freedoms and powers. Though many business leaders agreed with Roosevelt that the New Deal was necessary to save capitalism from itself, especially at a time of rising labor militancy and a collapsing economy, others were enraged, and believed that Roosevelt's plan would undermine American capitalism. Which is why a group of them plotted to overthrow his government.

On August 22, 1934, a little more than a year into Roosevelt's presidency and three days after Adolf Hitler had officially become

Führer of Germany, Smedley Darlington Butler, a former U.S. Marines general, and one of the nation's most honored and decorated military men, entered the lobby of the Bellevue Hotel in Philadelphia. A man named Gerald MacGuire, a World War I veteran who sold bonds for a living, was waiting to meet him. After a brief exchange of pleasantries, MacGuire told Butler he had been sent by a group of businessmen to ask the general to raise an army, seize the White House, and install himself as fascist dictator of the United States.[2]

Many business leaders at the time found fascism attractive, especially when they compared it to the "class hatred . . . preached from the White House," as Herbert Hoover characterized Roosevelt's New Deal. Benito Mussolini and Hitler had slashed the public debt, curbed inflation, driven down wages, and taken control of the trade unions in Italy and Germany, respectively. Roosevelt, on the other hand, had turned traitor to his class, they believed, and was now bent on destroying American capitalism. In its July 1934 issue, *Fortune* magazine extolled the virtues of fascism and the economic miracles wrought by Mussolini. Laird Goldsborough, the man who produced the issue, wrote, "The good journalist must recognize in Fascism certain ancient virtues of the race, whether or not they happen to be momentarily fashionable in his own country."[3]

Indeed, at the time, some major American corporations were reaping substantial profits by working for Adolf Hitler. Adam Opel AG, a German automobile maker owned and controlled by General Motors (which, at the time, was controlled by the du Pont family), was, with the help of GM executives, transformed in 1937 into an armaments concern. It manufactured trucks for the German Army, including three-ton "Opel Blitz" trucks, a crucial part of the blitzkrieg attacks on Poland, France, and the Soviet Union. It also built aircraft components, including engines for the Luftwaffe's Junker "Wunderbomber."[4] A recent GM television commercial boasts of the role of GM trucks in building roads and bridges to support the Allied campaigns during World War II—"some people say we were paving the road to victory," the ad states—but neglects to mention that the company helped build trucks for the enemy's armies as well.

IBM—a company where "if your customer needs help, you jump," according to Irving Wladawsky-Berger, vice president, technology and strategy—jumped when Hitler sought its technical assistance in running the Nazi extermination and slave-labor programs. IBM provided the Nazis with Hollerith tabulation machines, early ancestors of computers that used punch cards to do their calculations. Edwin Black, author of *IBM and the Holocaust,* says, "The head office in New York had a complete understanding of everything that was going on in the Third Reich with its machines . . . that their machines were in concentration camps generally, and they knew that Jews were being exterminated." IBM technicians serviced the machines, IBM engineers trained their users, and IBM supplied punch cards for the machines, according to Black, at least until 1941, when the United States declared war on Germany.[5]

IBM's motivation for working with the Nazis, says Black, "was never about Nazism . . . it was always about profit," which is consistent with the corporation's amoral nature. Corporations have no capacity to value political systems, fascist or democratic, for reasons of principle or ideology. The only legitimate question for a corporation is whether a political system serves or impedes its self-interested purposes. According to Peter Drucker—who says he "discussed it more than once with old Mr. Watson," the head of IBM at the time— Thomas Watson had reservations about working with the Nazis. "Not because he thought it was immoral," says Drucker, but "because Watson, with a very keen sense of public relations, thought it was risky" from a business perspective. In a similar spirit, Alfred Sloan, Jr., chairman of General Motors in 1939, seemed morally unconcerned about his company's work for the Nazis. The German subsidiaries were "highly profitable," he noted in defense of GM's investments in

Germany, and Germany's internal political affairs "should not be considered the business of the management of General Motors."[6] Though the assistance provided to the Nazis by U.S. corporations may seem shocking in retrospect, it should not be forgotten that many U.S. corporations today regularly do business with totalitarian and authoritarian regimes—again, because it is profitable to do so.[7]

Looking back on the 1930s, a time when some top American corporations unabashedly worked with fascist dictators and many businesspeople believed that the federal government was threatening the capitalist system, one can at least comprehend why a cabal of leading businessmen would hatch a plot to turn the country into a fascist dictatorship. Removing democracy likely seemed a defensible business plan, from their perspective, because democracy threatened to undermine the corporation's mission. And Smedley Butler was the obvious person for the job of removing it—or at least that is what MacGuire and his backers thought.

Butler had been a lifelong Republican and was a charismatic public speaker. A celebrated military hero—one of only four men to be decorated with the coveted Congressional Medal of Honor twice—the general had spent most of his military career protecting American business interests throughout Asia and Central America. He was also adored by veterans, for whom he had fought for better treatment and more generous benefits from government. Butler seemed ideally positioned to raise an army of veterans and lead them on a campaign to seize the White House.

MacGuire and Butler had already met several times before the Bellevue Hotel meeting. A year earlier, MacGuire had invited himself to Butler's Philadelphia home, claiming to be a representative of concerned veterans, and asked the general to deliver a speech at an upcoming American Legion convention. The speech, a copy of which MacGuire had with him, was designed to rally the veterans against Roosevelt's decision to abandon the gold standard, which, once done, would cost the banks dearly. Butler, confused about why veterans should be concerned with the gold standard, had refused MacGuire's request. A few months later, in September 1933, MacGuire had found Butler again, this time in New Jersey, where the general was delivering a speech to a Legion branch. The two men had met in Butler's hotel room, where MacGuire had once again pleaded with the general to deliver the gold standard speech at the Chicago convention. According to Butler, MacGuire scattered a mass of $1,000 bills on the bed and invited him to use them to finance his trip to Chicago. "You put that money away before somebody walks in here and sees that money around," Butler recalled telling MacGuire, "because I do not want to be tied up with it at all."[8]

When the two men met at the Bellevue Hotel several weeks later, Butler had already acquired the names and affiliations of the men MacGuire purported to represent, mainly from MacGuire himself. There was, Butler later stated, Grayson Murphy, head of a leading Wall Street brokerage firm and a director of Morgan Guaranty Trust, as well as of Anaconda Copper, Goodyear Tire, and Bethlehem Steel. Robert Clark, a wealthy banker whom Butler had actually met after demanding MacGuire produce some of his backers and who had told Butler that he was prepared to spend half of his $30 million fortune to protect the other half from Roosevelt, was another alleged backer of the plot, as was John Davis, the unsuccessful Democratic candidate for president in the 1924 election and later an attorney at J. P. Morgan & Co.

The meeting at the Bellevue Hotel took place in the closed-down hotel café at a table tucked away in a remote corner. MacGuire began by telling Butler that he had spent the past six months in Europe. Butler recalled the rest of the conversation as follows:

He said, "I went abroad to study the part that the veteran plays in the various set-ups of the governments that they have abroad. I went to Italy for two or three months and studied the position that the veterans of Italy occupy and the Fascist set-up of government, and I discovered that they are the background of Mussolini. . . . I then went to Germany to see what Hitler was doing, and his whole strength lies in organizations of soldiers, too. . . . Then I went to France, and I found just exactly the organization we are going to have. It is an organization of super soldiers." He gave me the French name for it, but I do not recall what it is. I never could have pronounced it anyhow. But I do know that it is a superorganization of members of all the other soldiers' organizations of France, composed of non-commissioned officers and officers. He told me that they had about 500,000, and that each one was a leader of ten others, so that it gave them 5,000,000 votes. And he said, "Now, that is our idea here in America—to get up an organization of that kind."[9]

MacGuire told Butler that his backers' plan was to create an American version of the Croix de Feu, the French soldiers' organization whose name Butler was unable to recall, and install the general at the head of it. With a powerful army behind him, the plotters anticipated, Butler could demand that Roosevelt make him a secretary of general affairs, a new position where he would serve as a kind of assistant president. From there, Butler could assume real power over the nation and the president would become a mere figurehead, on the contrived pretext that Roosevelt's health was failing. If Roosevelt refused to cooperate with the scheme, according to MacGuire, Butler's army would overthrow him.

Journalist Paul Comly French, who also spoke with MacGuire, corroborated Butler's story:

During the course of the conversation he continually discussed the need of a man on a white horse, as he called it, a dictator who would come galloping in on his white horse. He said that was the only way; either through the threat of armed force or the delegation of power, and the use of a group of organized veterans, to save the capitalist system.

He warmed up considerably after we got under way and he said, "We might go along with Roosevelt and then do with him what Mussolini did with the King of Italy."

It fits in with what he told the General, that we would have a Secretary of General Affairs, and if Roosevelt played ball, swell; and if he did not, they would push him out.[10]

The money was there, MacGuire boasted to Butler during their meeting, to raise and equip a veterans' army, $3 million in place and $300 million available if needed. His backers were already on the move, he said, putting together a front organization that would provide secret financial and practical support for the plot. The formation of the American Liberty League, an organization "to combat radicalism, to teach the necessity of respect for the rights of person and property, and generally to foster free private enterprise," was announced three weeks later. The league's treasurer, Grayson Murphy, was MacGuire's boss. Robert Clark was a major financial contributor, and men from J. P. Morgan and DuPont were the league's executives. John Davis was a member of the national executive committee. Financial backers included some of corporate America's major concerns: the Pitcairn family, Andrew Mellon Associates, Rockefeller Associates, E. F. Hutton Associates, William Knudsen of General Motors, and the V. Pew family.[11]

MacGuire and the plotters had made a fatal mistake in their choice of a leader, however. "With incredible ineptitude," states Jules Archer in *The Plot to Seize the White House*, "they had selected the wrong man."[12] The plot, and the men behind it, represented everything Smedley Butler now despised. Over the years his youthful passion for battles abroad had given way to an equally fierce desire to fight hypocrisy at home. He had come to believe that war was a product of corporate greed, that his men had fought for no higher ideal than profit. On August 21, 1931—a full two years before MacGuire first approached him—Butler had stunned an audience at an American Legion convention in Connecticut when he had said:

> I spent 33 years . . . being a high-class muscle man for Big Business, for Wall Street and the bankers. In short, I was a racketeer for capitalism. . . .
>
> I helped purify Nicaragua for the international banking house of Brown Brothers in 1909–1912. I helped make Mexico and especially Tampico safe for American oil interests in 1916. I brought light to the Dominican Republic for American sugar interests in 1916. I helped make Haiti and Cuba a decent place for the National City [Bank] boys to collect revenue in. I helped in the rape of half a dozen Central American republics for the benefit of Wall Street. . . .
>
> In China in 1927 I helped see to it that Standard Oil went its way unmolested. . . . I had . . . a swell racket. I was rewarded with honours, medals, promotions. . . . I might have given Al Capone a few hints. The best he could do was to operate a racket in three cities. The Marines operated on three continents.[13]

Butler was not about to add the United States to the list of countries where he had used military force to defend U.S. corporate interests from populist threats. On November 20, 1934, he revealed the plot to the House Un-American Activities Committee in a secret executive session in New York City. By that time the general had collected as much information as he could about the plot and had made sure his story was corroborated by the work of Paul French, who also testified before the committee. The committee vindicated Butler's story in all of its essential elements and submitted its findings to the House of Representatives on February 13, 1935:

> In the last few weeks of the committee's official life it received evidence showing that certain persons had made an attempt to establish a fascist organization in this country. . . .
>
> There is no question that these attempts were discussed, were planned, and might have been placed in execution when and if the financial backers deemed it expedient.
>
> This Committee received evidence from Maj. Gen. Smedley D. Butler (retired), twice decorated by the Congress of the United States. He testified before the committee as to conversations with one Gerald C. MacGuire in which the latter is alleged to have suggested the formation of a fascist army under the leadership of General Butler. . . .
>
> MacGuire denied these allegations under oath, but your committee was able to verify all the pertinent statements made by General Butler, with the exception of the direct statement suggesting the creation of the organization. This, however, was corroborated in the correspondence of MacGuire with his principal, Robert Sterling Clark, of New York City, while MacGuire was abroad studying the various forms of veterans organizations of Fascist character.[14]

With Butler having refused to cooperate with MacGuire and his backers and the committee's unwavering vindication of the general's story, the plot to seize the White House quickly unraveled.

"There was no doubt that General Butler was telling the truth," committee cochair John McCormack later recalled in a 1971 interview with Archer. "The plotters definitely hated the New Deal because it was for the people, not for the moneyed interests, and they were willing to spend a lot of their money to dump Mr. Roosevelt out of the White House." McCormack stated, "those fellows got desperate and decided to look into European methods, with the idea of introducing them into America. They sent MacGuire to Europe to study the Fascist organizations." How close was America's brush with fascism? Archer wanted to know. "Well," said McCormack,

> if General Butler had not been the patriot he was, and if they had been able to maintain secrecy, the plot certainly might very well have succeeded, having in mind the conditions existing at that time. . . . If the plotters had got rid of Roosevelt, there is no telling what might have taken place. They wouldn't have told the people what they were doing, of course. They were going to make it all sound constitutional, of course, with a high-sounding name for the dictator and a plan to make it all sound like a good American program. A well-organized minority can always outmaneuver an unorganized majority, as Adolf Hitler did.[15]

Today, seventy years after the failed coup, a well-organized minority again threatens democracy. Corporate America's long and patient campaign to gain control of government over the last few decades, much quieter and ultimately more effective than the plotters' clumsy attempts, is now succeeding. Without bloodshed, armies, or fascist strongmen, and using dollars rather than bullets, corporations are now poised to win what the plotters so desperately wanted: freedom from democratic control.

On July 24, 2002, nine desperate coal miners waited to be rescued from a watery hell 240 feet below a Pennsylvania cow pasture. Miraculously, they had escaped a torrent of water that had flooded their mine after they had mistakenly drilled into an adjacent mine shaft that was filled with water. The miners were finally rescued after spending seventy-eight hours in a cramped air pocket. President Bush proclaimed, when he flew into town one week later, that the miners' courage and perseverance reflected that of all

Americans in the aftermath of September 11, 2001. "It was their determination to stick together and to comfort each other," he said, "that really defines kind of a new spirit that's prevalent in our country—that when one of us suffers, all of us suffer; that in order to succeed, we've got to be united; that by working together, we can achieve big objectives and big goals."[16] It was, ironically as it turns out, similar sentiments that had originally animated Roosevelt's belief in the virtues of government regulation, including the regulation of coal mine safety.

In 1941, with Roosevelt in the White House, Congress substantially strengthened the regulatory regime for protecting coal miners' safety by granting to the federal Bureau of Mines the authority to enter and inspect mines for possible safety hazards. Though the bureau was almost thirty years old, its jurisdiction had previously been limited to collecting information and conducting research. Now, for the first time, it could actually enforce legislated safety standards. Further improvements would soon follow. In 1952, Congress enacted the Federal Coal Mine Safety Act, which gave the bureau new powers to issue and enforce violation notices, to close mines where inspectors found imminent dangers, and to require that mines be inspected on an annual basis. The act was strengthened in the late 1960s, and then replaced in 1977 with a new act, the Federal Mine Safety and Health Act, that consolidated protections for all types of mining, and created a new enforcement agency, the Mine Safety and Health Administration (MSHA), to take over from the Bureau of Mines. Annual mining fatalities dropped from 272 to 86 during the first decade of the new agency's operations.[17]

More recently, the Bush administration introduced measures that could have had the effect of rolling back protection of coal miners' safety. In his first budget George W. Bush sought cuts to staffing levels at the MSHA, but these were defeated by the then Democratic majority in

Congress. Then, in his 2003 budget, Bush sought a $4.7 million cut in the agency's coal enforcement program, to be realized through reduction of sixty-five full-time employees, the termination of a chest X-ray program to detect black lung disease in miners, and a reduction in inspection outreach activities, technical investigations, compliance follow-up, education, and training and technical assistance. With the new Congress and its Republican majority, these proposals seemed likely to be enacted, but after intense lobbying by the United Mine Workers of America (UMWA), the Senate Appropriations Committee voted to restore the $4.7 million to the MSHA budget. Bush's budget for 2004 now proposes a $6.3 million cut to enforcement of coal mine safety standards.[18] Even if no cuts end up being made, however, the "MSHA [due to earlier cuts] is unable to complete statutorily mandated inspections," its inspector general said in January 2002. According to United Mine Workers chief Joseph Main, the statutory requirement that a mine be inspected four times each year is seldom met, and inspections, when they do occur, tend to be rushed and ineffective.[19]

The Quecreek flood, it turns out, may have been caused by the miners' reliance on old inaccurate maps. The maps showed that the abandoned flooded mine that the miners drilled into, causing their own tunnel to flood, was located three hundred feet away from its actual location. Floods similar to the one at Quecreek had occurred at two other mines operated by Black Wolf Mining Company, the operator of Quecreek Mining, and a subsidiary of PBS Coals, within the two years preceding the Quecreek incident. It is reasonable to presume that an appropriately staffed and well-functioning agency might have ensured that the Quecreek miners had accurate maps and thus prevented their horrible ordeal.[20]

Funding cuts to the agencies responsible for enforcing regulatory laws are increasingly common across the regulatory system, not just in relation to mining. Their effect, if not always their intention, is to deregulate corporate behavior. Though legal standards are left in place, the gutting of enforcement mechanisms ensures that they are substantially weakened and sometimes entirely ineffective. Cuts to the agencies that regulate Alaska's oil fields and to the Department of Labor's budget (which have compromised effective enforcement of the Fair Labor Standards Act) are examples discussed earlier. Cuts to the Environmental Protection Agency,[21] the Occupational Safety and Health Administration,[22] and the Securities and Exchange Commission[23] have also recently been blamed for harm caused by inadequate oversight of corporate activities within those agencies' jurisdictions.

A second kind of deregulation involves the actual repeal of regulations. This phenomenon too is pervasive throughout the regulatory system. Laws designed to protect the public interest from corporate misdeeds are being scaled back and are sometimes disappearing altogether. There is no better illustration of the dangers of this trend than the Enron debacle.

When the lights first went out in California on December 7, 2000, an event that would occur almost forty more times over the next six months and wreak havoc on the state and its citizens, no one suspected that Enron was largely to blame. Overregulation was blamed by many for the suddenly short supply of electricity, and deregulation was proposed as the solution. "If there's any environmental regulations that's preventing California from having a 100 percent max output at their plants, as I understand there may be," stated President-elect George Bush in January 2001, "then we need to relax those regulations."[24] Republican Senator Phil Gramm, another Texan, blamed "those who valued environmental extremism and interstate protectionism more than common sense and market freedom" for the disaster.[25]

What eventually came to light, however, was that Enron's highly successful—and very expensive—campaign to eliminate government oversight of its operations had been a major factor in the electricity system's failure.[26]

Stripped down to its essentials, Enron's is the story of a corporation that used political influence to remove government restrictions on its operations and then exploited its resulting freedom to engage in dubious, though highly profitable, practices. Through the 1990s, the company and its officials, chiefly former CEO Kenneth Lay, dumped huge amounts of money into the political process to help transform an unremarkable pipeline company into a powerhouse energy trader. After lobbying successfully for deregulation of electricity markets in several states, among them California, it began a campaign to deregulate the trading of energy futures. In the early 1990s, it and several other energy companies sought to exempt themselves from the Commodity Exchange Act's requirement that energy traders disclose information about their futures contracts to the Commodity Futures Trading Commission (CFTC), the agency responsible for enforcing the act. Just over a week after Bill Clinton had defeated George Bush in the November 7, 1992 election the companies petitioned the CFTC, headed at the time by Wendy Gramm, to remove energy futures trading from its jurisdiction. Gramm, by that time a lame duck, as were the other Bush appointees on the commission, was also potentially in a conflict of interest—her husband, Texan Senator Phil Gramm, was a leading beneficiary of Enron's political largesse. She nonetheless brought the petition before her commission, which in January 1993 decided, by a vote of 2 to 1, in favor of Enron and the other petitioners. As a result, trading in energy futures was no longer subject to CFTC oversight.

It "sets a dangerous precedent," Sheila Blair, the lone dissenter on the commission, said of the decision at the time. It was "the most irresponsible decision I have come across," said congressman Glen English, an eighteen-year veteran of the House and chair of the

House subcommittee that governed Gramm's commission. Six days after she handed down her decision, on the day Bill Clinton took office, Wendy Gramm resigned from the commission. Five weeks later, she was appointed to Enron's board of directors.[27]

Though freed from CFTC scrutiny by the Gramm Commission decision, energy traders were still legally required to conduct trades in regulated auctions, such as on the New York Mercantile Exchange. Because these auctions reported prices, volumes, and other information to regulators, traders, such as Enron, remained under the watch of regulators. Enron attacked this problem head-on in 1999 by spending more than $1 million to lobby for repeal of the regulated-auction requirement. It was a tough challenge for the company—the President's Working Group on Financial Markets had only recently decided that energy futures trading should remain in regulated markets because supply and price manipulation would almost certainly occur if it did not. Enron persisted, however. It poured even more money into lobbying and got further assistance from its friend Senator Gramm, who introduced the Commodity Futures Modernization Act of 2000, which would repeal the regulated-auction requirement. The then chairman of the New York Mercantile Exchange, Daniel Rappaport, remarked at the time that "if this bill ever saw the light of day with full floor debate, it wouldn't have a chance to survive." The bill languished in the Senate, but then was passed by Congress, attached to an appropriations bill, after Senator Gramm reintroduced it under a different number and name. It was signed into law by then lame-duck President Clinton on December 21, 2000.[28]

Enron had won. It could now run its own auctions on its own trading floor, hidden from governmental scrutiny and the public view. It took full advantage of its new freedom by targeting California's energy markets for manipulation. In a series of brilliantly diabolical schemes, whose sinister character is best captured by Enron insiders' nicknames for them—"Death Star," "Get Shorty," and "Fat Boy"—the company helped manufacture an artificial energy shortage that drove the price of electricity, and consequently its profits, sky high. Thirty-eight blackouts plagued California over the six months after the Commodity Futures Modernization Act was signed by the president. Up until that point, and from the beginning of the energy crisis in May 2000, only one blackout had occurred. As Ralph Nader's Public Citizen organization concluded, "Phil Gramm's commodities deregulation law allowed Enron to control electricity in California, pocket billions in extra revenues and force millions of California residents to go hundreds of hours without electricity and pay outrageous prices."

On June 19, 2001, the crisis was brought to an end when the Federal Energy Regulatory Commission imposed strict price controls on California's electricity markets. Spot prices fell by more than 80 percent, and Enron, which had bet on prices remaining high, having had no reason to believe its manipulation of markets would be stopped, was left with billions of dollars of contracts now worth a fraction of what it had paid for them. The company began to bleed. Losses piled up. CEO Jeff Skilling quit, abruptly, very soon after the price controls were put in place, and Enron filed for bankruptcy four months later. Though numerous factors can be blamed for Enron's collapse, the losses it suffered as a result of its misdeeds in California rank high among them.

Enron may have been unique for the tactical brilliance it deployed in seeking to remove government oversight of its operations by influencing the political process. It was not unique, however, in using such a strategy. Though often accused of corrupting democracy with their money and influence, corporations have little choice but to seek influence when that is necessary for protecting and promoting their interests. Because regulations reduce profitability, strategies to remove them make good business sense. The executive who, out of principled concern for the integrity of the democratic process, refuses to be involved in political influence, fails his or her shareholders, as well as the corporation's legal mandate to promote its best interests. The job of a corporate executive is not to protect democracy but to manage its uncertainties and avoid the obstacles it presents.

Anne Wexler is one of Washington, D.C.'s top lobbyists, with a client list that includes major corporations, such as American Airlines, General Motors, and Roche, and an extensive network of contacts from her days at the helm of Bill Clinton's Office of Public Liaison. She was still gloating over a recent victory for one of her clients when we caught up with her for an interview. "Last night," she said, "the amendment which would have raised the [fuel efficiency standard] was defeated in the House . . . that was a victory for the automobile industry, including our client." The industry feared the amendment would restrict the production of highly profitable gas-guzzling sport-utility vehicles and spent millions of dollars to help defeat it. Its lobby against the amendment was typical of corporate lobbying more generally. When corporations lobby governments, their usual goal is to avoid regulation. Sometimes they seek to stop governments from introducing new or stronger regulations (as the auto industry did with the fuel efficiency standard); other times they pressure governments to repeal, weaken, or narrow the scope of existing regulations (as Enron did with the regulation of energy futures trading). Corporations lobby government, in other words, primarily for "defensive purposes," as Cato Institute chairman William Niskanen states, "largely in response to threats to their independence by government in the form of . . . regulation."[29]

Corporations began to take that threat seriously in the early 1970s. By then it was clear that the onslaught of regulation created over the previous decade—the "new social regulation," as it was called, composed of environmental, human rights, and workers' and consumers' safety regimes—had substantially curbed their freedoms

THE CORPORATION | 103

and powers, much as the New Deal had previously done. And though corporations had stood by idly during the 1960s and watched public opinion and political momentum turn against them, they now knew it was time to fight back. No coup was plotted this time. Instead, with a new "awareness that so many of the decisions that are made here [in Washington, D.C.] go directly to the bottom line," as lobbyist Wexler describes it, corporations began to mobilize politically. They set up offices in Washington, D.C., and created industry organizations, lobby groups, and industry-backed think tanks to assert their collective influence. The Business Roundtable, a highly influential association of top CEOs, was established in 1972 out of a belief among corporate heads "that the business sector in a pluralistic society should play an active and effective role in the formation of public policy" and that it was necessary to ensure that there "would be less unwarranted intrusion by government into business affairs."[30]

Business-government relations have undergone profound changes since the early 1970s[31]—a time when, as Niskanen describes it, only "relatively few corporations had much of a public role in federal politics . . . [and] most corporations did not have offices in Washington, did not have lobbyists here."[32] Today, all major corporations have offices in the nation's capital, as do the numerous industry groups, think tanks, and lobby organizations that represent their collective interests.

Another significant change in corporate-government relations since the 1970s has been the expanded role and influence of corporate donations within the electoral system. In the mid-1970s the Supreme Court extended First Amendment constitutional protection to corporate financing of elections, a decision that opened the door to corporations' near-complete takeover of the electoral process.[33] The logic of corporate election financing is clear. As Aristotle noted in *Politics,* "When money has been spent to get office, the purchasers may naturally be expected to fall into the habit of trying to make a profit on the transaction."[34] Or, as Anne Wexler puts it, "it's very hard [for a politician] to turn somebody down when they've given a hundred thousand dollars to [his or her] campaign. In terms of getting in the door and making your case, it's obviously easier."[35]

Corporate donations now fuel the political system and are a core strategy in business's campaign to influence government. To cite just a few examples:

- The coal industry gave roughly $1.5 million to political campaigns, with $1.3 million (84 percent) of that going to Republicans, during the 2002 election cycle alone. Since 1990, the industry has spent close to $11 million on political contributions, with $8.4 million (77 percent) going to Republicans, which may help explain why the Bush administration seems so determined to cut the MSHA's budget.[36]

- Corporations that contributed money to the GOP and Republican candidates were granted significant access to the Cheney Task Force, created by President Bush in 2002 to formulate a national energy policy. Enron gave more than $2 million between 1999 and 2002 and got four contacts with the task force; Southern Company gave more than $1.5 million and got seven contacts; Exelon Corporation gave close to $1 million and got six contacts; and so on. Heavy contributors received other kinds of benefits as well. Chevron, for example, proposed relaxation of regulations governing the granting of federal permits to develop energy projects and those relating to fuel supply. Its proposals were adopted in their entirety.[37]

- In 1999, Jim Nicholson, chairman of the GOP at the time, wrote to Charles Heimbold, Jr., CEO of pharmaceutical

company Bristol-Myers Squibb, asking for a $250,000 dona-
tion and stating, among other things, that "we must keep
the lines of communication open if we want to keep passing
legislation that will benefit your industry."[38]

After donating more than a million dollars to congressional
candidates, most of them Republicans, during the 2001
election cycle, Eli Lilly and Company found itself the beneficiary of a provision, buried in the Homeland Security Act,
that protected thimerosal manufacturers—of which it is the
only one—from lawsuits arising out of harm caused by the
drug's use. Thimerosal is a mercury-based preservative used
in children's vaccines that may be linked to the development of autism in children. The provision was eventually
removed in response to public indignation and political
pressure.[39]

Whether through lobbying, political donations, or public relations
campaigns, corporations seek to influence the democratic process for
much the same reason the anti-Roosevelt plotters sought to destroy
it—they want to ensure that governments do not restrict their freedoms and frustrate their self-interested missions. "Big corporations . . .
will do whatever they believe is necessary to survive and in some cases
that means seeking special favors from the government," according to
William Niskanen. The money they spend on the political process is a
business expense, an investment in creating a political environment
that promotes their profitability and thus helps them survive. Lacking
the legal license to spend shareholders' money without a reasonable
prospect of return, corporations spend money on politics for the
same reason they make other investments: to advance their own and
their owners' financial self-interest.[40]

From the public's perspective, however, "We are," as Harvard's

Joe Badaracco says, "evolving . . . towards a system where corporations have an enormous and arguably disproportionate influence
on our political system." Democracy requires, at a minimum, some
measure of equality of opportunity to participate in the political
process. Yet profound inequality is the result when corporations—
huge concentrations of shareholder wealth—exercise the same rights
as individuals within that process. Today, warns Robert Monks, we
face a "situation of great precariousness"; we are "dangerously close to
the co-optation of government by business." "Unless we are
extremely attentive to the inclination of business to dominate government," he says, "it could well be that the institution [of government]
will fade."[41]

Yet many corporate insiders seem to believe they are performing
a public service when they seek to influence the political process on
behalf of the companies that employ them.

"Educating people" is how Anne Wexler describes her work as a lobbyist for major corporations. "It is very difficult for a member of
Congress, who is a very busy person, to understand what every issue is,
every day," she says. "Our job . . . is to be sure that the folks who are
going to be making the decisions at least have an understanding of
what the issues are." Chris Komisarjevsky, CEO of public relations
giant Burson-Marsteller, also believes his work, some of which is aimed
at defeating proposed environmental and other public-interest regulations on behalf of corporate clients, serves an important public purpose: "What we do is based on the respect of an individual to have
information put at their disposal and then make the right decision. . . .
It's the respect for the individual to make the right decision which I
believe is at the root of communications and it is clearly at the root of
the way Burson-Marsteller practices its business."

"I don't think it's unfair at all," continues Komisarjevsky about
the claim that corporations have an unfair advantage in the political
realm. "Everybody has the same opportunity to garner resources to

share a point of view. . . . There are plenty of resources to help people share whatever their point of view is."[42]

Pfizer CEO Hank McKinnell similarly believes that he promotes the public good when he lobbies politicians on behalf of his company. "When I lobby, I try to change government policy in a way that's a win/win for . . . both [Pfizer and the public]." As for his company's political contributions—which McKinnell says "are very modest actually; these are not large amounts of money, and frankly, it's part of the way in which people participate in national policy debates"— these too are designed to promote the public good. "We hope to elect people who have supported policies which are good for the nation," he says. "We want to elect people who understand the needs of the nation and are going to strive to benefit us all . . . who support the right kinds of policies . . . who can participate in the political process wisely." His political donations, he says, do not "give us anything special in return." Does he believe he has undue influence over the political process? Not really. "I don't feel like I have very much power at all," he says, "I can try to influence the thought process and policy, but it's a very slow process."[43]

Yet where are the desperately needed countervailing lobbies to represent the interests of average citizens? Where are the millions of dollars acting in *their* interests? Alas, they are notably absent.

The beliefs shared by Wexler, Komisarjevsky, and McKinnell that lobbying and political donations are public services rather than undue influences over government are likely informed by a deeper belief about the proper relationship between business and government. Today, says Wexler, "corporations essentially feel that they're partners with government . . . they're not adversaries of government. . . . The attitude that business is a victim is basically disappearing. . . . People understand now that government's got to be a partner, and you've got to work with them. . . . Essentially, the business/government relationship is a symbiotic relationship."[44]

Pfizer's Hank McKinnell agrees. "The key to progress in the

future is partnership," he says. "The best way to succeed in almost any social endeavor is in partnership. If you say this is solely the job of the federal government or the state government or the municipality, you're missing what's really been proven to work, which is partnerships, between both the public and the private sector."[45]

The notion that business and government are and should be partners is ubiquitous, unremarkable, and repeated like a mantra by leaders in both domains. It seems a compelling and innocuous idea—until you think about what it really means.

Partners should be equals. One partner should not wield power over the other, should not regulate the other, should not exert sovereignty over the other. Partners should share the same mission and the same goals. They should work together to solve problems and plan courses of action. Democracy, on the other hand, is necessarily hierarchical. It requires that the people, through the governments they elect, have sovereignty over corporations, not equality with them; that they have authority to decide what corporations can, cannot, and must do. If corporations and governments are indeed partners, we should be worried about the state of our democracy, for it means that government has effectively abdicated its sovereignty over the corporation.[46] A partnership between big business and government is what the plotters of the 1934 coup were after. They wanted Smedley Butler, a representative of big-business interests, to become Franklin Roosevelt's "partner" in governing the United States—a secretary of general affairs, or assistant president, who would quickly parlay his position into dictatorial power. Today corporations stand next to, rather than under, democratic governments in much the same way the plotters had planned for Smedley Butler to stand next to Roosevelt. Their leaders believe they have a legitimate role, as partners with government, in governing society.

By corollary, government is believed to have a less legitimate role in governing corporations. As stewards of the public interest, along with their government partners, corporations should be left free to regulate themselves—or at least that is the argument made by proponents of deregulation. "While some regulation is necessary to ensure that certain standards—minimal standards—are maintained," says Pfizer's Hank McKinnell, "in most cases best practices in industry are well ahead of government regulation, and in fact we have many examples of where excessive regulation has damaged industry." Corporations can regulate themselves now, according to Douglas G. Pinkham, president of the Washington, D.C.-based Public Affairs Council, and should be "given the freedom to deal with a concern [such as workers or the environment] in a constructive way that maybe doesn't involve government regulation, to create a voluntary code." In a similar spirit, BP's John Browne, complains that "there is still something of a belief that solutions lie fundamentally in regulation and control" in Europe and that even in the United States, a majority of people, according to one survey, believe that "companies needed regulation and could not be trusted to manage their own activities responsibly." Today, "regulations, central control, is not the direction people are going," says fellow oilman Jim Gray. "We have to be responsible at the other end, we in business, not to take advantage of circumstances."[47]

Yet business is all about taking advantage of circumstances. Corporate social responsibility is an oxymoron, I argued earlier, as is the related notion that corporations can, like their government counterparts, be relied upon to promote the public interest. Corporations have only one duty: to promote their own and their owners' interests. They have no capacity, and their executives no authority, to act out of a genuine sense of responsibility to society, to avoid causing harm to people and the environment, or to work to advance the public good in ways that are unrelated to their own self-interest. Deregulation thus rests upon the suspect premise that corporations will respect social and environmental interests without being compelled by government to do so. No one would seriously suggest that individuals should regulate themselves, that laws against murder, assault, and theft are unnecessary because people are socially responsible. Yet oddly, we are asked to believe that corporate persons—institutional psychopaths who lack any sense of moral conviction and who have the power and motivation to cause harm and devastation in the world—should be left free to govern themselves.

Corporations Unlimited

"It was one of the worst things I've seen in my lifetime." Carlton Brown, a normally unflappable commodities broker, was deeply troubled by what he had seen on September 11, 2001. "All I could think about was getting them the hell out," he says. "Before the building collapsed, all we were thinking was, let's get those clients out"—out of the gold market, that is. Brown was mainly concerned about clients who might get trapped in the gold market, which he knew would close once the World Trade Center towers collapsed. When the airplanes hit the towers, says Brown, "the first thing you thought about was 'Well, how much is gold up?'" Fortunately, he says, "in the next couple of days we got them all out . . . everybody doubled their money." September 11 "was a blessing in disguise, devastating, you know, crushing, heart-shattering. But . . . for my clients that were in the [gold] market, they all made money," he says. "In devastation there is opportunity. It's all about creating wealth."[1]

The corporation too is all about creating wealth, and it is a highly effective vehicle for doing so. No internal limits, whether moral, ethical, or legal, limit what or whom corporations can exploit to create wealth for themselves and their owners.[2] To "exploit," according to the dictionary, is to "use for one's own selfish ends or profit" (*The New Lexicon Webster's Encyclopedic Dictionary of the English Language*). Over the last century and a half, the corporation has sought and gained rights to exploit most of the world's natural resources and almost all areas of human endeavor. As early as 1932, Adolf Berle and Gardiner Means observed in *The Modern Corporation and Private Property*,

> Following the lead of the railroads, in the last part of the Nineteenth century and the early years of the Twentieth, one aspect of economic life after another has come under corporate sway. . . . In field after field, the corporation has entered, grown, and become wholly or partially dominant. . . . On the basis of its development in the past we may look forward to a time when practically all economic activity will be carried on under the corporate form.[3]

That time has come. Today practically all economic activity *is* carried on under the corporate form. One large barrier remains, however, to corporations being in control of everything: the public sphere.

The twentieth century was unique in modern history for the widely held belief that democracy required governments to protect citizens' social rights and meet their fundamental needs. Essential public interests, and social domains believed to be too precious, vulnerable, or morally sacred to subject to corporate exploitation, were inscribed by law and public policy within protective boundaries. Human beings could not be owned and children could not be exploited, either as workers or as consumers. Institutions essential to human health and survival (such as water utilities and health and welfare services), human progress and development (such as schools, universities, and cultural institutions), and public safety (such as police, courts, prisons, and firefighters), were deliberately placed beyond the corporation's exploitative grasp, as were precious natural domains, which were turned into parks and nature reserves.

The resulting public sphere, which exists to greater and lesser degrees in all modern nations, is now under attack. Historically, corporations have been hostile to it, as, from their perspective, it is little more than a collection of unwarranted exclusions from vast profit-making opportunities. Particularly over the last two decades, they have waged a determined campaign to push back its exclusionary boundaries. Through a process known as privatization, governments have capitulated and handed over to corporations control of institutions once thought to be inherently "public" in nature. No part of the public sphere has been immune to the infiltration of for-profit corporations. Water and power utilities, police, fire and emergency services, day care centers, welfare services, Social Security, colleges and universities, research, prisons, airports, health care, genes, broadcasting, the electromagnetic spectrum, public parks, and highways have all, depending on the jurisdiction, undergone, or are being considered for, full or partial privatization.[4]

As a result, we are moving toward a new kind of society, one that eventually could look similar to the model proposed by privatization advocates, such as economist Milton Friedman, who recommends that only 10 to 12 percent of total income—compared to what he estimates as 40 to 50 percent in the United States today—should come from government. Nothing but the most basic functions—the judicial system, the armed forces, and relief of the most extreme cases of poverty—Friedman says, should be within government's control. "The private area would be much larger," he says, "and it would be run largely by private for-profit enterprises." Many economists and policy makers agree with Friedman. Cato Institute chairman William Niskanen, for example, believes that "there are very few functions"—the only one he could think of was the military—that should remain in the public sphere. And Michael Walker, an economist who heads the Fraser Institute, Cato's Canadian partner, responded with an enthusiastic "Absolutely!" when asked whether he believed every square inch of the planet should be under private control.[5]

Such views may yet prevail, and, in the not-too-distant future, the public sphere could be reduced to a quaint historical anomaly.

"The classic investment opportunity is where there's a problem," according to investment banker Michael Moe. "The larger the problem, the larger the opportunity." And "there is no larger problem today"—and hence no larger investment opportunity—"than how to better educate our populace." Inspired by that belief, Moe helped raise more than a half a billion dollars to finance Edison Schools, a publicly traded for-profit company that operates schools on behalf of local governments and plans eventually to own and run its own schools. Edison Schools is the largest education management organization (EMO) in the United States, with 133 schools and 74,000 students currently under its control. It, along with roughly forty other EMO corporations, reflects a growing trend in the United States toward privatization of kindergarten through twelfth grade (K–12) education.[6]

Because the "education market" combines a large problem with a small corporate presence, says Moe, it is poised, much as health care was thirty years ago, to expand rapidly in the coming years. The industry is in the first inning of a nine-inning game that could go into extra innings, he says. In 2001 alone, for example, the number of EMOs in the United States increased by 70 percent. Conservatively, Moe estimates, 10 percent of the $800 billion education industry will be run by for-profit corporations in ten years' time, compared to 1 percent today. Government, much like other businesses, he says, now wants to outsource its operations, and it is likely in coming years to transform its role in education from an "owner-operator of schools . . .

to be more of a general contractor." Milton Friedman agrees. "I've been involved in this movement now for forty-five years," he says of his advocacy of privatized schools, "and it's in the last five years or so that we've really started to break the ice jam and get moving." In the not-too-distant future, he predicts, corporations like Edison Schools will "develop into enterprises that will run their own private schools," rather than just operating government-owned schools.[7]

No doubt huge opportunities await corporations such as Edison Schools that manage to infiltrate K–12 education in any significant way. It's "almost unimaginably vast," says Edison chairman Benno Schmidt, Jr., of the potential for growth in the industry. "Education is bigger than defense, bigger than the whole domestic auto industry. . . . In fact, only health care has a larger segment of the American marketplace." In other countries too, there are potentially bright futures for corporate schools, adds Moe, who cites Canada and the United Kingdom as just two examples of the many "countries around the world [that] are turning more toward market-driven mechanisms to reform their education systems."[8]

Backers of for-profit schools have used political muscle to promote the growth of their industry. Two of Edison's largest investors, Boston financier John Childs and Gap chairman Donald Fisher, recently donated $670,000 and $260,800, respectively, to the Republicans. They must have been pleased when President Bush pledged $3 billion in federal loans to fund new charter schools and subsidize students who wish to attend private schools, policy changes that will expand the markets for EMOs. Other big-money supporters of Bush also have major stakes in the education industry. Leading businessmen, such as Amway founder Richard De Vos, industrialist David Brennan, and Wal-Mart's John Walton, have supported Bush and spent millions of dollars promoting state voucher systems, which will create lucrative markets for EMOs once they are adopted.[9]

Despite their enthusiasm for privatized schools, proponents have no solid evidence to support their claims that such schools perform better, in terms of children's learning outcomes, than comparable public schools. Indeed, Edison's claims to that effect have been questioned by independent researchers at Western Michigan University who found that "Edison students do not perform as well as Edison claims in its annual reports on student performance."[10] The company has been criticized for other alleged exaggerations, such as inflating the numbers of schools it runs by counting each of the K-5, 6-8, and 9-12 grade divisions as separate schools in settings where they are actually all administered by one principal and housed in one building.[11]

But that is not the worst of Edison's troubles. Recently, shares in Edison Schools, which had reached a high of $21.68 on the Nasdaq stock exchange, plummeted to less than one dollar. To save money in running its Philadelphia schools, the company sold off textbooks, computers, lab supplies, and musical instruments. It also moved its executives into schoolrooms in the hope of saving $9,000 a month in rent on their corporate offices (upon learning about the move, the school board quickly ordered the executives out of the schools). Edison founder and CEO Chris Whittle further proposed that the company use unpaid Edison students to do the work of paid school employees. "We could have less adult staff," he is reported to have told a group of Edison principals as he described his plan to have each of six hundred students in a school work one hour a day at administrative tasks, thus making the work of seventy-five adults redundant.[12]

Proponents defend the privatization of schools, and privatization more generally, as theoretically correct, even while, in the real world, it often goes awry. Playing on people's self-interest in material gain, they say, echoing the premise of laissez-faire economic theory, is the surest route to promoting the public good. "People tend to react to economic incentives as a reason to do things," says Edison Schools financier Jeffrey Fromm, explaining why he thinks for-profit schools should outperform their public counterparts. Motivated by a desire to make money, teachers in for-profit schools will teach better, administrators will administer better, and corporations will provide their customers—parents, teachers, school boards—with what they want and need. Therefore, says Fromm, "the for-profit incentive can have a positive impact on schools," even though corporations "have to think . . . really only about one bottom line." Corporations can "provide the ability for change to be infused into the educational system," he believes, because the "Darwinism among business in a capitalist economy . . . if unleashed on the education system, will tend to produce better education in the U.S."[13]

Privatization thus makes the most of our inevitably selfish and materialist nature. "We owe our daily bread not to the benevolence of the baker but to his concern for his own interest" is how Milton Friedman, paraphrasing Adam Smith, explains the virtues of privatization. By corollary, public institutions are inherently flawed, according to Friedman and other privatization proponents, because they rely on an unrealistic—that is, not entirely selfish and materialistic—concept of human nature. "The big difference," Friedman told me when I asked him what separated his views from John Kenneth Galbraith's, "is whether you are really willing to accept the idea that civil servants are pursuing the interest of the community at large, rather than their own self-interest. That's the big divide. That's the divide between Galbraith and myself."[14]

Though privatized services might by some measures and in some contexts prove more effective than public ones, privatization is flawed as a general and long-term solution to society's problems. Philosophically, it rests upon a distorted and incomplete conception of human nature. Self-interest and materialistic desire are parts of who we are, but not all. To base a social and economic system on these traits is dangerously fundamentalist. At a more practical level, privatization is flawed for its reliance on for-profit corporations to deliver the public good. Unlike public institutions, whose only legitimate mandate is to serve the public good, corporations are legally required always to put their own interests above everyone else's. They may act in ways that promote the public good when it is to their advantage to do so, but they will just as quickly sacrifice it—it is their legal obligation to do so—when necessary to serve their own ends (as Edison's Philadelphia debacle demonstrates).[15] No doubt privatization opens up new areas for corporations to exploit for profit, which is why they zealously promote it. From the public's standpoint, however, we have to ask what kind of society we create when we put corporations in charge of the very sinews of our society—the institutions that define who we are, that bind us together, and that enable us to survive and live securely.

These concerns are not confined to privatization, however; they also extend to a closely related, though less formal process—the commercialization of society—which also involves corporations infiltrating areas of society from which, until recently, they were excluded.

The annual Vancouver Children's Festival was once a respite from commercialism. So I was taken aback when, on a recent visit to the festival with my son, we found ourselves in the middle of a mock Kia car dealership after entering the grounds through the main gate. Shiny new vehicles were seductively positioned on the grass, banners with Kia logos fluttered in the breeze, and chippy young Kia staff roamed the grounds giving away free stuff to kids. The festival had permitted the display in exchange for Kia's sponsorship dollars. My son wanted to play on the cars, and I had to pry him away so we could attend a concert by children's performer Raffi—a concert, it turned out, that would never happen. Raffi, appalled, he told me later, by "what appeared to be a car dealership" on the festival grounds, refused to play and withdrew from the festival. "I was just completely floored by this corporate visibility, this . . . gross commercialization," he said. "It was distressing to the max for me, and I didn't feel I could perform in that environment." So at my son's insistence we went back to the cars, where he nagged me persistently to buy him an SUV but settled for an inflatable dinosaur with a Kia logo on it.[16]

Then, during the National Hockey League Stanley Cup play-offs, my son nagged me again, this time to buy him a 24-pack of Labatt Blue beer. He absolutely had to have the plastic Stanley Cup replica that came with the 24-pack, a promotion he had learned about from an advertisement run frequently during the games. Labatt must have known that young children would be watching the Stanley Cup play-offs with their parents—it's a national ritual in Canada—and also that most adults would not be enticed to abandon their preferred brand of beer to obtain a plastic Stanley Cup replica. Therefore, it seems reasonable to assume that part of the company's aim was to get my son to get me to buy its beer—which it did.

In buying that beer (and being nagged to buy the Kia SUV) I was an unwitting victim of the Nag Factor, a brilliant new marketing strategy that takes manipulation of children to the extreme. Lucy Hughes, who serves as director of strategy and insight for Initiative Media, the world's largest communications management company, is one of the creators of the Nag Factor, a solution to a problem that has vexed marketers for years: How can money be extracted from young children who want to buy products but have no money of their own? Though "you can manipulate consumers into wanting and therefore buying your products," says Hughes, young children present unique challenges. For them, she realized several years ago—and this is the crucial insight behind the Nag Factor—advertisements must be aimed not at getting them to buy things but at getting them to nag their parents to buy things.[17]

To that end Hughes and her colleagues at Initiative Media, with the help of child psychologists, developed a scientific breakdown of different kinds of nags that children use and the differential impacts they have on different kinds of parents: "We found . . . that the way a child nags isn't always the same. That there's one of two ways. That they nag either with persistence or they nag with importance. When we talk about nagging with persistence, it's really whiny: 'Mommy, I really, really want the Barbie Dream House, wah, wah, wah, wah.' . . . Nagging with importance is that the child has associated some sort of importance to this product: 'Mommy, I need the Barbie Dream House so Barbie and Ken can live together and have children and have their own family.' . . . The way the child nags to the parent will have an impact on whether or not the parent will buy that product."[18]

The effectiveness of each kind of nag depends upon which of four types of parents is the target. "Bare necessities" parents, one of the largest groups, tend to be affluent and upscale but unresponsive to a child's whining. They want a good reason for buying something for their child. So, says Hughes, "we will try to get the kids to nag them with importance to show them the value or benefit this product has to them, why it's important to the child. And in the right circumstances the parent will be receptive to it." The other three groups of parents may be more susceptible to persistent whining. The smallest group, "kids' pals," tend to be younger parents who buy products, such as computer games and remote control toy trucks, for themselves as much as for their kids. "Indulgers" are working moms who buy things for their children to ease their guilt about not spending enough time with them. "Conflicted" parents, usually single moms, feel they shouldn't be buying frivolous things for their children but do so anyway; they say they don't like impulse buying, but they do it anyway; and they oppose advertising aimed at their children but welcome its assistance in helping them decide what to buy for them.[19]

The fate of entire corporate empires could depend upon marketers' abilities to get children to nag their parents effectively. "With McDonald's," for example, says Hughes, "parents wouldn't be going there unless their child nags." Chuck E. Cheese's? "Oh, my goodness," says Hughes. "It's noisy, and there's so many kids. Why would I want to spend two hours there?" Hughes, who says her company "wanted to be the first . . . [to] actually quantify the impact" of children's nagging, found that "anywhere from 20 percent to 40 percent of purchases would not have occurred unless the child had nagged their parents. . . . We found, for example, a quarter of all visits to theme parks wouldn't have occurred unless a child nagged their parents. Four out of ten visits to places like Chuck E. Cheese's would not have occurred. . . . We saw the same thing with movies, with home video, with fast food. Children's influence on what products the parents are buying is huge."

Children's influence extends well beyond children's products, even to high-end adult items, such as cars. "There are," says Hughes, "many features in a car that really do appeal to kids"[20]—which explains Kia's marketing efforts at the Vancouver Children's Festival, as well as its tie-in deals with blockbuster kid videos, such as *The Lord of the Rings* (a deal that, according to Kia, is designed to "build showroom traffic by leveraging the highly anticipated VHS/DVD release of the popular film") and *Shrek*. Kia is not alone in targeting children, however.[21] Nissan sponsors the American Youth Soccer Organization, Chrysler uses glossy kid-friendly pop-up books in direct mailing campaigns, and increasingly, kids are prominently featured in the car advertisements of all companies.[22]

"From a marketing point of view, it's pretty powerful stuff," says marketer Julie Halpin of the trend toward harnessing children's influence to sell adult products. "The toy and candy manufacturers have always been there and always will be. But we have a financial services client. Whoever thought a kid agency would have a financial services client?" Indeed.[23]

"Kids are amazing when they watch TV," marvels Hughes, "they're paying attention to the advertising. . . . How many people actually pay attention to the advertising? Among parents it's probably quite thin, quite small."[24] Targeting children makes a lot of sense from a marketing perspective, as it allows advertisers to bypass media-savvy parents and engage the considerable persuasive power children wield over their parents. Children are also easier to manipulate than adults. Lucy Hughes and her industry colleagues would likely agree with the experts that young children are particularly susceptible to media manipulation—that, as the American Academy of Pediatrics states, "young children under 8 years of age developmentally are unable to understand the intent of advertisements and, in fact, accept advertising claims as true. Indeed, the youngest viewers, up to age 8, cannot distinguish advertising from regular television programming."[25] For marketers and the corporations they work for, children's susceptibility to advertising is exactly what makes them such appealing targets. Within the psychopathic world of the corporation, vulnerability is an invitation to exploit, not a reason to protect.

Children, as "tomorrow's consumers . . . represent a huge market today" and therefore are "fair game" for corporations, says Lucy Hughes. Or, as another advertising executive puts it, "They aren't children so much as what we like to call 'evolving consumers.' "[26] "Is it ethical? I don't know," Hughes says of her work but then quickly states, as though the question about ethics is irrelevant, that her company's role is simply "to move products, and if we . . . move products . . . then we've done our job." Even Raffi, as staunch a critic of children's marketing as there is, feels compelled to acknowledge, though with regret, that "targeting children for increased sales is just part and parcel of what the laws of the land allow corporations to do. . . . The CEOs of corporations are doing what they're paid to do, which is to increase their per-share profit."[27]

Raffi is right about the law. In 1981, the Federal Communications Commission (FCC) lifted restrictions on children's advertising that it had put in place during the 1960s, reflecting its new preference for market solutions over regulatory ones. Television, according to then FCC chairman Mark Fowler, was just another household appli-

ance, a "toaster with pictures," and did not require special regulation.[28] Not surprisingly, children's advertising exploded once the ban
was lifted. As Harvard Medical School expert Dr. Susan Linn says,
"The average American child sees 30,000 commercials a year on television alone. . . . Comparing the marketing of yesteryear to the marketing of today is like comparing a BB gun to a smart bomb. The
advertising that children are exposed to today is honed by psychologists. It's enhanced by media technology that nobody ever thought
was possible. And also it is everywhere. They can't escape it. It finds
them in every nook and cranny of their life."

Pitching junk and fast food directly to children is one of the more
controversial tactics of children's marketers. Children crave food that
is bad for them and would, as parents well know, eat and drink little
else but candy, soda pop, and fast food if left to their own devices.
Corporations exploit this vulnerability with advertisements that make
sugary and high-fat foods irresistible to children and that undermine
parents' attempts to control their children's diets. In one Frito-Lay's
potato chips television advertisement, for example, three boys in a
school lunchroom excitedly pull bags of the chips out of their lunch
boxes, while a fourth boy, who must make do with only a banana, is
unhappy and shunned by the others—at least until he is given a bag
of the chips, in exchange for his banana, by a monkey. Even a three-
year-old would get the message: food that is good for you, a banana, is
bad; junk food, such as potato chips, is good. There are no limits on
what marketers will do to get children to crave junk food. Books
aimed at very young children use M&M's or Cheerios to help them
learn to count, reflecting industry wisdom that if you get kids young,
you've got them. "Babies are . . . having this experience of cuddling
with caretakers or parents [while they read them a book]," says Dr.
Linn, "and they're associating those warm cuddly wonderful feelings
with candy or with breakfast cereal."[29]

Critics blame marketing tactics like these for the epidemic levels of childhood obesity and the recent steep rise in related health problems among children. According to Linn, "Kids are being inundated with all of these images about high-fat foods or foods that are not particularly good for them. And the commercials have messages that say, 'Eat this and you'll feel better. Eat this and you'll be happy. Eat this and you'll be cool.' "[30]

Verity Newnham, speaking on behalf of a group of Australian physicians and researchers, describes the consequences:

> The aggressive marketing of fast food and confectionery to children does influence their dietary choices early in life, and it puts them at greater risk of becoming obese or overweight later in life. A major concern is childhood diabetes. [General practitioners] are seeing more children than ever before with type II diabetes, and that's a disease associated with poor diet and lack of exercise. Children can be extremely vulnerable to television advertising promoting fast food.[32]

A recent lead editorial in *The Lancet,* a prestigious medical journal, stated that "the soaring increase in obesity and type II diabetes among children is a public-health crisis, plausibly linked to the 'toxic environment' created in large part by the food industry." "It is time," the editorial concluded, "to return parents, teachers, and public-health professionals to their rightful roles as the real experts on children."[32]

In the meantime, from the perspective of marketers and corporations, there is always "opportunity in devastation" (to borrow a phrase from commodities broker Carlton Brown). With the epidemic levels of childhood obesity and close to one third of girls now wearing size 14 or larger, one marketer sees that "another opportunity [for the apparel industry] is clothing for plus-sized girls."[33] With the diet food and drug industries also benefiting from obesity, much profit, not just weight, is being gained as a result of the obesity epidemic. Industry representatives defend their tactics and blame irresponsible parents and other factors for the ill effects of junk and fast food on children. "The issue of overweight and obesity among some Americans is complex and multifaceted," says Tom Foulkes, spokesperson for the U.S. National Restaurant Association. "Common sense and personal responsibility must prevail, and that includes parental responsibility."[34] Jill Holroyd, vice president of research and communications at the Canadian Restaurant and Foodservices Association, adds, "The kids aren't driving themselves to the restaurants." "The real issue in our view," she says, "is personal responsibility. Parents have a responsibility to make sure their children are consuming a balanced diet and getting enough physical activity."[35]

According to Harvard business ethics expert Joe Badaracco, "On the question of advertising to young kids, I'm inclined to say that it's fine so long as it doesn't work very well." The problem, however, is that it does work well. Junk-food marketers' claim to innocence is about as plausible as the tobacco industry's long-standing position that cigarette advertising does not increase smoking. Marketers such as Lucy Hughes work hard to design campaigns that encourage children to nag their parents to buy junk food and to take them to fast-food restaurants. It is more difficult for a parent to say "no" to a child when the child has been urged by advertisers to question the parent's authority over food and is persuaded that he or she *needs* the advertised product. Under these conditions, the result of saying "no" is often petulance, sulking, acting out, and family conflict—which is why so many parents are prone to just put the kids in the car and drive to McDonald's. With the industry actually working to incite children to punish their parents for saying "no," its blaming parents for saying "yes" has more than a ring of hypocrisy to it.[36]

Fortunately, some people in advertising are honest about what they do. "I'm sucking Satan's pecker" is how Chris Hooper, a highly successful television ad director and voice-over artist, describes his work for the likes of McDonald's, Coca-Cola, and other major corporations. Hooper says his job is to create "images that are trying to sell products to people that they don't really need" and that "encourage very sophomoric behavior, irresponsible, hedonistic, egotistical, narcissistic behavior." Despite this he carries on, taking some comfort from his belief that other people in his industry share "this strange discomfort with what they're doing." "You know," he says, "if I had to do another McDonald's commercial, I would. I would because—I know I sound like . . . a Nazi or something—if I didn't do it somebody else would." Hooper salves his conscience by doing free anticorporate advertising spots. It was he, for example, who did the voice-overs for the television advertisements that were part of Ralph Nader's presidential campaign.[37]

Children's minds, not just their bodies, are ill served by the exploitative marketing practices of corporations, says Steve Kline, a communications expert who specializes in children's culture. Kline believes that "promotional and synergistic saturation marketing," a prevalent practice in the toy industry today, is causing a "diminishment of the imagination of the child." Corporate tie-in toys—such as Play-Doh's McDonald's Happy Meal molds, Mattel's Barbie dolls that work at McDonald's drive-throughs, or Burger King's free (with a meal) *Men in Black* toys, or any number of television show products (G.I. Joe and Rescue Heroes toys) and movie products (*Star Wars* and *Spider-Man* toys)—turn children's play into "a highly repetitive reproduction of the scripts provided by the toy merchandisers," Kline says. As a consequence, children are losing their abilities to "make meaning for themselves," "to go off on their own and . . . construct their own little world and negotiate it amongst themselves."[38]

What children really need, says Kline, are toys that encourage "creative destruction," the process of imagining, creating, destroying, and re-creating something, and that "give them a sense of mastery [and] help them explore the physical laws of the world." Corporations are unlikely to make such toys, however, when the profits from synergistic marketing are so high. The toy companies are "clearly selling more toys" now, says Kline. "Toy sales boomed after the initial launch of those tie-in programs." Even LEGO, the quintessential "creative destruction" toy company, adopted the tie-in strategy, driven to it by bottom-line concerns (and despite Kline's protests when he worked as a consultant for the company), and began to make LEGO sets based on characters and scenes from popular children's movies, such as *Star Wars* and *Harry Potter*.[39] (Old-style "creative destruction" LEGO, in the meantime, is now being used in management workshops to stimulate the creativity and imaginations of corporate executives.[40])

Kline worries that, as children's worlds become increasingly defined by profit-driven synergies among megacorporations, a kind of corporate "enclosure of childhood" is taking place, with children living more and more of their lives inside "brand enclosures." "Children now," says Kline, can no longer "imagine that the world hasn't been totally reconstructed by the corporation . . . that there are ways of being outside of that commercialized space." We are "producing kids as consumers" first, he says, and becoming less good at creating "competent citizens . . . good, moral and virtuous human beings." Susan Linn agrees with Kline, adding that, with the hypercommercialization of their worlds, we are teaching children that it's all about "me first" and failing to instill in them fundamental skills of democratic citizenship: "cooperation . . . living in a society . . . and working and playing with other people."[41]

There are indeed few places today where children can escape the encroaching influence of corporations. Even their schools have become platforms for corporate marketing and propaganda, as cash-starved school boards, in exchange for money and products,

- Provide corporations advertising space on scoreboards, rooftops, bulletin boards, walls, computer screen savers, textbook covers, and school Web sites

- Enter into contracts with corporations to sell their products exclusively in school vending machines and lunchrooms (Coca-Cola and Pepsi are notorious for doing this)

- Enter into sponsorship agreements (Wells Fargo Bank, for example, paid $12,000 to get its name onto an Arizona high school athletic conference)

- Accept strategic philanthropy (such as my son's school program that invites students to bring in labels from a local dairy company's products, which the school then exchanges for donations from the company)[42]

Corporations have even infiltrated school curricula with curriculum kits, usually offered to schools for free, that promote their products (such as the school program on nutrition sponsored by McDonald's that uses a Big Mac to illustrate the four food groups);[43] and their perspectives (such as Procter & Gamble's classroom Decision Earth program, which states that "clear cutting removes all trees . . . to create new habitats for wildlife. P&G uses this economically and environmentally sound method because it most closely mimics nature's own processes. Clear cutting also opens the floor to sunshine, thus stimulating growth and providing food for animals").[44]

In many schools, television advertisements are a central part of students' daily fare. Channel One, a project of Edison Schools' founder, Chris Whittle, produces ten-minute news programs followed by two-minute advertising sequences for schools that agree, in three-year contracts with the company, to ensure that at least 90 percent of their students watch the program daily. In exchange, schools receive from the company a satellite dish, two VCRs, a television for each classroom, and wiring and maintenance facilities. Though some states have barred Channel One from their classrooms, the company still claims to reach 40 percent of all middle school and high school students in the United States. Proponents of Channel One point to the free equipment and exposure to news students get, and claim, along with tobacco and junk-food advertisers, that the advertising has no effect on students (one wonders if they make similar claims to prospective buyers of advertising slots). Studies demonstrate, however, that exposure to the shows increases students' product evaluations and desires to buy the advertised products, and also fosters consumer-related attitudes of materialism, results that may be partly explained, according to one study, by the "implicit endorsement of these products by the schools, that is, by permitting them to be advertised in school."[45]

Corporations become involved with schools for the same reason they do everything else—to promote their own and their owners' financial interests. "If there's a cardinal rule in preparing sponsored material," states Ed Swanson of Modern Talking Pictures (an educational marketing company), "it is that it must serve the needs of the communicator first." "The kids we're reaching are consumers in training" is how another educational marketing executive, Joseph Fenton of Donelley Marketing, describes the benefits to corporations of becoming involved with schools. "You want to reach consumers at their most formative point."[46]

Schools are being transformed into commercial enclaves by the various forms of advertising and promotion that corporations are using within them. They are, however, just microcosms of the wider commercialized world. Advertising is now inescapable, whether on our television or computer screens, huge outdoor billboards and electrical signs, wrapped around buses and subway cars (sometimes covering even their windows), or at museums, concerts, galleries, and sporting events, which increasingly seem like little more than shills for their corporate sponsors. Beyond these tangible signs of encroaching commercialism, however, an even more subtle process is under way: the places where we interact as social beings, our public spaces, are increasingly commercialized.

"PUBLIC SPACE," proclaims a plaque in the AT&T Plaza in New York, "Owned and Maintained by AT&T."[47] The "street"—a term that denotes not only streets but other public places such as plazas and town squares—occupies a central place in the democratic imagination. It is a public urban space, a place where people meet and congregate, where they rally, protest, march, picket, shout through megaphones, convey various forms of information, and simply enjoy their freedom just to be in public. The idea of freedom of speech draws much of its evocative power from the street, whether through images of protesters in Tiananmen Square, soapbox orators at Speakers' Corner in London's Hyde Park, or civil rights and labor marches through downtown streets.[48]

The street, however, is disappearing as suburban town centers give way to shopping malls and downtown sidewalks are replaced by commercialized skywalks and tunnels. As one commentator observes:

> Sidewalks are changing; they are moving indoors into private property. During the last several decades, [we] have witnessed the erosion of traditional streets where public life transpired. The automobile, the skyscraper, the dispersed residential suburb, and the shopping mall have contributed to the demise of a pedestrian-oriented, outdoor street life in our city cores. . . . Civic life now occurs indoors on privately owned, publicly used, pedestrian places in the form of above-ground "skywalks" between buildings, ground-level office and retail complexes, atriums and shopping malls, and below-ground shop-lined tunnels.[49]

In Toronto's downtown core, for example, ten kilometers of tunnels connect 1,100 shops and services, sixty-three buildings, nineteen shopping malls, five subway stations, four hotels, the stock exchange, and city hall. Thirty-six principal corporations own the various buildings that make up the underground network, which is used by approximately a hundred thousand pedestrians each day.[50]

More than eighty other North American cities have similar enclosed pedestrian systems, though sometimes they are elevated skywalks rather than tunnels.[51] Almost all of downtown Minneapolis, for example—hundreds of shops and services, four major department stores, government buildings, and corporate headquarters—are connected by more than seven miles of skyways, each segment built, owned, and maintained by the companies (and sometimes government agencies) whose buildings they connect. The skyways are lined with advertising, much of it provided by CityLites USA—the self-proclaimed "providers of skyway advertising," which boasts that its "backlit advertising program [in Minneapolis] makes it possible to reach up to 1,000,000 upscale decision-makers each week."[52]

Urban tunnels and skywalks, along with suburban malls, are places designed and used for public interaction but controlled by private owners, generally large corporations, which control what happens and who can be on their premises. Security guards and surveillance equipment are ubiquitous because, as one commentator points out, "The proprietors must maintain an atmosphere conducive to business, which necessitates prohibiting those members of the public and activities they perceive as detracting from this objective"[53]—such as, for example, picketers, protesters, leafleters, and homeless people. Because malls, tunnels, and skywalks are private property, citizens' exercise of rights to free speech and assembly can be more easily curtailed in these places than on comparable public property.[54] They also tend to be decorated and designed in ways that create environments comfortable for middle-class and upscale consumers but no one else.[55]

On the residential side, gated neighborhoods, walled off from the surrounding areas and regulated through networks of covenants relating to use and services, are now home to as many as 4 million people in the United States. They represent, in the words of one study, "a trend away from increased governmental control over land use and governmental provision of services and toward an increased reliance on privately created controls and privately supplied services" and "provide a new and more potent way to exclude unwanted persons and uses from the company of those rich enough to afford the increased control and privacy supplied in such developments."[56]

Public space is overtly commercialized when urban streets are replaced by private tunnels and sidewalks, suburban town centers with shopping malls, and municipalities with gated communities There are, however, covert forms of commercialization as well, some so subtle that you don't even know they are happening.

Imagine that you are walking along an out-of-the-way trail in a national park. A group of young hikers is standing at the side of the trail talking to one another in loud, excited voices. You cannot help but overhear them. "They would be talking about the great backpack they are wearing," says Jonathon Ressler, CEO of marketing firm Big Fat, "how [with other backpacks] your back hurts after you hike 84,000 miles . . . [but] with this backpack it has a special da-da-da-da . . . it's really comfortable. Boom," says Ressler, they "have just delivered the message" to you—and you have no idea that you were just pitched a product by a group of professional actors working for Big Fat.[57]

Undercover marketing, the name of this technique, "is happening everywhere," according to Ressler, the man credited with its invention: "It happens in bars, it happens at soccer games, it happens in shopping malls, it happens in subways, it happens in the movie theater. . . . The beauty part is if [the operatives] are doing it well, you don't even know it's happening, so there's stuff going on all around you all the time—which I know is kind of scary, but it is going on all around you all the time."

In fact, says Ressler, undercover marketing is inescapable. On a typical day, "by the time you go to bed you've probably received eight or nine different undercover messages," he says. As you leave your apartment building in the morning, you may notice a bunch of boxes from an on-line or mail-order retailer at the doorman's feet. "Wow! A lot of people must be ordering from that company," you think. "What you don't know," says Ressler, "is that we paid the doorman to keep those empty boxes there."

Then, while you're waiting for the bus, "you hear some people having a kind of loud conversation about a musical act, and they're kind of passing the headphones back and forth and going, 'Wow, this is great! Hey, do you know that I heard this CD is really hard to find, but I heard they sell it at store X.' "

Next you get to work, and you find the office fridge is stocked with a certain brand of water. You drink some. " 'Wow! That's pretty good water,' " you think, says Ressler. "Who knows? Maybe someone placed the water there." On your lunch break, you go to the park and sit on a bench. People next to you "are talking about . . . a hot restaurant they heard about and you think, 'Hmm, I have a date Friday night. Maybe I should go there.' "

When you get back to your apartment building and take the garbage down to the compactor room, you find that "there are a bunch of those boxes from that on-line company . . . ," says Ressler. "'Wow, people must really be ordering from . . . this on-line retailer,'" you think.

You go out to a bar. As you're waiting in line, you notice that the doormen have a box of Brand X soft drink at their feet. They are drinking it and handing it out to people in the line. Then, once inside, you are standing at the bar waiting to order a [drink]. Someone—"what we call 'leaners,' " says Ressler, "they kind of lean over because the bar is crowded"—taps you on the shoulder: "Would you mind getting me a Brand X drink?" she asks. You, if you "are even remotely human . . . are going to say, 'Hey, what is Brand X? I've never heard of it,' " says Ressler, "And bang!" The message that Brand X is great quickly spreads, beginning with you, through the rest of the bar. "Send in three leaners into a busy bar," says Ressler, "within an hour everybody's ordering that drink."[58]

"The whole key to undercover marketing is never knowing that it's going on," says Ressler. The practice is premised entirely on deception, which is why undercover operatives must sign confidentiality agreements—if someone asks them whether they are doing undercover marketing, "technically they would have to be dishonest and say 'no,' " says Ressler—yet it is perfectly acceptable within the corporation's amoral universe. Indeed, Ressler says he is proud of Big Fat's commitment to honesty—"what we are telling you is true," he says.[59] Notwithstanding Ressler's rosy view of it, however, undercover marketing, with deception at its core, is another example of how unrestrained corporations—not just Ressler's Big Fat, but the corporations that hire him as well—can be in their search for profit. More than that, however, undercover marketing demonstrates how deep the commercialization of society now runs.

"The corporation has essentially replaced the church in terms of who you are," says Edison Schools financier Michael Moe. It wants the same thing as the church, he says: "obedient constituents that . . . pay [their] dues and follow the rules." Human nature is neither static nor universal. It tends to reflect the social orders people inhabit. Throughout history, dominant institutions have established roles and identities for their subjects that meshed with their own institutional natures, needs and interests: God-fearing subjects for the church, lords and serfs for feudal orders, citizens for democratic governments.[60]

As the corporation comes to dominate society—through, among other things, privatization and commercialization—its ideal conception of human nature inevitably becomes dominant too. And that is a frightening prospect. The corporation, after all, is deliberately designed to be a psychopath: purely self-interested, incapable of concern for others, amoral, and without conscience—in a word, inhuman—and its goal, as Noam Chomsky states, is to "ensure that the human beings who [it is] interacting with, you and me, also become inhuman. You have to drive out of people's heads natural sentiments like care about others, or sympathy, or solidarity. . . . The ideal is to have individuals who are totally disassociated from one another, who don't care about anyone else . . . whose conception of themselves, their sense of value, is 'Just how many created wants can I satisfy? And how deeply can I go into debt and still get away with satisfying created wants?' If you can create a society in which the smallest unit is a person and a tube, and no connections to people, that would be ideal."[61]

Chomsky says that the "main driving force" behind privatization is "not just profit for Wall Street" but also reinforcement of the corporation's particular conception of humanity. Privatization of the Social Security system, for example, he says, is designed, in part, "to undermine the very dangerous principle on which Social Security rests, namely . . . that you care about whether a widow down the street has something to eat. You're not supposed to do that. You're supposed to only gain wealth, forgetting about all but self. . . . Same with schools. [With privatization] you're undermining the social solidarity that the public system relies on, that is the idea that I care whether the kid down the street goes to school. Well, make sure to undermine that because you're supposed to be out for yourself and no one else."[62]

"From the point of view of the corporation," adds philosopher Mark Kingwell, "the ideal citizen is a kind of insanely rapacious consumer," driven by a "kind of psychopathic version of self-interest."[63] A century and a half after its birth, the modern business corporation, an artificial person made in the image of a human psychopath, now is seeking to remake real people in *its* image.

Chris Barrett says he was "willing to do anything really" for the corporation, First USA, that sponsored his life and the life of his friend Luke McCabe. Luke, for his part, says he would have tattooed his body with First USA's logo if the company had asked him to. Such a tattoo, adds Chris, "would be a good thing when you have kids and they ask you, 'Daddy, what does that mean?' And you can tell them some great stories. Like our parents had war stories and stuff to tell us, we have our corporate sponsorship story." "Exactly," says Luke, who, when asked where he would put the tattoo, says he would "have to wait for the company to tell me that."[64]

Chris and Luke are the world's first corporate-sponsored human beings. The two teenagers had planned to attend college in California but then learned, on a recruitment visit to the University of San Diego, that it would cost them a prohibitive $40,000 a year. Discouraged, they returned to their hotel room and turned on the television. Tiger Woods was on, playing golf in his Nike cap. "We figured, you know, he probably gets like millions of dollars just to wear the hat on a press conference or something like that," which gave Luke an idea. He and Chris could go one step further than Tiger Woods, he realized. They could offer up their lives, not just their golf games, for a corporation to sponsor.[65]

The two created a Web site, ChrisAndLuke.com, on which they undertook to become living advertisements for the corporation that would pay their college tuition. More than fifteen corporations asked to be the one. Chris and Luke chose First USA, a Bank One company and the largest Visa card vendor in the world. College students are a lucrative market for the company.[66]

In return for its sponsorship dollars, First USA asked Chris and Luke to promote the company's credit cards to students on college campuses—to tell them, as Chris describes it, that "you need a credit card . . . [and also that] you need to learn how to use it properly." Beyond that, Chris and Luke were obliged by their contracts with the company to obey the law—"We can't go out there and get arrested. We can't kill anyone," says Chris—and to maintain at least a C average in their college studies. Not everything was explicitly spelled out in the contract, however. For example, the agreement was silent on whether the two could participate in anticorporate demonstrations.

When asked about that, Chris inferred that "Since we are corporately sponsored . . . maybe we could go there and help out other . . . students and let them know that maybe the corporation isn't as bad as they think it is." "Exactly," added Luke. "These people, such as the ones who are at the anticorporation things, just focus on maybe one or two bad things, and they don't see the good things that the corporations are doing for society."[67]

Chris and Luke have no desire to protest against corporations, so it is unlikely they would find themselves constrained by their sponsorship deal. Indeed, with their lives sponsored by a corporation, they have mainly good feelings about the institution.

LUKE: I have a lot of faith in the corporate world because it's always going to be there, so you may as well have faith in it because if you don't then it's just not good.

CHRIS: People just have to understand that the corporations are trying to do their best, I think. And they're all in there to help out the community and each country that they're in.

LUKE: I mean, it's definitely a positive thing when you can have big corporations spending their money just little bits here and there, on, you know, helping kids with their education. Or, you know, helping other people in need in any sort of way . . . as long as they, you know, continue to send a little bit to charity or help kids with education and stuff, I think it's very good.[68]

Chris believes that he and Luke have "contributed to the corporate takeover [of society] in a positive way." Corporate sponsorship, he says, has the potential to solve all kinds of social problems, even homelessness. One day in New York City he saw a homeless man watching a television set he had rigged up at his spot on the street. Passersby would stop, intrigued, and watch the man watching TV. Some would have pictures taken of themselves standing next to him. There was a real opportunity here, Chris thought to himself. The homeless man could find a corporation to sponsor him. Polaroid, for example, could promote its cameras by hiring a photographer to take pictures of people posing with him. He would receive a sponsorship fee from the company, and the posers would get free pictures. The homeless and many others can take inspiration from Chris and Luke's story, says Luke, because it demonstrates "that anyone can basically do whatever you want just as long as you have the heart and the desire to have it follow through and do all that it can do."[69]

Chris and Luke also "symbolize the increasing normalization and acceptance of commercialization in virtually every area of life," however, as commentators Alex Molnar and Joseph Reaves point out.[70] The idea that some areas of society and life are too precious, vulnerable, sacred, or important for the public interest to be subject to commercial exploitation seems to be losing its influence. Indeed, the very notion that there *is* a public interest, a common good that transcends our individual self-interest, is slipping away. Increasingly, we are told, commercial potential is the measure of all value, corporations should be free to exploit anything and anyone for profit, and human beings are creatures of pure self-interest and materialistic desire. These are the elements of an emerging order that may prove to be as dangerous as any fundamentalism that history has produced. For in a world where anything or anyone can be owned, manipulated, and exploited for profit, everything and everyone will eventually be.

6

Reckoning

Over the course of the twentieth century the world stumbled, halt-ingly and unevenly, toward greater democracy and humanity. New nations embraced democratic ideals, and governments in extant democracies expanded their domain over society and the economy. Social programs and economic regulations, such as Roosevelt's New Deal and later initiatives in the United States, were created as part of a broad midcentury movement by Western governments to protect their citizens from neglect by the market and from exploitation by corporations. Beginning in the latter part of the century, however, governments began to retreat. Under pressure from corporate lobbies and economic globalization, they embraced policies informed by neoliberalism. Deregulation freed corporations from legal constraints, and privatization empowered them to govern areas of society from which they had previously been excluded. By the end of the century, the corporation had become the world's dominant institution.

Yet history humbles dominant institutions. Great empires, the church, the monarchy, the Communist parties of Eastern Europe were all overthrown, diminished, or absorbed into new orders. It is unlikely that the corporation will be the first dominant institution to defy history. It has failed to solve, and indeed has worsened, some of the world's most pressing problems: poverty, war, environmental destruction, ill health. And growing numbers of people—activists, Main Street Americans, the globe's poor and disenfranchised, and even business leaders—believe that rationalized greed and mandated selfishness must give way to more human values. Though the collapse of corporate capitalism is not imminent, people are increasingly uneasy with the system. The hard question is, What do we do now about, and with, the corporation?

On November 25, 1997, I watched through my office window as thousands of students spilled out of their classrooms and dormitories and marched across the University of British Columbia campus to confront a wall of police. The students were protesting against the Asia Pacific Economic Cooperation (APEC) summit, a meeting of world leaders, among them Bill Clinton and Indonesia's since-disgraced Suharto, who had gathered to advance the free trade agenda of economic globalization. I ventured outside—Constitution in one hand, library card in the other (it identified me as a law professor at the university)—to try to protect the students' civil rights from overzealous police. My efforts were futile, which came as no surprise.

The real surprise was that the protest had happened at all. Most students in mid-1990s North America were building investment portfolios, not social movements, I had thought. Yet here they were, thousands of them, braving pepper spray and police batons to fight for ideals. Even more unusual, the students were protesting against corporations—against their destruction of the environment, exploitation of workers, and abuses of human rights. For the first time since the Great Depression and after years in the shadows of other issues—civil rights, the Vietnam War, race and gender politics—the corporation was back in the spotlight of political dissent. Throughout the late

1990s and early 2000s, protesters continued to dog the architects of economic globalization wherever they met. Soon after the 1997 APEC protest in Vancouver, Seattle was rocked by a massive demonstration—the "Battle of Seattle," as it was dubbed by the media—prompted by a meeting of the World Trade Organization in that city. Similar protests soon followed throughout North America and Europe, most recently at the G8 meeting in Geneva in 2003.

Though some business leaders dismissed the antiglobalization protesters as ignorant, marginal malcontents, most of them understood that thousands of people in the streets, risking injury and even death for a cause, reflected an anger that runs wide and deep in society. "It would be a grave mistake to dismiss the uproar witnessed in the past few years in Seattle, Washington, D.C., and Prague," warned *Business Week.* "Many of the radicals leading the protests may be on the political fringe. . . . Yet if global capitalism's flaws aren't addressed, the backlash could grow more severe."[1]

Ira Jackson, a former Boston banker and head of the John F. Kennedy School of Government's Center for Business and Government at Harvard, warns that the antiglobalization protests are a sign that business may be overplaying its hand. "We've won," he says of capitalism's triumph over communism, but growing resentment toward the corporate system could snowball into "a potential backlash that will be felt well beyond the mean streets of Seattle, Davos, and Prague." This is no time, he says, for business to "binge at the Ritz." Though "capitalism has no competition and capitalism rules . . . it's leaving many behind," and that could become a source of "resentment and a potential backlash."[2] With half the world's population living in poverty and the earth spiraling toward ecological catastrophe, Karl Marx's prophecy that capitalists would eventually hang themselves on their own excesses will come true, says Jackson, unless corporations change their ways. Marx and Engels's "Communist Manifesto" was seductive, he says, because, like the Bible itself, it was a moral treatise. The problem with capitalism is that "we have a global theology without morality, without a Bible." And that's dangerous, he warns—"we're not going to be able to exist in a global context if we are the bastards of our business." Capitalism needs the moral equivalent of the "Communist Manifesto," he says, "a manifesto for capitalism."[3]

Prior to Enron's collapse and the spate of scandals that followed, Harvard Business School professor Joe Badaracco observed that the antiglobalization protests, though significant for what they were, had not yet "resonated . . . with middle America." "If [among other things] there's scandals involving politicians and companies," however, he said, then middle America could join the antiglobalization protesters in their anger toward corporations. The scandals have arrived, and people's distrust of corporations is running high, perhaps as high as it did during the Great Depression.[4]

Recently, three of the world's top business thinkers—Harvard's Robert Simons, McGill's Henry Mintzberg, and Oxford's Kunal Basu—joined forces to pen a manifesto for the corporation. "Capitalism is facing a crisis," they warned. Scandals on Wall Street are "merely the tip of the black iceberg," beneath which lies "a culture that is increasingly defined by selfishness" and that threatens to destroy business, "the very thing we cherish." CEOs, they say, "have learned to repeat almost mindlessly," like a mantra, that "corporations exist to maximize shareholder value"; they are trained to believe self-interest is "the first law of business." And the notion that "a rising tide lifts all boats" is believed by businesspeople to "rationalize what otherwise looks like self-serving behavior," despite its profound implausibility (the facts belie the concept, according to the professors, who point out that "at the height of a decade-long economic boom, one in six American children was officially poor and 26% of the workforce was subsisting on poverty-level wages . . . [and] more than 30% of US households have a net worth—including homes and investments—of less than $10,000"). "The recent backlash against globalization," say the professors, "is due in no small part to the promises that capitalism hasn't kept to poor people in poor countries—those whose boats have not been lifted."[5]

Many businesspeople, and others too, share the professors' views. But what is the remedy for the corporation's current afflictions? In the past, at least during the last century, people turned to government when they lost faith in corporations. Today, however, many business leaders insist that government regulation is no longer an option for curtailing corporate harms. They champion the market instead as the most capable and appropriate regulator of corporate behavior.

"What we need is not more intrusive government," says Ira Jackson. "When government is in retreat, when public confidence in public institutions is so low, when capitalism and corporations are so powerful," the market, not government, is where solutions lie. "The customer and the consumer and the employee are the kings and the queens of the new capitalism, and we have to start exercising our authority and opportunity responsibly." Business leaders are not "a bunch of socialists in drag" when they embrace social responsibility, he feels, nor do they do it "because government is putting a gun to their head" or "because they've suddenly read a book about Transcendental Meditation and global morality." Rather, "they understand the market requires them to be there, that there's competitive advantage to be there." That is why BP's John Browne is Jackson's ideal CEO: "He's not wearing his ethics on his sleeve, and he's not on a moral hobbyhorse. And he doesn't believe that BP was created so that he can give out more philanthropy at the end of the day. What he and others are purporting to do and the reason they've embraced these new principles [of social responsibility] as business practices is that the market has changed."

Browne and other socially responsible business leaders understand that profit and conscience are not contradictions, says Jackson; that there is synergy between the two—"the opportunity for one and one to equal five or seven or nine."[6]

Many among the business elite echo Jackson's views. Chris Komisarjevsky, CEO of Burson-Marsteller, for example, says, "Corporate social responsibility is a mandate that companies have today. They don't have any choice. The fact of the matter is that when you look at the research, our research as well as other research you'll find that . . . those people who shape opinions . . . are saying to companies, 'Yes, we want you to earn a return, but we want you to do it right. And we want you to do it in a responsible way. We don't want you to abuse the environment. We don't want you to abuse ethics. We don't want you to abuse people's rights. We want you to do it properly, and we're going to hold you accountable for it.' "

Pfizer chief Hank McKinnell agrees. "If you define your mission as to maximize profit to the expense of all others," he says, "the 'all others' will treat you as a problem." And BP's John Browne believes that people's angst about corporations—the "quiet monster living in the public mood," as he calls it—can be tamed by corporate social responsibility. "If we're going to win back public acceptance and trust," he says, "we have to be progressive."[7]

Robert Monks too shares Jackson's belief that solutions lie with the market, rather than with more government regulation—"There is no need for government intervention," he says, as "the market can and will respond appropriately if it has the right information"—but he would rely on stock markets instead of consumer markets as vehicles to check corporate abuse.[8] Because so many people now own company stock, usually through their pension plans, shareholders can serve as "a good proxy for the public good," he says, and use their power of ownership to protect society and the environment from corporate misdeeds:

Increasingly the two [pension-plan shareholders and the broader
public] are one and the same. . . . In a very real sense, [pension-plan
shareholders] *are* the public. Like all ordinary people, pensioners
not only want to receive payments sufficient to afford a decent standard of living, but also to live in a world that is civil, clean, and safe.[9]

Therefore, Monks believes, if shareholders become an "effective,
informed, competent counter force to whom management must be
accountable," which is what he advocates, much of what citizens
might otherwise seek through the political process will be available to
them as shareholders. The idea, which Monks calls fiduciary capitalism, is to "restore ancient values of ownership that preceded the corporate form, and that seem to have eluded corporations in the long
modern era."[10]

Whether, as Monks suggests, shareholders are a "proxy for the
public good" or, as in Jackson's model, consumers play that role, the
central idea is the same: corporations can be, and should be, controlled, at least to a large degree, by markets rather than government
regulators. People's decisions about what products or what shares to
buy are, within these models, expected to have a *political* character,
to serve as effective public-interest constraints on corporate behavior.
The models—and Jackson's and Monks's prescriptions are examples
of two broader ideas known, respectively, as "consumer democracy"
and "shareholder democracy"—are not entirely implausible.
Corporations do sometimes modify their behavior in positive ways to
please or placate shareholders and consumers. They fall far short,
however, of providing effective and reliable substitutes for government regulation.

One premise of democracy is that, as citizens, all people are
equal, at least within the political sphere. Everyone has one vote,
regardless of his or her wealth or social position, and that means, in
relation to corporations, that every citizen has an equal say about

how these powerful entities must behave. Moving regulation of corporations from government to the market immunizes them to the effects of citizens' participation in the political process and leaves their control to an institution where one *dollar*—not one person—equals one vote. "At least in a democracy each person is formally equal," says political economist Elaine Bernard, executive director of the Trade Union Program at Harvard University. "The humblest citizen, the most prestigious citizen still only has one vote. But when we move that power over to the marketplace, the humblest and the wealthiest are totally asymmetrical. And one has such immense power that they can literally crush the other completely and utterly and fully. So that's one of the reason historically we've always felt the need to regulate markets."[11]

To say, as Jackson does, that consumers are the kings and queens of the new capitalism conveniently ignores the fact most of the world's population is too poor to participate in the consumer economy—as Jackson himself acknowledges in recognizing that "three billion of us still live in poverty." And even those who do participate in consumer markets are likely to have radically unequal amounts of disposable income, meaning that some of them have many "votes" while others have very few—hardly a formula for anything worth calling democracy. Moreover, it is dubious to presume, as Jackson must, that consumers make decisions about what to buy with social or environmental purposes in mind. Typical is the woman Charles Kernaghan describes meeting in the toy department of a Wal-Mart store. When he asked her if she was concerned about where and how the toys had been manufactured, she replied, "I feel very uncomfortable . . . I've heard so many horrible stories; but what can I do, my kids want these toys." Harvard Business School expert Debora Spar confirms Kernaghan's anecdotal experience when she says that there is no evidence that "when [people] walk into the store . . . [their] buying practices will change" because of social and environmental concerns.[12]

Like Jackson's model, Monks's proposal to rely upon shareholders as a "proxy for the public good" presumes that one dollar (or, more accurately, one share) equals one vote. And though it may be true that in the United States roughly half of the population owns some corporate stock and thus can participate in a shareholder "democracy," the other half are entirely disenfranchised. And even among those who do own shares, and thus have "votes," most own relatively few, meaning that they have very little voting power. When developing countries, where very few people own any shares at all, are considered, the case for shareholder democracy is further weakened. Moreover, even though people who own shares in companies may have concerns about social and environmental issues, their decisions to buy, hold, or sell those shares are likely to be driven mainly by financial self-interest rather than social and environmental concerns. Indeed, Monks's own work as a shareholder activist is focused exclusively on protecting the long-term financial interests of his clients. When asked whether he had reduced harms caused by corporate externalities at the many companies he has helped reform, his simple answer was "No."[13]

Finally, even if significant numbers of consumers and shareholders were prepared to consider social and environmental concerns when making their decisions, a large problem still remains: How do they get the necessary information to do this effectively? Corporations have no incentive to reveal their misdeeds to the public, and the nongovernmental organizations that monitor their activities, though valiant in their efforts and ever more effective with the Internet at their disposal, nonetheless operate on shoestring budgets and lack the legal authority to compel corporations to disclose information. They cannot serve as substitutes for regulatory agencies, which have (or should have) the necessary resources and legal powers to inspect sites, compel disclosure, and enforce standards. According to Harvard's Debora Spar, though corporate misdeeds are occasionally revealed through the work of nongovernmental organizations and the media, the process is still sporadic and insufficient, more like a highly mobile spotlight on corporations than a fixed and powerful floodlight. "You're going to need to have some combination of moral and market norms *and formal government sanctions*," she says. "Ultimately you can't rely on the media and public pressure to tell corporations what to do."[14]

Charles Kernaghan, who sifts through garbage dumps in the developing world in search of clues about where factories are hidden and what is going on inside of them, is well aware of the limitations of nongovernmental organizations, such as his own National Labor Committee. He agrees with Spar that formal government sanctions are necessary and believes that effective government regulation is the only hope for stopping corporate abuse. His organization, and others like it, he says, can complement the democratic process but not replace it. They can provide citizens with education and information that will enable them to demand that governments pass laws against corporate abuse. But getting those laws in place must be the ultimate goal. "The global sweatshop economy will not be ended without enforceable human rights and worker rights standards, it cannot be done," he says. "It will never be done on the back of voluntary codes and privatization and monitoring. Never. It has to be laws."[15]

Many activists agree with Kernaghan that enforceable laws, enacted by government—regulations—must be at the heart of any effective strategy to curtail corporate harms and exploitation. Simon Billenness of Boston's Trillium Asset Management, a socially oriented investment firm that recently joined forces with Greenpeace and other environmental groups to spearhead a shareholders' resolution to stop BP from drilling on Alaska's coastal plain, says the belief that nongovernmental solutions can replace government regulation is "just a bunch of crap." "Shareholder resolutions," he says, though useful for drawing public attention to corporate misdeeds, "are [not], in any way, a substitute for effective government regulation." "Social investors and other activists can . . . [nip] at the heels of . . . companies," he continues, but, in the end, corporations must be "subject to democratic control, regulation if you want."[16]

When, in 1933, Supreme Court Justice Louis Brandeis likened corporations to "Frankenstein monsters," there was more to his observation than rhetorical flair. Governments create corporations, much like Dr. Frankenstein created his monster, yet, once they exist, corporations, like the monster, threaten to overpower their creators. The regulatory system was designed to keep the Frankenstein monster on a chain and stop it from causing harm, as Justice Brandeis reasoned in the judicial opinion in which he drew the Frankenstein analogy.[17] Regulations—such as those that protect the environment from destruction, workers from death and injury, and consumers from faulty and dangerous products and exploitative advertising—require corporations, by law, to be socially and environmentally responsible, rather than trusting and hoping that they will be. They reflect decisions about appropriate standards for corporate behavior that are made by an institution—government—whose sole purpose, unlike the corporation's, is to protect and promote the public interest and reflect the people's will. Government regulation, unlike market-based solutions, combines authority, capacity, and democratic legitimacy to protect citizens from corporate misdeeds. Through it, governments can pursue social values—such as democracy, social justice, citizens' health and welfare, environmental integrity, cultural identity—that lie beyond the narrow goals of self-interest and wealth maximization that dictate the behavior of corporations and markets.

Milton Friedman, who believes "we need a great deal more deregulation," is, he boasts, "noted . . . for the phrase that 'there is no free lunch.' " The phrase has application here. There is no free lunch with deregulation. No doubt costs are created by regulation, and benefits are derived from deregulation's removal of those costs. Corporations become more profitable when relieved of regulatory restrictions that prevent them from externalizing their costs; consumers sometimes benefit from lower prices; governments, and thus taxpayers, save money when they are able to cut the budgets of regulatory agencies. In most cases, however, the costs saved by deregulation only reappear elsewhere—a point underlined by earlier stories of victims of corporate misdeeds who might have been, or might yet be, saved from their ordeals by effective regulation: Norma Kassi and her Gwich'in People, Patricia Anderson and her family, Wendy Díaz and the young women she works with, Don Shugak, the Quecreek miners, sweatshop workers in New York and Los Angeles, and children made sick or obese by unhealthy food pitched to them on television.[18]

Regulations are designed to force corporations to internalize— i.e., pay for—costs they would otherwise externalize onto society and the environment. When they are effective and effectively enforced, they have the potential to stop corporations from harming and exploiting individuals, communities, and the environment. Deregulation is really a form of *dedemocratization,* as it denies "the people," acting through their democratic representatives in government, the only official political vehicle they currently have to control corporate behavior.

Despite that, a growing number of activists, not just businesspeople, eschew government solutions. They believe, with some justification, that government has lost its capacity to contain corporate power. People should confront corporations directly, in the streets and through nongovernmental organizations and community coalitions, they say, rather than relying on governments to forge solutions. "We should be directly pointing the finger at businesses, not even bothering with the governments," says Anita Roddick,[19] reflecting a widely held view that is also expressed by antiglobalization activist and pundit Naomi Klein: "We see corporations as the most powerful political entities of our time, and we are responding to them as citizens, citizens to political organizations. . . . The corporation has become the new site of protest. . . . Rather than protesting on the doorsteps of governments on Sunday afternoon when no one is there, they're protesting outside of the Niketown on Fifth Avenue."[20]

Though the movement against corporate rule would be impossible, even senseless, without robust nongovernmental institutions, community activism, and political dissent, the belief these can be a *substitute* for government regulation, rather than a necessary complement to it, is dangerously mistaken. Many among the corporate elite and their defenders would likely sing "Hallelujah" the day activists against corporate abuse abandoned government. That is, after all, what many business leaders want: replacement of government regulation of corporations with market forces, perhaps shaped by the oversight of nongovernmental organizations (with no legal powers) and the demands of conscientious consumers and shareholders (with minimal effects). In this scenario, corporations get all the coercive power and resources of the state, while citizens are left with nongovernmental organizations and the market's invisible hand— socialism for the rich and capitalism for the poor, to borrow a phrase from George Bernard Shaw.

There is little democracy in a system that relies on market forces and nongovernmental organizations to promote socially responsible behavior from corporations. Benevolent corporations, like benevolent tyrants, may be better than malevolent ones, but, as Noam Chomsky observes, it is "better to ask why we have tyranny than whether it can be benevolent." Corporations are not democratic institutions—their directors and managers owe no accountability to anyone but the shareholders that employ them. The belief that corporate benevolence and social responsibility can and should be achieved through market forces, to the point where government regulation becomes unnecessary, is premised on a dangerous diminishment of the importance of democracy. Democratic governments, despite all their flaws, are, at least in theory, accountable to the whole of society.[21]

Admittedly, the actual practices of the regulatory system fall short of the democratic ideals that inform it. "Regulatory capture," a term coined by economist George Stigler in the 1960s to describe corporations' domination of regulatory agencies through lobbying and selective information sharing, is endemic; many corporations regularly breach regulatory laws, confident that they won't be caught or that, if they are, the financial benefits derived from the breach will exceed the costs of the fines assessed against them; regulatory agencies tend to be understaffed, unaccountable, and peopled by bureaucrats—many of whom are drawn from the industries being regulated—who see themselves as partners with industry, rather than its overseers; and the standards established by regulatory laws often are reactive, rather than preventive, and too weak to stop corporations from causing serious harm to people and the environment.[22]

More generally, the democratic system as a whole ill serves its animating ideals. Broad public participation in self-government is absent, as people's participation is limited to occasional voting, and close to half the population does not even do that; politicians are unduly pressured and influenced by corporate money and increasingly deprived of meaningful decision-making powers, as deregulation and privatization roll back government's domain; the public sphere is shrinking, and social inequality is rampant. Despite all of this, however, as Chomsky states, "Whatever one thinks of governments, they're to some extent publicly accountable, to a limited extent. Corporations are to a zero extent. . . . One of the reasons why propaganda tries to get you to hate government is because it's the one existing institution in which people can participate to some extent and constrain tyrannical unaccountable power."[23]

Though the existing regulatory system, and the political system as a whole, are flawed and fall short of the democratic ideals that sustain them, they have the potential—which governance by a combination of corporations, the market, and nongovernmental institutions does not—to govern society democratically. Now is the time to reinvigorate, not abandon, democratic institutions, and to craft them into truer reflections of the ideals upon which they were founded.

But is it too late for that? Is government now so dominated by corporate power that it will never be able to regain control of corporations? Sometimes it feels that way. The evidence of corporate domination is everywhere—the sheer size of corporations, some of whose economies dwarf those of small nations, the transnational scope of their operations, and their control of society and influence over government. There is surface appeal to the argument that economic globalization, and corporate domination more generally, have put corporations beyond government's grasp, possibly forever. However, that argument ignores one crucial fact—namely, that the corporation depends entirely on government for its existence and is therefore always, at least in theory, within government's control.

The corporation was originally conceived as a public institution whose purpose was to serve national interests and advance the public good. In seventeenth-century England, corporations such as the Hudson's Bay Company and the East India Company were chartered by the crown to run state monopolies in the colonies of England's empire. During the eighteenth and early nineteenth centuries too, in both England and the United States, corporations were formed primarily for public purposes, such as building canals and transporting water. The modern for-profit corporation, programmed solely to advance the *private* interests of its owners, differs profoundly from these earlier versions of the institution. Yet in one crucial respect it remains the same: it is, as it has always been, a product of public policy, a *creation* of the state.

The state is the only institution in the world that can bring a corporation to life. It alone grants corporations their essential rights, such as legal personhood and limited liability, and it compels them always to put profits first. It raises police forces and armies and builds courthouses and prisons (all compulsorily paid for by citizens) to enforce corporations' property rights—rights themselves created by the state. And only the state, in conjunction with other states, can enter into international trade deals and create global institutions, such as the World Trade Organization, that, in turn, limit its ability to regulate the corporations and property rights it has created.

Without the state, the corporation is nothing. Literally nothing.

It is therefore a mistake to believe that because corporations are now strong, the state has become weak. Economic globalization and deregulation have diminished the state's capacity to protect the public interest (through, for example, labor laws, environmental laws, and consumer protection laws) and have strengthened its power to promote corporations' interests and facilitate their profit-seeking missions (through, for example, corporate laws, property and contract laws, copyright laws, and international trade laws). Overall, however, the state's power has not been reduced. It has been redistributed, more tightly connected to the needs and interests of corporations and less so to the public interest. Thus, it is only partly true to say, as Daniel Yergin and Joseph Stanislaw do in *The Commanding Heights*, that "the general movement away from traditional state control of the commanding heights [of the economy] continues, leaving it more to the realm of the market."[24] While that statement captures the diminishing role of the state in protecting citizens from corporations, it ignores the expanding role of the state in protecting corporations from citizens.

The question is never *whether* the state regulates corporations—it always does—but *how*, and in whose interests, it does so. Beguiled by the "natural entity" conception of corporations, the notion that they are *independent* persons, we tend to forget that they are entirely *dependent* upon the state for their creation and empowerment. That, in turn, "destroy[s] any special basis for state regulation of the corporation that derive[s] from its creation by the state," as historian Morton Horwitz describes the ideological effects of the natural entity theory.[25]

The New Dealers understood this. They knew that the natural entity theory and related laissez-faire doctrines undermined the legitimacy of regulations designed to promote the public interest. So they discarded those ideas and revived earlier conceptions of corporations and markets as creations of government. "The freedom from regulation postulated by *laissez-faire* adherents is demonstrably nonexistent and virtually inconceivable," wrote one New Deal supporter in 1935. "Bargaining power exists only because of government protection of the property rights bargained, and is properly subject to government control."[26] Such ideas had been around even before the New Deal. Robert Hale stated in 1922 that "The dependence of present economic conditions, in part at least, on the government's past policy concerning the distribution of the public domain, must be obvious. *Laissez faire* is a utopian dream which never has been and never can be realized."[27] The Norris-LaGuardia Act, the most important piece of New Deal labor legislation, rehearsed similar logic in its preamble as justification for restrictions on employers' property rights:

> Whereas under prevailing economic conditions, *developed with the aid of governmental authority for owners of property to organize in the corporate and other forms of ownership association,* the individual worker is commonly helpless to exercise actual liberty of contract and to protect his freedom of labor, and thereby to obtain acceptable terms and conditions of employment.[28]

Corporations cannot exist without the state, nor can markets. Deregulation does not scale back the state's involvement with corporations; it simply changes its nature.

As a creation of government, the corporation must be measured against the standard applicable to all government policies: Does it serve the public interest? The nineteenth-century judges and legislators who refashioned the corporation into a self-interested institution never really abandoned that idea. Rather, with laissez-faire ideas dominant at the time, they embraced a new conception of what the public interest required. It would best be served, they thought, if individuals, including corporations, were enabled to pursue their self-interest unimpeded by government.

Out of that belief developed a kind of circular logic—still in place today—that justified (and justifies) governments' facilitation of the interests of corporations. To wit, if serving corporations' interests advances the public good, then the public good is advanced when corporations' interests are served. Or, as Charles Wilson, a former president of General Motors and secretary of defense, told a U.S. Senate subcommittee in the 1930s, "What is good for General Motors is good for the country." More recently, Dr. Harriet Smith Windsor, secretary of state for corporations in Delaware, a state whose major industry is manufacturing corporations (half of Fortune 500 and NYSE companies are incorporated there; 27 percent of the state's $2.3 billion yearly revenue is derived from incorporation business), rehearsed a similar logic when she observed, "Our laws are geared to help business, to meet their needs"; her assistant secretary of state, Rick Geisenberger, added, "We write our laws in a way that enables businesses to flourish and people to access capital." That is good public policy only if you presume that what's best for business is best for the public—a presumption that drives much public policy today.[29]

However, the fact that corporate law and policy rest upon a *conception* of the public good, albeit a narrow one, only confirms that the *concept* of the public good remains the ultimate measure of the corporation's institutional worth and legitimacy. As a concrete reflection of this, most corporate law statutes include provisions that permit governments to dissolve a corporation, or seek a court order to dissolve it, if the government believes that the corporation has grossly violated the public interest. Charter revocation laws, as these provisions are known, have always been a part of corporate law. They suggest a government can destroy a corporation as easily as it can create one, and symbolize the obvious, though easily forgotten, idea that in a democracy corporations exist at the pleasure of the people and under their sovereignty. As New York Attorney General Eliot Spitzer remarked in reference to these laws, if "a corporation is convicted of repeated felonies that harm or endanger the lives of human beings or destroy our environment, the corporation should be put to death, its corporate existence ended, and its assets taken and sold at public auction."[30]

Charter revocation laws are a "well-kept secret," according to law professor Robert Benson, who, using California's charter revocation law, recently petitioned that state's attorney general to dissolve the Union Oil Company of California (Unocal) by revoking its charter:

> The people mistakenly assume that we have to try to control these giant corporate repeat offenders one toxic spill at a time, one layoff at a time, one human rights violation at a time. But the law has always allowed the attorney general to go to court to simply dissolve a corporation for wrongdoing and sell its assets to others who will operate in the public interest.[31]

Benson listed Unocal's alleged transgressions in his 127-page application to the attorney general: the company had collaborated on a pipeline project with the outlaw Burmese military regime, which had allegedly used slave labor on the pipeline and forced whole villages to relocate; it had allegedly collaborated on projects with Afghanistan's former Taliban regime, which was notorious for its violations of human rights long before the United States waged war against it; it had, the application claimed, persistently violated California's environmental and employee safety regulations. The application was rejected by the attorney general's office five days after it was filed.

Benson never really expected to succeed with his application. Though governments often resort to charter revocation laws to dissolve small corporations for technical infractions (California suspended 58,000 corporations for tax evasion and failure to file proper statements in 2001–2;[32] Delaware revoked roughly half that number in the same period[33]), the remedy is not used to punish large corporations for major infractions. Even Enron was spared this corporate death penalty and continues to exist as a corporate entity. "I never saw the biggest payoff of filing charter revocation suits as being able to get rid of Unocal or any specific company," says Benson. "I saw the payoff as changing the climate of public opinion against corporate malfeasance, and I think we helped do that."[34] Corporate charter revocation laws, he says, symbolize the fact that corporations are our creations and that we—the people—still have the power to control them.

The time has come to use that power, not only by activating charter revocation laws but also, more generally, by subjecting corporations to robust democratic controls. The corporation is not an independent "person" with its own rights, needs, and desires that regulators must respect. It is a state-created tool for advancing social and economic policy. As such, it has only one institutional purpose: to serve the public interest (and not some circular conception of the public interest that equates it with the interests of business). We must work to ensure that that is what corporations do. But how can the corporation, which is currently constituted as a psychopathic institution, be made to respect and promote the public interest?

The question of what to do about, and with, the corporation is one of the most pressing and difficult of our time. There are no easy answers—no blueprints for change—and we should be wary of people who offer them. As a society we have created a difficult problem for ourselves. We have over the last three hundred years constructed a remarkably efficient wealth-creating machine, but it is now out of control. Though solutions to this problem must ultimately be democratically fashioned by "the people," not by a law professor sitting in front of his computer, I do want to conclude with some general thoughts about how we might move forward.

To begin with, tinkering with corporate governance is not enough. Though post-Enron proposals for the reform of corporate governance and measures such as those found in the Sarbanes-Oxley Act are likely to strengthen managers and directors' accountability to investors, they will do little to improve corporate accountability to society as a whole. Broader reforms, such as tighter restrictions on acquisitions and mergers, representation of stakeholders (union representatives, for example) on boards of directors, and laws that permit or require executives to consider stakeholder interests in their business decisions (so-called constituency statutes), though desirable, are unlikely to strengthen corporations' accountability to society in significant ways.

At the other extreme, proposals based upon visions of corporation-less futures leave unsolved the problem of what to do about and with corporations right now. Though it may be true that "millions of people are saying not only do we not need [corporations], we can do it better, we are going to create systems that nourish the earth and nourish human beings," as activist Vandana Shiva states, a corporation-less future is, for now, too remote a possibility to plan for. As Harvard Business School pundit Joe Badaracco says, "This institution, the corporation, is going to be around for a very long period. It may have rough sledding for a decade or two—it did, arguably, a decade or two ago—but I think its resilience has already been demonstrated and the opportunities for it to grow even stronger are really astonishing." It seems reasonable to presume, and plan for the fact, that the corporation—though vulnerable, as all other dominant institutions have been, in the longer sweep of history—will remain present and powerful in society in at least the medium-range future.[35]

What about remaking the corporation, changing it into a nonpsychopathic entity? That is what proponents of social responsibility and ethical management claim they are doing. Yet, despite their often good intentions, they are profoundly limited by the corporation's legal mandate to pursue, without exception, its own self-interest, as I have argued in previous chapters. To reform the corporation meaningfully, that mandate would have to be changed. Corporations would have to be reconstituted to serve, promote, and be accountable to broader domains of society than just themselves and their shareholders. Such corporations already exist, and we deal with them on a daily basis. The U.S. Postal Service, a self-supporting corporation wholly owned by the U.S. federal government, is one example, as its legislated mission indicates:

> The Postal Service shall have as its basic function the obligation to provide postal services to bind the Nation together through the personal, educational, literary, and business correspondence of the people. It shall provide prompt, reliable, and efficient services to patrons in all areas and shall render postal services to all communities.[36]

Public-purpose corporations operate in numerous other public-service domains—transportation, utilities, broadcasting, and security and rescue services, to name a few examples—and are, as I suggested in Chapter 4, preferable to for-profit corporations for delivering key public programs and services.

But should all corporations become public-purpose corporations? Is that the solution to our current corporate woes? Such a solution, even if desirable, is currently too utopian to be realistically proposed. Perhaps someday we shall understand how truly to democratize economic relations, and widespread use of public-purpose corporations may be a key part of the plan. In the meantime, however, in the near- to medium-range future—in terms of what we can do tomorrow, next week, and next year—realism dictates presuming that the corporation's constitution will remain much as it is: self-interested to the point of psychopathy. It bears stating here that the corporation is an institutional reflection of the principles of laissez faire capitalism. Changing it must be understood as part of a larger project of economic change.

The challenge for now is to find ways to control the corporation—to subject it to democratic constraints and protect citizens from its dangerous tendencies—even while we hope and strive in the longer term for a more fully human and democratic economic order. Improving the legitimacy, effectiveness, and accountability of government regulation is currently the best, or at least the most realistic, strategy for doing this. To that end, I offer the following general prescriptions:

IMPROVE THE REGULATORY SYSTEM

- Government regulation should be reconceived, and relegitimated, as the principal means for bringing corporations under democratic control and ensuring that they respect the interests of citizens, communities, and the environment.

- Regulations should be made more effective by staffing enforcement agencies at realistic levels, setting fines sufficiently high to deter corporations from committing crimes, strengthening the liability of top directors and managers for their corporations' illegal behaviors, barring repeat offender corporations from government contracts, and suspending the charters of corporations that flagrantly and persistently violate the public interest.

- Regulations designed to protect the environment and people's health and safety should be based upon the precautionary principle, which prescribes that corporations be prohibited from acting in ways that are reasonably likely to cause harm, even if definitive proof that such harm will occur does not exist.

- The regulatory system should be reformed to improve accountability and avoid both "agency capture" and the centralized and bureaucratic tendencies of current and past regimes. Local governmental bodies, such as city councils and school and park boards, should play greater roles in the regulatory system, as they are often more accessible to citizens than federal and state agencies and more willing and able to forge alliances with citizen groups around particular issues (as they have done effectively in relation to, among other things, restrictions on advertising in schools, urban sprawl, "box" retailers, and environmentally damaging practices).

- The roles of trade unions and other workers' associations in monitoring and regulating the behavior of corporations should be protected and enhanced, as should those of environmental, consumer, human rights, and other organizations that represent interests and constituencies affected by what corporations do.

STRENGTHEN POLITICAL DEMOCRACY.

- Elections should be publicly financed, corporate political donations phased out, and tighter restrictions imposed on lobbying and the "revolving door" flow of personnel between government and business. Though corporations have a place in representing their concerns to government and cooperating with government on policy initiatives, the special status they currently enjoy as "partners" with government endangers the democratic process. At a minimum, their influence should be scaled back to a degree more commensurate with that of other organizations, such as unions, environmental and consumer groups, and human rights advocates.[37]

Electoral reforms that would bring new voices into the political system and encourage disillusioned citizens to return to it, such as proportional representation, should be pursued.

CREATE A ROBUST PUBLIC SPHERE.

Social groups and interests judged to be important for the public good or too precious, vulnerable, or morally sacred to subject to corporate exploitation, should be governed and protected by public regimes. Inevitably, people will debate the extent to which such groups and interests should be immune to corporate exploitation, the kinds of measures that should be used to protect them, and what groups and interests should be protected—children's minds and imaginations, schools, universities, cultural institutions, water and power utilities, health and welfare services, police, courts, prisons, firefighters, parks, nature reserves, genes and other biological materials, and public space are all likely candidates—but these are healthy debates to have, far healthier than the increasingly prevalent presumption that no public interest exists beyond the accumulated financial interests of individual corporations, consumers, and shareholders.

CHALLENGE INTERNATIONAL NEOLIBERALISM.

- Nations should work together to shift the ideologies and practices of international institutions, such as the WTO, IMF, and World Bank, away from market fundamentalism and its facilitation of deregulation and privatization. The current ideological biases of these institutions are not written in stone. Indeed, their original mandate, formulated at Bretton Woods, reflected the economic theories of John Maynard Keynes, and thus a very different orientation than they have today.

Most important, we must remember the most subversive truth of all: that corporations are our creations. They have no lives, no powers, and no capacities beyond what we, through our governments, give them.

"We live in a world full of fear, people are afraid of the dark, people are afraid of losing their jobs, people are afraid of speaking, people are afraid of giving their opinion, people are afraid of acting," according to Oscar Olivera, a union official who led a popular uprising against privatization of the freshwater system in Cochabamba, Bolivia. "It's time that we lose our fear . . . [and] develop the capacity to unite, to organize, and to recover our faith in ourselves and in others." That is what Olivera and the people of Cochabamba recently did.[38]

It all began when the Bolivian government, under pressure from the World Bank to privatize water utilities, contracted with Aguas del Tunari, the major shareholder of which is Bechtel subsidiary International Water Ltd., to run the water system of Cochabamba, a water-starved region in central Bolivia. At the time, Cochabamba was served by an old and decaying system that did not reach areas of the countryside where many peasants lived. Aguas del Tunari, when it took over the system, raised rates, to up to three times what they had been, and began charging peasants for water they drew from their own wells. The government, in compliance with its contract with the company, passed a law that prohibited people from collecting water from local lagoons, rivers, and deltas, and even rainwater. The company confiscated people's alternative water systems, without compensation, and placed them under its control. All of these actions, including the rate increases—which imposed severe hardships on many people, according to Olivera—were justified by the company as necessary to meet contractually mandated profit levels.[39]

People organized in the city and in the countryside, with the help of Olivera and others, and demanded that the company leave, which it did, eventually, but only after bloody confrontations between citizens and the police and military. "We started to see many injured youths, young people at sixteen or seventeen years old who lost arms, legs, were left paralyzed, had brain and nervous system injuries, had one young man, Victor Hugo Daza, killed . . . and there had been five people killed in the countryside," recalls Olivera. "It was a victory at a real great cost."

It was still a victory, however, and not just for water, according to Olivera, but for "the struggle for justice, the struggle for democracy, and the struggle for the change of the living conditions of the people.

We saw this incredible capacity of people to organize, to unify and to be in solidarity with each other. . . . At one point it was so strong, and people were coming together so much . . . there were a hundred thousand people in the streets, and there were people from all sectors of society, rich and poor, peasants, women, seniors, young people. And the incredible thing was that people were really starting to feel powerful, feeling that they had the power to make decisions, to make decisions about the water. And finally they did decide about the water. And I think for the first time in a long time, young and old had the chance to taste, to really savor democracy, because as we

have always said, democracy is about who makes decisions. . . . The
only sovereign is the people, and no one else.

The water corporation was deprivatized and returned to the people
of Cochabamba. Olivera now dreams of making it a truly "social corporation that really involves people in . . . decision making and [solv-
ing] their problems." Already, he says, the nonprofit corporation, with
a board of directors composed of local officials and representatives
from unions and professional associations, is "not only transparent,
but more just, more efficient, and encouraging of participation of the
people in the solution to their problems."[40]

Corporate rule is not inviolable. When people unite and organize
and have faith in themselves and one another, their dissatisfaction
can become a powerful source of vulnerability for corporations and
the governments that support and empower them. No doubt the corporation is a formidable foe, but, as Olivera says, "small battles are
being won around the world," including his and the people of Cochabamba's. Restoring broad democratic control over the corporation is a
large battle, but it is one that must be fought.

Corporate rule must be challenged in order to revive the values and
practices it contradicts: democracy, social justice, equality, and compassion. The corporation and its underlying ideology are animated by
a narrow conception of human nature that is too distorted and too
uninspiring to have lasting purchase on our political imaginations.
Though individualistic self-interest and consumer desires are core
parts of who we are and nothing to be ashamed about, they are not all
of who we are. We also feel deep ties and commitments to one
another, that we share common fates and hopes for a better world. We
know that our values, capacities, aesthetics, and senses of meaning
and justice are, in part, created and nurtured by our communal attach-
ments. We believe that some things are too vulnerable, precious, or

important to exploit for profit. "We don't have to see ourselves primarily as rapacious producers and consumers of goods who function in ways that are competitive and self-interested," as philosopher Mark Kingwell says. "Humans have organized themselves by and large for vast stretches of what we call civilization in other ways."[41]

The best argument against corporate rule is to look at who we really are and to understand how poorly the corporation's tenets reflect us. "We are basically organisms of feeling, of empathy," says scientist and activist Dr. Mae-Wan Ho. "When other people suffer, we suffer. We want a safe, equitable, just, and compassionate world because it is a matter of life and death to us." Dr. Vandana Shiva, another scientist turned activist, notes that "in every period of history" people have risen up against systems that are "based on illegitimate measures" and that deny people "the right and freedoms . . . to live and survive with dignity." No social and ideological order that represses essential parts of ourselves can last—a point as true of the corporate order as it was for the fallen Communist one. We only have to remember who we are and what we are capable of as human beings to reveal how dangerously distorted is the corporation's order of narrow self-interest.[42]

"How does a free people govern themselves?" asks Richard Grossman of the Boston-based Program on Corporations, Law and Democracy. "I mean, in a sense this is all not about the corporation. It's about us as human beings . . . our role on the earth, our temporal span, our life span, what are we to do with ourselves; how we come together with other people to govern ourselves . . . to live in harmony with other creatures on the earth, to live in harmony with the earth itself, to live in harmony with the future generations . . . including the children of men and women who work in corporations? It's really about us."

That is why I am optimistic—because it really is about us.

Interview with Noam Chomsky, October 24, 2000

1.

Mark Achbar: I find I have this very complex relationships with corporations and their products. They clothe me, feed me, entertain me, inform me, transport me and medicate me. I try to make responsible consumption choices. But the fact remains that I use their products from the minute I wake up to the minute I fall asleep. And to make this film, I was even forced by federal and provincial funding agencies to create a for-profit corporation which now employs me. I feel inescapably surrounded by this institution. At times grateful to it, yet at the same time resentful and often overwhelmed by its ubiquity. Has the corporation become the dominant institution of our time?

Noam Chomsky: The dominant role of corporations in our lives is essentially a product of the past century. Corporations were originally associations of people who were chartered by a state to perform some particular function. Like a group of people who want to build a bridge over the Charles River, or something like that, municipalities were corporations. Now that began to slowly change in the nineteenth century. By the end of the century there were huge market failures. And it became obvious to everyone that somebody was going to have to administer markets or the society would collapse.

Naturally private power wanted to administer them themselves, not have it under public control. So there were many attempts made, mergers, trusts, cartels were tried, as is true of all major industrial countries. What emerged in the United States is the corporate system as it took shape in the early twentieth century, mostly through radical judicial activism. There's not much legislation behind it—sometimes a state entered with its own rules.

So the state of New Jersey in 1889, I think it was, agreed to eliminate all constraints on corporations. Charters had had constraints. New Jersey let them come in without constraints. So there was of course a big flood of corporate money across the river. And that's why you have things like Standard Oil of New Jersey and so on. And then it started a race to the bottom, everyone had to do the same thing.

After a short period of time the conditions on corporations, the conditions of their charter, had dissolved. The courts accorded corporations the rights of persons. That's a very sharp attack on classical liberalism in which rights are inherent in people—people of flesh and blood, not corporate entities like states or something like that. In fact this grew out of a kind Hegelian concept of the rights of organic entities over individuals.

Actually it had three major outgrowths in the twentieth century. One is Fascism, another is Bolshevism and other is Corporatism. They're rather similar in their character and the reasoning behind them. And in fact the corporate system was supported by progressives for pretty much the same reason they supported the other two if you look back. The corporations were given the rights of immortal persons. But they were special kinds of persons; persons who had no moral conscience.

You expect a human being to care about others or something like that. These are a special kind persons who are designed, again by law, to be concerned only for their stockholders. And not say what are sometimes called their stakeholders, like the community or the work force or whatever. And that's not a law of nature, that's a very specific decision. In fact it's a judicial decision.

So they're concerned only for the short-term—actually it turns out to be short term—profit of their stockholders who are very highly concentrated. I mean it's not little people around. So for example, by now about close to half the stock is owned by about 1% of the population. And the bottom 80% of the population hold about 4% of the stock.

And the corporations are interlinked. Like a bank will own a big piece of one corporation. I mean, it's a massive system of highly concentrated power, given the rights of immortal persons but without the responsibility of persons. And the courts then proceeded to take another step and that is to identify the corporation more and more closely with the management. Instead of the association of people— the owners—being the corporation it was the management that was the corporation, and the directors.

Actually that's very similar to what happened in other tyrannical systems of the twentieth century. So if you look at the history of Bolshevism, for example, this was part of the very early critique of Bolshevism made by left wing Marxists like Rosa Luxemburg and Trotsky before he bought into the system. They predicted that the Bolshevik system was going to transfer power from the working class to the party to the central committee, and then to the maximal leader. This is indeed exactly what happened, and in fact it happened very quickly.

The corporate system is going down the same path. So the corporation was identified in the law, created by the courts, mostly with the top leadership. They become immortal persons. In the modern period, the last, the period that's very misleadingly called globalization, the last twenty years or so, corporations even get rights far beyond those of people.

So for example if General Motors operates in Mexico they're supposed to have what's called National Treatment. They have to be treated like a Mexican person. On the other hand, if a Mexican person of flesh and blood comes to New York and says, "I'd like to be treated like everyone else," he'd be lucky if he gets out alive.

So in fact corporations can effectively sue governments. I mean, a little maneuvering, but in effect they can sue them and they win. You and I can't do that. And of course they're just phenomenal in scale. And since one of their main goals is to administer markets, they want to limit competition, make sure they can control pricing and so on. They tend to move towards a kind of oligopoly, a small number of corporations that dominate some domain.

And if you look over the last fifty years, particularly in the last ten or twenty years, when it's been sharply accelerating, most spheres of economic life are moving towards not monopoly but oligopoly. They don't like monopoly because if you have a monopoly you start getting public service requirements. So for example, when AT&T, which was private, monopolized the telephone system, they were simply forced by legislation to provide services that they didn't want to provide. They had to provide services for isolated rural communities and to poor people in the cities and so on. They'd much rather get rid of those people.

Every corporation knows, in fact there's a rule, there's a law, a rule taught in the business schools called the 80/20 rule: 20% of your customers give you 80% of your profits. And if you can figure out a way to get of the other 80% you're better off. By now there are ways to do that one. One of the effects of high tech is you can monitor the people who purchase very closely, and you can adjust services in such a way that it's only the high spenders who get any services.

So you call the telephone company to ask a question, and they instantly know if you are a high spender, or a low spender. High spender usually means business. If you're a high spender you get treated very nicely and so on. If you're a low spender they essentially want to get rid of you. So you get put on lists and then they lose your call and so on.

And that's very carefully calculated. I mean, there was a big study in *Business Week* about it but it's perfectly natural. Because, remember, these are amoral institutions. In fact they are private tyrannies which are amoral and required to be amoral. They want to avoid monopoly because then they get public service requirements. But they want to be very limited in number so that they can have what are called "strategic alliances". They can effectively act together.

You look at the automobile industry. There are now a few major corporations worldwide and they're interlinked. They have common products and they trade—there's a degree of competition but they don't want it to be too much. Same in every other domain. There's a lot of talk about media concentration which is true, but of course it's just one aspect of what's going on all over the economy. And these are very natural tendencies for tyrannical systems that are unaccountable to the public. And are private only in the sense that they're unaccountable.

I mean it's not private in a sense that say Thomas Jefferson would have understood, or Adam Smith or anyone like that, and the same is true of international trade. I mean it's not a free trade system. It's a kind of a mercantilist system. But a kind of corporate mercantilist system with an awful lot of what's called the trade internal to a particular corporation. Or involves things like what's called outsourcing. You get very cheap labour somewhere which is ununionized and you can get rid of it when you don't like it. And you've run it but it's essentially centrally administered.

These are the kind of systems that have evolved through the twentieth century for a variety of reasons. Not economic law or anything like that; economic laws would apply just as well if the workers or the community controlled the business.

These are particular decisions about how to concentrate power. The decisions are made in the context of hugely concentrated economic power. This concentration of power decisively influences the political process, and the judicial process and so on. So these things converge in a kind of a natural way towards particular kinds of oppressive hierarchical systems which have very little concern with people.

The goal for corporations is to maximize profit and market share. And they also have a goal for their target—namely, the population. They have to ensure that the human beings who they're interacting with, you and me, also become inhuman. You have to drive out of people's heads natural sentiments like care about others, or sympathy, or solidarity. Which are also incidentally again the foundations of classical liberalism, Adam Smith and David Hume and others. That has to be driven out of people's heads.

They have to be turned into completely mindless consumers of goods that they do not want. You have to develop what are called "created wants". So you have to create wants. You have to impose on people what's called a philosophy of futility. You have to focus them on the insignificant things of life, like fashionable consumption—I'm just basically quoting business literature, and it makes perfect sense.

The ideal is to have individuals who are totally disassociated from one another, who don't care about anyone else. My sense of value is just how many created wants can I satisfy. And how deeply can I go into debt and still get away with satisfying created wants. If you can create a society in which the unit, the smallest unit, is a person in a tube and no connections to people, that would be ideal.

We have huge industries, public relations industries, monstrous industry advertising and so on. They are designed to try to mold people from infancy into this desired pattern. They try to ensure that they don't have strange thoughts about caring about each other, or caring about the future generations and so on. That you don't want, because it interferes with the goal of simply maximizing power, profit, market share and domination.

So there's a move towards a particular social form that doesn't have anything to do with—in fact it would horrify—any classical liberal if he showed up. And incidentally, when these systems did begin to take shape a century ago, they were very sharply condemned by conservatives. It's a breed of people that doesn't exist anymore but they did at that time. A conservative meant classical liberal. They were condemned as a kind of a reversion to feudalism, or even as a form of communism which was not unreasonable. If by communism you mean Bolshevism, yeah, it was rather similar in conception.

Their advocates like, say, progressives like Woodrow Wilson, who was a big proponent of corporatizition, nevertheless pointed out correctly that this is the end of freedom. It's the end of private enterprise. It's the end of freedom; it's a new America in which people will not be working for themselves but will be servants of corporate entities. And he thought well that's a good way to go but that's what's happened. And then we see the developments of the past century intensifying in the last ten or twenty years.

Mark Achbar: There are a number of factors that people chose to focus on when criticizing the corporations. Some like Richard Grossman emphasize the importance of "personhood", which you mentioned. Others like Michael Albert point to the hierarchical division of labour within corporations. Our particular entrance point is the institutionalization of self interest. The amoral character of the corporate firm. What do you identify as the sort of central flaw or danger in the institution of the corporation?

Noam Chomsky: Well, as far as dangers of corporations, every factor you mentioned is a danger. I mean, a corporation is an unaccountable tyranny which internally is as close to totalitarian as any institution that humans have created. Power flows from the top. At every level you get orders from above and you transmit them down below. At the very bottom are people who, if they're able to, can rent themselves to the corporation. Working people 150 years ago without benefit of radical intellectuals regarded this as a kind of slavery. They had to rent themselves to private tyrannies to survive and bitterly opposed that.

And for outsiders, those that were not part of the system, you have the constructed choice, carefully constructed choice, of purchasing their product. And there's a huge effort that goes into making sure that those choices are very limited and you don't even think in other terms. Now that's why advertising is so focused on infants. They try to convert people into a particular kind of creature who is only going to try to satisfy the wants that are constructed for them.

So that's . . . these are . . . I don't know if you call them flaws or not—they're properties of the system. It's a hierarchical, tyrannical, basically unaccountable system. There's a limited accountability through public institutions. Whatever one thinks of governments they are publicly accountable to a limited extent. Corporations are to a zero extent. I guess one of the reasons why propaganda tries to get you to hate government is because it's the one existing institution in which people can participate to constrain tyrannical, unaccountable power. So you can have EPA regulations and so on. They're pretty much toothless because the distribution of power is such that the corporation is going to dominate the regulatory institutions. In fact they often help create the regulatory institutions because it controls some of their destructive and predatory characteristics—keeps things sort of organized.

But apart from that, and of course as in any totalitarian system—I mean, even with Stalin—there's interchange up and back. Nothing is totally rigid. So there were ways in the Stalin system for pressures to come from the bottom and reach the top. Yes of course any system is going to have leakage like that. But it's about as totalitarian as you can find.

And if you happen to think that human beings should be free and independent and make their own choices, and associate with one another voluntarily, well these are flaws. If you think that people should be slaves and a system of rigid hierarchy, these are benefits. So it depends on what your values are.

To the extent that markets function they have properties which are flaws from the point of view of human survival. So if you think human survival is of value then there are obvious flaws in the functioning of markets. In theory, a market is supposed to reflect individual choices. Of course that's far from true because of the construction of the choices and so on. But that's the theory.

In theory a free market is supposed to reflect individual choices. You have a vote, I have a vote, the next guy has a vote. And we vote in the market and that determines what happens. But there are people that don't vote like the next generation, for example. They're not alive so they don't vote in the market. Now that means they can't express their preferences about the world in which they would like to live.

For example, should the world exist? Maybe they would like the world in which they're going to be born to exist, to be survivable. Well maybe so, but they don't have a vote in the market. This is what's called an externality. It's something you don't count when you make business decisions, like whether the next generation will be able to survive. And you don't because they don't have a vote in the market. Your goal, in fact your legal responsibility, is to ignore those things.

If you spell this out it has huge effects. This falls under the rubric of what's called sustainable development. You can not, in principle, have a system of sustainable development under corporate tyrannies that respond to a limited market because they can't pay attention to that.

For example, suppose you had three automobile companies and so a limited competition. One of them decided to put resources into the kind of technology that would make it possible for the next generation not to die of poisoning or something and the other two didn't. Well the first one wouldn't be around long enough to succeed because the others would not be wasting money on dealing with externalities but rather putting their resources into short-term gain. So they'd win out the competition.

And that's an inherent dynamic in the system. It shows up in all kinds of ways. Like in financial institutions, for example, which have overwhelming force in the modern economy. They just, the last twenty years in particular the amount of wasted capital that flows in speculative markets is just astronomical. So they have an enormous degree of power. The system has been designed to grant them enormous power.

Well there are things that they don't worry about, like when you lend money. Suppose a bank lends money. It cares about one thing, its own profits. Now there's a property called systemic risk. The risk that if the market crashes somewhere it's going to be contagious. And there is that phenomena. It's monstrous in fact. But the investor doesn't think of it, can't. You know you think about your own risk. You cannot think about the cost to others, or the fact that contagion may destroy a system. That's not part of your calculations. That's another externality.

So the system is sort of built to magnify extremely dangerous properties. And this happens all over the place. I mean, what are called the externalities dominate life. Well those are things, properties that are inherent in this minimally competitive, tyrannical system. And yes, they are flaws if your values happen to say you'd like a different world.

There are other kinds of flaws and they led to a big struggle to impose the industrial system in the first place. It wasn't imposed easily. To try to drive independent farmers into mills, let's say, was not easy. Take right where we are, eastern Massachusetts, where the American Industrial Revolution sort of began.

You go back to say the mid-nineteenth century, there was a very lively independent working class press run by young women from the farms called Factory Girls. Artisans from the town, you know, shoe makers, Irish immigrants and so on. And it's interesting reading. I mean they very bitterly condemned what they called, 150 years ago, the new spirit of the age. Again, wealth forgetting all but self. And that's the doctrine of the modern system.

They recognized it, they condemned it. It was the new spirit of the age then. They said it was totally dehumanizing. They did not want to be the kind of people who would gain wealth forgetting all but self. Namely, what they're taught to be. And by now a huge indoctrination system tries to force them to be. They regarded it as degrading, destructive of culture of independence of freedom. They described themselves as being the subjects of a monarchical or feudal system, losing their rights as Americans.

There is a big battle about this and the same thing happened in England to some extent, then elsewhere where industrial systems were opposed. South Korea for example recently saw tremendous resistance to the imposition of these systems of coerced and controlled labour. And it shows up in all kind of ways. The union movement is one example of it. Sometimes it just shows up in personal distress.

So one of the features of contemporary economic systems is what's called imposing flexibility in labour markets. That's considered a wonderful thing. Labour markets are supposed to be flexible. It's a fancy way of saying you don't know when you go to sleep at night whether you have a job tomorrow morning. And that contributes to efficiency. Anybody who's taken an economics course understands that you get more efficiency if people have no security. They don't know what's going to happen to them tomorrow. And then you can move them around, it's just like a tool.

If you had to worry about whether the tool was going to be happy it would be inefficient. If the tool can be treated just like a piece of metal you use it if you want, you throw it away if you don't want it.

And you can cut a piece off of it and so on—it's much more efficient. So if you can get human beings to become tools like that it's more efficient by some measure of efficiency. An ideological measure but a measure. A measure of which is based on dehumanization. You have to dehumanize it—that's part of the system.

So if you can get labour market flexibility then you get a kind of efficiency. But of course at a cost. For example one of the costs is mental illness. The International Labour Organization just did a study in which they found that the incidence of mental illness among workers has increased very sharply. Which they attribute plausibly to workers' insecurity.

On the other hand you can look at this as a game. So like when Allan Greenspan at the Federal Reserve tells Congress about what a wonderful economy he's running now, he attributes a good part of it to what he calls "growing worker insecurity" because then people are afraid to ask for better wages, or more benefits. And profits go up and inflation stays down and you get a fairy tale economy except for the population but they're tools. They're tools of production and units of consumption. So they're doing their job if that's what they do.

2.

Mark Achbar: Given that corporations are private tyrannies and antithetical to democracy, even if a corporation could be socially responsible, would we want it to be? And do you think corporations are preaching social responsibility today because they fear their legitimacy is being questioned? But are there historical precedents for this embrace of corporate social responsibility?

Noam Chomsky: Well, corporate or social responsibility has plenty of historical precedents. The concept of benevolent tyranny for example goes way back in history. Even some of the most brutal, some of the most extreme tyrants happened to be benevolent. They did good things for people. Take maybe the worst monster of history, Hitler. Under Hitler there was a kind of social revolution which provided benefits to a good part of the German population. In fact that's part of the reason why Hitler was one of the most, maybe the most, popular leader in German history until things started to go wrong.

The West regarded both Hitler and Mussolini the same way. Of course they destroyed the parliamentary system. They destroyed the political opposition. They carried out torture. They invaded other countries. But they were still being praised in the internal documents in the State Department and in the British Foreign Office for their astonishing achievements, raising the level of the masses and so on. "This admirable Italian gentleman", as Roosevelt called Mussolini, was being praised by him up till 1939. And with some justice.

I mean, they were doing some things for the people. And all the way back in history, yes, there have been benevolent tyrants. And benevolent tyrants I suppose are better than murderous tyrants. On the other hand, if you ask, well, would I like the tyrant to be benevolent, it's clearly the wrong question. If the choice is between a benevolent slave owner and a malicious slave owner I suppose it's better to have a benevolent slave owner.

But the question is, do we want a slave owner? Should the slave owner have the choice as to whether to be benevolent or not? Well the same is true of corporations. When you look at a corporation, just like when you look at a slave owner, you want to distinguish between the institution and the individual. So slavery, for example, or other forms of tyranny are inherently monstrous.

The individuals participating in them may be the nicest guys you can image. Benevolent, friendly, nice to the children, even nice to their slaves. Caring about other people. I mean, as individuals they may be anything, but in their institutional role, they're monsters, because the institution is monstrous. And the same is true here.

So an individual CEO, let's say, may really care about the environment. Or about poor children. Since they have such extraordinary resources, they may even devote some of their resources to that without violating their responsibility, the monstrous responsibility to be totally inhuman. But of course within limits. The institution allows only a certain amount.

For years, it's not recent, there's been talk about what's called the "soulful corporation"—full of love for people and everything. The concept comes right out of the academic profession I should say. And of course you could have a soulful slave system too. It's not actual contradiction, it's just ludicrous.

The pressure on corporations to become more socially responsible comes from the fact that they're worried that their legitimacy will be challenged. After all their rights or even existence are not graven in stone—they can be dismantled. And in fact most states have laws which *require* that sometimes they be dismantled.

In the state of California, for example, there's cases going through the courts where law professors, and others, are demanding that the Attorney General fulfill his legal responsibility to remove the charter of, in this case Unocal, because of great crimes that they've committed in California and in Burma and elsewhere. And if the courts refuse to accept this responsibility, it is for political, not legal, reasons. On pure legal grounds, let alone moral grounds, well yeah, corporate crime should be punished. It rarely is but it should be punished like other crime.

If the corporation is carrying out criminal activities, which often it is, it should have its charter removed and be eliminated. Put under public control. Well the distribution of power is such that corporate criminals aren't punished or very rarely punished. Corporate crime is far worse than street crime but essentially unpunished. But corporate managers are concerned.

And one of the ways of expressing the concern is to try to show that you're socially responsible. So, take, say, the Student Anti-sweatshop

Movement which has put a lot of pressure on the corporations to try to look nice. You want to be able to sell your sneakers in college campuses so you have to look like a nice guy. Corporations are indeed imposing codes of responsibility which conceivably had a certain effect. But to the extent that they do it's because they're under constant pressure. Pressure is eliminated, the codes go.

In fact there's a lot of fraud involved. There was just a major case that even hit the newspapers; I think it was the textile and sneaker manufacturers, that kind of thing. Clothing corporations did have a code and they hired a big accounting firm, PricewaterhouseCoopers, to monitor their overseas factories. And—big surprise—Pricewaterhouse put out a glowing report about how wonderful they are. But they made a mistake—they allowed a speacialist to come along, Dara O'Rourke, a young faculty member at MIT (and incidentally, a former student in undergraduate classes of mine).

He is a specialist in environmental issues, labour issues, in particular in Asia, where they were working. So they allowed him to tail along. And he did a very close detailed analysis of what was actually going on in the factories they looked at, and the things that Pricewaterhouse wasn't investigating. Like, for example, do the factories use carcinogenic chemicals and are employees forced to work eighty-hour weeks and so on. They didn't ask about that but he did. And all sorts of other things.

He published a very critical paper which, to their credit, the *New York Times* had a pretty good story about from their reporter who covers labour issues, Steven Greenhouse. Well that's what you'd expect. They're going to be monitored by systems like Pricewaterhouse which are basically inside the system. If they allow outside monitoring you're going to find something else. If they allowed the workers themselves to speak you'd get a totally different picture.

It's the activists in the rich countries who have some clout. Now they have a responsibility to make sure that these codes are implemented, but a deeper responsibility to eliminate the slave system itself. So that the people instituting the codes have no right to do it. Just like a slave, you could impose codes of responsibility on slave owners. And if you force them, threaten to take away the institution unless they act responsibly toward their slaves, you might get them to do it, which is an improvement but not wonderful.

It's kind of like when Amnesty International appeals, and I think they're right, like I sign the appeals. They appealed to the most brutal tyrant, politely, not to torture his citizens. Okay that's nice. And I sign it too, yeah please don't torture your citizens so much. And that's a good thing to do but without illusions. What you really want to eliminate is the tyrant. And the ability of the tyrant to make the decision as to whether to torture or not.

And the same is true in this case. Pressure on corporations will make them act soulful. A striking example today is the tobacco manufacturers. They can't conceal any longer the fact that they're mass murderers. Some of the major mass murderers of the twentieth century. I mean the numbers are colossal and they knew it all along. And they have consciously been killing people.

So now they're putting on a huge propaganda campaign to show what nice guys they are. You know, they take little old ladies and help them walk across the street and do all the kinds of things we were taught to do when we were Boy Scouts and so on and so forth. And it's transparent why: they want to try to overcome the image of mass murder.

But the fact is that being mass murderers was inherent in their nature. They had to. Again, the CEOs might have been very nice people. But the institutional structure was such that, yes, they became mass murderers and they had to. And this goes way back. I mean, you get some of the most decent people, you know, people of the greatest integrity and honour of modern times right in the middle of this.

Take somebody like John Stuart Mill. It would be hard to think of anyone who's a figure of greater honour and integrity and intelligence. He was, implicity, defending major atrocities and massive narco-trafficking, which was the core of the British Imperial system at the time. He certainly knew about it but was lavishly praising the perpetrators, with incredible absurdities. The only way Britain could enter the Chinese market was to force Indian opium on to China so they'd become addicts. And then Britain would make the profits and they'd be able to enter the market.

John Stuart Mill is right in the centre of this. He was an official of the East India Company, Secretary of Correspondence. He was writing all these magnificent praises of Britain right when they were carrying out some of their worst—and well-publicized—atrocities in India, and conquering more of India in the hope of gaining a monopoly over opium production. It's like Pueblo Escobar, the Columbian drug lord, being one of the great men of the twentieth century. Well you know that's part of history. And it reveals very graphically the sharp disassociation between individual benevolence and integrity and institutional behaviour—including the common behaviour of "public intellectuals"—which are quite different things.

Mark Achbar: What about the ordinary worker who's caught up in that system and their moral conscience? I mean, I get the feeling that there's a lot of perfectly moral people who are participating. And it's as if the corporate structure gives everyone licence to behave in this way.

Noam Chomsky: Well it's a fair assumption that every human being, real human beings, flesh and blood ones, not organic entities like corporations, but every flesh and blood human being is a moral person. You know we've got the same genes, we're more or less the same. But our nature, the nature of humans allows all kinds of behaviour. I mean, every one of us under some circumstances could be a gas chamber attendant and a saint. Depends on all sorts of things, which are not written in your genes.

But people have a fundamental moral nature. I don't doubt that very few people would steal food from a starving child if there was no policeman around. Those that would do it are really pathological. I mean, there's some pathological extremes. But ordinarily people wouldn't behave like that.

They do behave like that on a massive scale, massive scale. But they're unaware of it and there's a huge doctrinal system designed to make them unaware of it. And even to make them think that the starving child is really stealing from them so we're the victims. That's what propaganda and regimentation are all about. And it sort of works and it erodes the moral character. It prevents you from looking at what you yourself are doing, or what your leaders are doing (for which you share responsibility in a free society), and worry about somebody else. You see that all the time.

To move to some other domain, take war crimes trials. There are plenty of war criminals around . . . nice to have criminal courts that go after them. But it's always someone else. We never put our own criminals on trial. In fact they're immune from trial—you can't even raise the question whether they're criminals.

It is appalling to raise the question whether they're criminals. Yeah, they are, and they have hideous criminal records. But you know that can't even be discussed. I mean it's outlandish. You are driven out of polite society if you raise such a question. That's again the way institutions protect themselves and a good part of the role of respectable intellectuals—not just media and PR agencies—is to protect the institutions from exposure, practices that go back to the earliest recorded history and are probably close to a cultural universal.

So the people can be very moral. But they're acting within institutional structures, constructed systems in which only certain options are easy to pursue. Others are very hard to pursue.

Mark Achbar: You talked about secret documents that show sympathy for fascism but Mussolini was on the cover of *Fortune* magazine in 1934. There was a military coup against the US government alleged by Smedley Butler, alleged to have been plotted by Remington, Goodyear, Morgan Investment and Dupont. Why was business so enamoured with fascism?

Noam Chomsky: *Fortune* magazine, I think it was *Fortune*, had a front cover in the early thirties, maybe 1932, which said something like "the Wops are unwopping themselves". It was super racist of course and that continued. But here's these wops, kind of real low-life but finally they're getting unwopped by this wonderful dictator who destroyed the parliamentary system and sent dissidents to prison and was torturing people. But he was making the economy work. And in fact US investment shot up in Italy. Mussolini was greatly admired all across the spectrum. I've mentioned that Franklin D. Roosevelt admired him, and the State Department. Business loved him, investment shot up.

And suddenly when Hitler came in, in Germany the same thing happened there, investments shot up in Germany. He had the workforce under control. He was getting rid of dangerous left-wing elements. Investment opportunities were improving. Germany received I think, more investment, US investment, than I think any country in Europe, maybe even England. And this incidentally continued right up to the war and probably after the war through subsidiaries. It's hard to make sure of the details.

Yeah, because the opportunity for profit making was fine. You didn't have to worry about workers getting out of control. You didn't have to worry about left-wing movements threatening to institute democracy. There were no problems. These are wonderful countries. And this continues in the post-war period. I mean, the targets of investment and the most honoured people are typically the most brutal—take Suharto—in the latter part of the twentieth century it's hard to find anyone who compares with them as an utter monster.

He came into power in 1965 with a huge mass murder. The CIA compared it to the crimes of Stalin and Hitler and Mao in fact. It was reported pretty accurately, and elicited utter euphoria. You look back at the newspapers at the time they described it, it was a "staggering mass slaughter" and "boiling blood bath". And it was wonderful. You couldn't contain the euphoria. The Indonesian "moderates" who carried out the staggering mass slaughter were highly praised by liberal commentators and media, and the US government was praised for keeping its involvement secret, so as not to embarrass the moderates who provided this "gleam of light in Asia", as James Reston of the *Times* called it. Investment went in, it's a country with very rich resources, and now corporations could gain access to them. It was called "a paradise for investors". Labour was super-cheap, thanks to force and violence. And it pretty much stayed like that, for most of the population, along with huge torture and other domestic atrocities, unmatched corruption, aggression and slaughter that comes about as close to genocide as anything in the modern period. Always supported by the US, from the Ford and Carter administrations and particularly through the Reagan years, when Paul Wolfowitz was one of his most effusive supporters.

In 1995 he was welcomed to Washington. The Clinton administration called him "our kind of guy", a really nice fellow. One of the most horrible human rights records in the late twentieth century, but perfectly open to exploitation and robbery. So fine—what's your problem? In fact they only turned against him when he actually did commit a crime. He lost control and he started dragging his feet on IMF orders.

Well, he soon got a dressing-down from the head of the IMF, with a very insulting picture circulated in Asia but not here. Soon after, he got a phone call from Secretary of State Albright saying that the United States had decided that it was time for a "democratic transition". And four hours later he handed over power to his vice-president. I don't mean to suggest it was simple cause and effect. There were other things going on. But it symbolizes the relations of power. All of this has to be kept under the rug. It was sometimes mentioned that the "democratic transition" that followed, for which of course US propagandists took credit, was the first since 1958. But you'd have to look hard to find any mention of the fact that 1958 was when the Eisenhower administration intervened to overthrow the parliamentary regime, partly in fear that it was becoming too democratic, permitting a party of the poor to function. There's fine scholarly work on it, in particular by Audrey and George Kahin (the founder of modern Southeast Asia scholarship in the US). But it clearly tells the wrong story.

So yes it was nice to have a democratic transition after he had committed a real crime. But not when he was just killing tens of thousands of people and leaving corpses in the street, as he boasted, to terrorize the rest. And just destroying, carrying out genocide, well that was all fine. In fact we contributed to it, as did England, and plenty of others, though the US-UK took the lead, with great vigor and enthusiasm. He was, after all, "at heart benign", as the London *Economist* explained while ridiculing the reports of propagandists like the Church and Human Rights organizations that were telling the truth —as they later quietly conceded, after Suharto had lost favor.

And the same in case after case after case. So it's not that Hitler or Mussolini before the war were something out of the ordinary. It is pretty much the norm, a fairly normal example of how things work, for institutional reasons. Now, I don't say that the people involved were rotten people any more than John Stuart Mill was a rotten person because he was defending murderers and narco-traffickers. No, that's just your institutional role. Your life as a human being can be quite different.

I remember when Klaus Barbie—you know the butcher of Lyon, Nazi gangster—was finally extradited by France from Bolivia, it must have been mid-eighties, and brought back to France for trial. I was listening to the BBC or something and they interviewed his daughter. And his daughter was saying she just didn't believe any of the things that were being said about him. He was the nicest father. He was really sweet with the kids. He was nice to his wife. I mean, he gave candy to children.

Which is probably all true. He was also a brutal torturer and murderer. At first for the Nazi's, then for the Americans. We took him over at the end of the Second World War, and he continued his work under US control, pretty much as before, same targets, as his US military supervisor explained in a letter to the *New York Times*. Namely, trying to suppress and destroy the resistance and the Communist Party. And, yeah, at the same time he's probably nice to his kids.

Mark Achbar: Today corporations are getting into the business of prisons, welfare, schools, universities, daycare, medical care, old-age homes. Is there some kind of inherent problem with allowing the for-profit principles of the corporation to run institutions that provide a necessary public service? And I'd like to hear your general response, but we're also specifically interested in K-12* at public education.

Noam Chomsky: Well you know any tyrannical system is going to want to maximize its control over the society. So anything that is under some public accountability it will want to get rid of. It is extremely important to eliminate public accountability, and also to drive out of people's head the idea that they care about anyone else. Those are very important goals.

What's called privatization, another misleading term, is an effort to achieve these ends. Privatization does not mean you take a public institution and give it to some nice person. It means you take a public

---

* K-12 refers to schooling from kindergarten to the end of secondary school.

institution and give it to an unaccountable tyranny. The corporate tyranny, which is more massive than a public system to begin with.

So you take, say, the water system of Bolivia and hand it over to Bechtel, for example. Bolivia is not much of a democracy, but there is some kind of role for the public in influencing what happens, some minimal kind. So poor people had water. If you give it to Bechtel they do exactly what the World Bank tells Bolivia to do and what they themselves do automatically—they charge user fees.

That's the way to be rational—charge user fees. It's also the way to make profit. And in Bolivia it happened to have the consequence that most of the population didn't get any water, but after all, nothing can work perfectly. And then next thing that happened is near revolution combined with public protest in the rich countries. So Bechtel had to pull out.

Well that's privatization. And we're seeing it right now with schools and social security. They are very striking examples. There are all kinds of completely fraudulent scams being constructed about the crisis, alleged crisis of social security. I mean there's no serious social security crisis. The claims are mostly fraud.

There's a major effort, however, to make people believe that the system is in crisis. This is the usual precursor to privatization, to make the system not function. You want to privatize the railroads? First we'll make sure they don't work. Everybody hates them and so on, then you can hand them over to private enterprise. And they'll work even worse. As recently happened in Britain under Major.

Same with Social Security. You try to get people frightened about it in ways so fraudulent that it's astonishing they can get away with it. And then hand it over to Wall Street which is hoping to make a killing (though that's not a primary issue, and they of course deny it—they want to kill the system out of benevolence). The effects on the population will probably be bad. But the main purpose, I think, the main driving force behind it is not profit for Wall Street, but rather to undermine the very dangerous principle on which Social Security rests. Namely, the principle that you care whether a widow down the street and her children have something to eat. You're not supposed to do that—you're supposed to only "gain wealth, forgetting all but self", You know—the "New Spirit of the Age" that working people denounced 150 years ago. Social Security tends to enhance human qualities, and therefore must be destroyed.

There's more, of course. Social Security is meaningless for the wealthy, scarcely a little icing on the cake. But it is of critical importance to working people, the poor, the disabled, dependents, the large majority. And it is administered so efficiently that there is nothing in it for the corporate sector. Compare the health care system, which is facing a very real crisis—which is a factor in the minimal problems faced by Social Security. The US has the most inefficient system in the industrial world, far higher per capita costs than elsewhere and some of the worst health outcomes—in no small measure because it is privatizing, hence has huge administrative costs, many layers of bureaucratic control, lots of paper work and supervision, etc.—costs that are really much higher than what economists measure, because they don't count the costs transferred to doctors and patients, or to those who can't get medical care and drugs. But even the official numbers are awful enough. However, health care is effectively rationed by wealth: for the rich, there's the best care in the world, and others have to learn "responsibility". So there is no health care crisis that has to be dealt with—except by ensuring that big pharma makes even greater profits and that medical support for those who are not wealthy enough is reduced. The non-crisis of Social Security demonstrates that Social Security must be "reformed"—meaning dismantled. The very serious crisis of the health care system demonstrates that we should make it worse. It all makes good sense, if we accept the basic doctrines.

Same with schools. There are problems in the schools and I don't think there's a big question about the basic way to improve them.

You put more money into them. Make teacher's salaries better, have smaller class sizes—there are a lot of things you can do to improve schools. But if you hand them over to private enterprise and they run for profit then you are undermining the social solidarity that the public school system relies on: the idea that I care whether the kid down the street goes to school. Well make sure you undermine that because you're supposed to be out for yourself and no one else: the "New Spirit of the Age" that the business world has been seeking to impose for 150 years, with increasing effort and sophistication, by now with huge industries. You should be a slave of the propaganda system and the commercial system. Can't care about anyone else.

Once the schools are under private control they can be used more effectively for useful purposes, like indoctrination to try to convert children into regimented creatures oriented towards consumerism. Following orders and so on. It makes good sense if you're trying to increase profit. By some measures of efficiency that can be devised it may even turn out to be more efficient. Test scores maybe, though I doubt it.

The whole privatization pressure is kind of an interesting one. It's always been there, but it took off in the Thatcher-Reagan years, after 1980. Around then you were getting tremendous propaganda about the need for privatization. And for poor countries it's just forced on them.

So these are IMF conditionalities. Do you want to have access to international markets and capital? You've got to privatize. You don't have any choices. In the richer countries you have to sort of convince people.

There was a major study done, I think it was in 1993, by two well-known Cambridge University economists, international economists. It was done for UNCTAD, the UN organization that deals with economic issues. It's quite an interesting study. One thing they pointed out is that there was no academic work, no scholarly work, showing that privatization had benefits. This was pure ideological doctrine. I mean maybe it has benefits, maybe it doesn't, but there was no basis for it.

So the pressure behind it was something else. And it's obvious what it was. The pressure was, for one thing, more power to the private tyrannies, hence reducing the ever-present threat of democracy. And for another, undermining human sentiments, again all to the good. It takes serious work to tell whether public institutions are needed, or more or less inefficient or corrupt than private ones. And there's unlikely to be any general answer.

It depends. For example, a Swedish public institution is going to be better run than a Peruvian one. The same is true of a Swedish corporation and a Peruvian corporation, and for obvious reasons. But public institutions have many side benefits. For one thing they may purposely run at a loss. They're not out for profit. They may purposely run at a loss because of the side benefits. The externalities, not measured. They can take account of externalities.

So for example, if a public steel industry runs at a loss it's providing cheap steel to other industries. Maybe that's a good thing for the society. Public institutions can have a counter-cyclic property. So that means that they can maintain employment in periods of recession which increases demand, which helps you get out of recession.

Private companies can't do that. In a recession they throw out the work force because that's the way you make money. And there are lots of other side effects like these which aren't calculated by economists. Not because they couldn't be calculated, but because these considerations are, by choice, mostly out of the heavily ideological constructed system called economics, which largely keeps to market doctrines that are often quite remote from reality. You measure certain things and not other things. But if you start measuring those things well you know you have all kinds of other calculations.

Plus the fact that public institutions are accountable to the extent that the country is democratic. I mean no country is very high on that ranking and some are very low but they're all somewhere. The public has some effect on public institutions. And to the extent that the country allows public expression and organization and so on, there can be a significant public impact on what publicly owned institutions do.

On the other hand, there may be benefits from private competition. You really have to look case by case. It has to be shown, and you have to recognize that the competition is not among people. Tyrannical entities are competing, tyrannical entities which are interlinked in many ways and dependent on state power—of which they are the "tools and tyrants", as James Madison warned, long before they reached anything remotely like their current form. Tyrannies that have no right to exist anyway.

3.

Mark Achbar: It seems to me that there's something extreme and very strange about the fact that a corporation can have and own genes, and even entire life forms. It seems like the ultimate in privatization.

Noam Chomsky: The patenting of life forms and now genes is in an extreme case of the perversity of the contemporary system. One feature is its radical anti-market tendencies. Patenting altogether is interference with markets. And the modern patent regime that was imposed under the World Trade Organization rules reaches new levels of protectionism, far beyond anything that preceded. If the US had been compelled to follow those rules, we'd probably still be pursuing our comparative advantage in exporting fish and fur—not cotton, since slave labor is an extreme market interference. The new system imposed on the "developing world" is also designed to impede growth. That's what product patents are about. Their point is to prevent other people from figuring out smart ways of making the same product, hence guaranteeing monopoly pricing rights to private tyrannies.

Furthermore the corporations that are getting the patents on life forms and genes are, for the most part, heavily subsidized by the public.

They receive a huge public subsidy for research and development and so on. So what you get is that the public is paying for the monopolization of the technology of the future. And even for interfering with growth. And it is also paying to be propagandized since the corporations do a ton of advertising, of course—not to provide information but to delude and control. That's hardly controversial.

When you get to genes and life forms it's particularly extreme. No one knows much about what the genes do, and it may even be the wrong question but you think maybe they'll be used for some things, some day. And I'll own them so I'm going to own genes or I'm going to own somebody's blood or something like that.

Furthermore on top of all of this it's sheer robbery. I mean when they patented life forms they are using the knowledge, and expertise, that's been gained over thousands of years by experimentation, and research, and achievements of what we call indigenous societies that don't have our form of ownership control.

This is mostly work done by women. I mean that the knowledge and techniques have been transmitted from mother to daughter over long periods of time. Techniques of breeding, what should be grown where, what's useful for this purpose and so on. A big pharmaceutical company comes in and just steals all that—they don't pay anything for it. And since there's no technical ownership in the Western sense you don't have to pay people for the fact that for thousands of years they've been developing these things and figuring out what to do.

You just steal it from them. Then you make a minor modification of it and you patent the modification. And then they have to buy it back from you because your market power is so extreme that they're going to have to go to you for seeds or whatever. So it's a combination of extraordinary robbery, I mean profound immorality, and the probable undermining of economic growth. It's quite apart from the whole moral question of the right to own life forms. Again that's a value question, but it looks kind of outlandish to me.

Notes

Introduction

1. Interviews with Hank McKinnell and Joe Badaracco.

2. The interviews were taped for a documentary film, *The Corporation,* that is based on this book. I wrote the film and am also cocreator of it with Mark Achbar, who is also coproducer (with Bart Simpson) and codirector (with Jennifer Abbott). Interviews were conducted by Mark Achbar, Dawn Brett (an associate producer, as I am too), or myself. For most of those I did not personally conduct, I was involved in formulating questions and strategies. I am indebted to Achbar, Abbott, Brett, and Simpson, as well as to Big Pictures Media, the company that produced the film, and the broadcasters, agencies, and other investors who financed it.

3. Lawrence E. Mitchell, *Corporate Irresponsibility: America's Newest Export* (New Haven: Yale University Press, February 19, 2002).

1: The Corporation's Rise to Dominance

1. Tom Hadden, *Company Law and Capitalism* (London: Weidenfeld and Nicolson, 1972), 14.

2. John Carswell, *The South Sea Bubble* (London: Cresset Press, 1960), 42 ("Spaniards"), 55 ("profits").

3. Ibid., 173

4. Ibid.

5. Hadden, *Company Law and Capitalism,* 16.

6. Carswell, *The South Sea Bubble*, 210.

7. Especially in high-technology companies, where stock options are widely used to compensate employees, failure to account for them unduly inflates reported earnings, sometimes by hundreds of millions of dollars. Yet, despite criticism of the practice by investor groups, accounting bodies, and the likes of Alan Greenspan and Warren Buffett, the federal government seems reluctant to stop it. Why? Likely because powerful business interests unduly influence what government does. True, many large companies—Coca-Cola, General Electric, Home Depot, Dow Chemical Company, and General Motors—now voluntarily count stock options as compensation expenses, but these are not companies that make significant use of the practice. Business interests lobbied hard and successfully in the early 1990s to block attempts by the Financial Accounting Standards Board (the body responsible for setting accounting standards) to fix the problem and are likely to prevail over any future attempts at reform in this area.

8. The Sarbanes-Oxley Act, Pub. L. No.107–204, 116 Stat. 745, was signed into law by the president on July 30, 2002. Among other things, the act limits the extent to which an accounting firm can serve as both an auditor of and consultant to the same corporation. That practice, which contributed notoriously to Arthur Andersen's complicity in Enron's misdeeds, generates an obvious conflict of interest. An accounting firm that wants to protect its lucrative consulting contracts with a corporation has every incentive to cooperate with, rather than oversee, the corporation's financial reporting; obviously that compromises its ability to audit the corporation objectively. The Sarbanes-Oxley Act, and regulations created under it by the Securities and Exchange Commission (SEC), though imperfect and containing some wide loopholes, do go some of the way toward remedying the problem by barring a firm from auditing a client for which it provides certain kinds of consulting services. It also enhances the powers of corporations' audit committees, requires CEOs and CFOs to certify financial reports (and face up to ten years in prison for "knowing" falsification and twenty years for "willing" falsification), and strengthens disclosure requirements. Several problems are likely to limit the act's effectiveness, however. First, the SEC has discretion to allow a firm to provide consulting services to an audit client on the prohibited list, so long as "it is reasonable to conclude that the results of these services will not be subject to audit procedures" when the client is audited. Second, certain services are not on the prohibited list, such as routine preparation of tax

returns, a lucrative practice for accounting firms and one that clearly has a direct impact on audited financial statements. Third, the SEC is "ludicrously underfinanced," as Paul Krugman states in "Business as Usual," *The New York Times,* October 22, 2002, and thus may not be effective in ensuring firms comply with the act. Fourth, the SEC has, according to some critics, watered down the act's requirements (see, e.g., Fulcrum Financial Inquiry, "Through Rule-Making, SEC Continues to Weaken Sarbanes-Oxley," January 27, 2003, available at www.fulcruminquiry.com).

9. Hadden, *Company Law and Capitalism,* 13.

10. John Lord, *Capital and Steam Power,* 1925, available at www.history.rochester.edu/steam/lord.

11. Scott Bowman, *The Modern Corporation and American Political Thought: Law, Power and Ideology* (University Park, Pa.: Pennsylvania State University Press, 1996), 41.

12. 1825 is the year Scott reports this statement as having been made by a businessman at a fictitious meeting of businessmen in a Scottish tavern. Walter Scott, *The Waverley Novels—The Betrothed, vol. 19* (Philadelphia: John Morris & Co., 1892) (I would like to thank Miranda Burgess for bringing this work to my attention).

13. The prerevolutionary history of the American corporation is inseparable from that of the English corporation. As Chief Justice John Marshall acknowledged in the 1819 case of *Trustees of Dartmouth College v. Woodward:* "Our ideas of a corporation, its privileges and disabilities, are derived entirely from the English law."

14. Bowman, *The Modern Corporation and American Political Thought,* 41–42.

15. Paddy Ireland, "Capitalism Without the Capitalist: The Joint Stock Company Share and the Emergence of the Modern Doctrine of Separate Corporate Personality," *Journal of Legal History* 17 (1996): 63.

16. Cited in ibid., 62.

17. Cited in ibid., 65.

18. Select Committee on the Law of Partnership, 1851, B.P.P., VII, vi (as cited in Rob McQueen, "Company Law in Great Britain and the Australian Colonies 1854–1920: A Social History," Ph.D. thesis, Griffith University, p. 137). For further discussion of the relationship between limited liability and middle-class investment capital, see Ronald E. Seavoy, *The Origins of the American Business Corporation, 1784–1855: Broadening the*

Concept of Public Service During Industrialization (Westport, Conn.: Greenwood Press, 1982); Phillip Blumberg, *The Multinational Challenge to Corporation Law: The Search for a New Corporate Personality* (Oxford: Oxford University Press, 1993); "Report of the Select Committee in Investments for the Savings of the Middle and Working Classes," 1850, B.P.P., XIX, 169.

19. Cited in McQueen, "Company Law in Great Britain and the Australian Colonies 1854–1920," p. 75.

20. Cited in Barbara Weiss, *The Hell of the English: Bankruptcy and the Victorian Novel* (Lewisburg, Pa.: Bucknell University Press, 1986), 148.

21. Morton Horwitz, "Santa Clara Revisited: The Development of Corporate Theory," in *Corporations and Society: Power and Responsibility,* ed. Warren Samuels and Arthur Miller (New York: Greenwood Press, 1987), 13.

22. Interview with Dr. Harriet Smith Windsor.

23. Roland Marchand, *Creating the Corporate Soul: The Rise of Public Relations and Corporate Imagery in American Big Business* (Berkeley: University of California Press, 1998), 7.

24. Cited in Edward Herman, *Corporate Control, Corporate Power* (Cambridge, England: Cambridge University Press, 1981), 7 ("tie" and "witnesses").

25. Stewart Kyd, *A Treatise on the Law of Corporations (1793),* vol. 1, p. 1, as cited in Ireland, "Capitalism Without the Capitalist," 45–46.

26. John George, *A View of the Existing Law of Joint Stock Companies* (1825), p. 29, as cited in Paddy Ireland, "Capitalism Without the Capitalist," 45.

27. University of Chicago law professor Arthur W. Machen, as quoted in Horwitz, "Santa Clara Revisited," 51.

28. *Santa Clara County v. Southern Pacific Railroad,* 118 U.S. 394 (1886). Between 1890 and 1910, business interests invoked the Fourteenth Amendment 288 times before the courts, compared to 19 times by African Americans, according to Mary Zepernick of the Program on Corporations, Law and Democracy in an interview. And in the name of the Fourteenth Amendment, beginning with its 1905 decision in *Lochner v. New York,* the Supreme Court fashioned a jurisprudence that, over the next three decades, would bar states from enacting various kinds of regulatory measures, such as maximum-hour and minimum-wage protections for workers. In 1937, President Roosevelt, fearful that the Court might thwart his New Deal with its antiregulatory bias, threatened to pack it with five new judges, all of them

New Deal sympathizers, prompting it to adopt a more deferential posture toward government. More recently, however, courts have once again begun to recognize corporations' rights under the Constitution and strike down laws that, in their view, offend them.

29. Marchand, *Creating the Corporate Soul*, 8 ("human" and "general"), 4 ("affection"), 76 ("directly").

30. Ibid., 139.

31. Kim McQuaid, "Young, Swope and General Electric's 'New Capitalism': A Study in Corporate Liberalism, 1920–33," *American Journal of Economics and Sociology* 36 (1977): 323.

32. Jeffrey L. Rodengen, *The Legend of Goodyear: The First 100 Years* (Fort Lauderdale, Fla.: Write Stuff Syndicate, 1997).

33. *Louis K. Liggett Co. et al. v. Lee, Comptroller et al.,* 288 US 517 (1933), 548, 567.

34. Gerard Swope, *The Swope Plan: Details, Criticisms, Analysis* (New York: Business Bourse, 1931), 22. Cited in E. Merrick Dodd, "For Whom Are Corporate Managers Trustees?," *Harvard Law Review* 45 (1932): 1145–1163. Dodd also quotes economic historian Charles Beard's wry observation about Swope and his plan: "Mr. Swope spoke as a man of affairs, as president of the General Electric Company. No academic taint condemned his utterance in advance; no suspicion of undue enthusiasm clouded his product. As priest-kings could lay down the law without question in primitive society, so a captain of industry in the United States could propose a new thing without encountering the scoffs of the wise or the jeers of the practical (1155)."

35. Adolf A. Berle and Gardiner C. Means, *The Modern Corporation and Private Property* (New York: Harcourt, Brace & World, 1968), 4 ("princes), 312–13 ("cupidity"), 312 ("survive"); Dodd, "For Whom Are Corporate Managers Trustees?," 1157. The corporation's prestige was partly restored by the outbreak of World War II. Corporations were widely believed to be key to defeating fascism; they were called "arsenals of democracy" at the time, for having transformed their operations in ways that would meet the needs of a nation at war. The war, however, had also strengthened ties between workers and the institutions they looked to for protection: government and organized labor, which were now more powerful than ever. In response, business began a systematic campaign during the postwar years to become a powerful, well-organized political presence. Corporate lobbying and campaign financing were used to help foster a political climate that

viewed corporations as benevolent, responsible, and best left alone by government, and an all-out public relations campaign, led by the National Association of Manufacturers, was launched to help convince Americans that individualism, competition, and free enterprise were synonymous with the American Way. See Elizabeth A. Fones-Wolf, *The Selling of Free Enterprise: The Business Assault on Labor and Liberalism 1945–1960* (Urbana: University of Illinois Press, 1994). The campaign really picked up steam beginning in the 1970s, however, as is discussed in Chapter 4.

36. Quoted in Richard Gwyn, "The True Allegiance of Canadian Corporations," *Toronto Star*, April 28, 1999.

37. See, for discussions of globalization, Anthony Giddens, *Runaway World: How Globalisation Is Running Our Lives* (London: Profile Books, 1999); Joseph E. Stiglitz, *Globalization and Its Discontents* (New York: W. W. Norton and Company, 2002); Alan Tonelson, *The Race to the Bottom: Why a Worldwide Worker Surplus and Uncontrolled Free Trade Are Sinking American Living Standards* (Boulder, Colo.: Westview Press, 2000); Saskia Sassen, *Losing Control: Sovereignty in an Age of Globalization* (New York: Columbia University Press, 1996); William K. Tabb, *The Amoral Elephant: Globalization and the Struggle for Social Justice in the Twenty-first Century* (New York: Monthly Review Press, 2001); Gary Teeple, *Globalization and the Decline of Social Reform into the Twenty-first Century* (Toronto: Garamond Press, 2000); William Greider, *One World, Ready or Not: The Manic Logic of Global Capitalism* (New York: Simon & Schuster, 1997).

38. See, for discussions of the WTO and its impact (and globalization more generally), Stiglitz, *Globalization and Its Discontents*; Charles Derber, *People Before Profit: The New Globalization in an Age of Terror, Big Money and Economic Crisis* (New York: St. Martin's Press, 2002); Noreena Hertz, *Silent Takeover: Global Capitalism and the Death of Democracy* (New York: Free Press, 2002).

39. WTO Press Release, "WTO Adopts Disciplines on Domestic Regulation for the Accountancy Sector" (December 14, 1998), available at www.wto.org (WTO News: 1998 Press Releases).

40. Ibid., Article III. The stated "legitimate objectives" are protection of consumers, quality of the service, professional competence, and integrity of the profession.

41. Ibid.

42. See supra, note 8, for description of the act.

43. Anthony DePalma, "WTO Pact Would Set Global Accounting Rules," *The New York Times,* March 1, 2002; Murray Dobbin, "We Must Fight the Enron Virus," *The Globe and Mail* (Toronto), February 7, 2002, A19.

44. See, for discussion of examples, Debi Barker and Jerry Mander, "Invisible Government. The World Trade Organization: Global Governance for the New Millennium?," San Francisco: International Forum on Globalization, October 1999; Lori Wallach and Michelle Sforza, *The WTO: Five Years of Reasons to Resist Corporate Globalization* (New York: Seven Stories Press, 2000); Derber, *People Before Profit;* Hertz, *Silent Takeover.*

45. See WTO Appellate Body Report: "United States, Import Prohibition of Certain Shrimp and Shrimp Products: Recourse to Article 21.5 of the DSU by Malaysia," October 22, 2001, available at www.wto.org (doc. # 01-5166).

46. See WTO Appellate Body Report, "European Communities, Measures Affecting Meat and Meat Products," January 16, 1998, available at www.wto.org (doc. # 98-0099).

47. Examples discussed in Ralph Nader, "Notes from Nader: The Chill Factor: Consumer Safeguards Under Fire," *World Trade Observer,* Seattle, Wash., 1999, available at depts.washington.edu/wtohist/world_trade_obs/issue3/nader.htm.

48. Stiglitz, *Globalization and Its Discontents,* 20.

49. Helmut Maucher, "Ruling by Consent," *Financial Times,* December 6, 1997, 2, as cited in Belen Balanya, Ann Doherty, Olivier Hoedeman, Adam Ma'anit, and Erik Wesselius, *Europe Inc.: Regional and Global Restructuring and the Rise of Corporate Power* (London: Pluto Press, 2000), 136.

50. Interviews with William Niskanen, Ira Jackson, and Sam Gibara. As Jonathan Chait recently observed about the Bush administration in *The New Republic,* "Government and business have melded into one big 'us' " (as cited by Paul Krugman, "Channels of Influence," *The New York Times,* March 25, 2003). Robert Monks says, "Particularly since the Berlin Wall came down in 1989, it probably is clear that the heads of large corporations have more impact on your life and the lives of citizens around the world than the head of any country."

51. Interviews with Chris Komisarjevsky and Clay Timon. For an excellent critical discussion of branding and its implications for society, see Naomi Klein, *No Logo: Taking Aim at the Brand Bullies* (Toronto: Knopf Canada, 2000). More generally, the notion that corporations are persons—individuals—

has served throughout history to obscure, in both law and public opinion, the fact that corporations exercise the *collective* economic power of vast numbers of shareholders and thus are profoundly more powerful than the rest of us.

52. Interviews with Clay Timon and Samir Gibara.

Chapter 2: Business as Usual

1. Interview with Tom Kline. The documentary crew was from Mark Achbar's Big Picture Media company and was making the film version of this book. See supra, Introduction, note 2.

2. Interview with Sonia Gerrardo.

3. Interviews with Hank McKinnell and Tom Kline.

4. Interview with Hank McKinnell ("planet"); www.pfizer.com ("generous" and "innovative").

5. Quoted in Princeton University Development Offices, "Princeton Receives Grants to Address Greenhouse Problem," available at www.princeton.edu/cfr/FALLOO/BPAmoco.html.

6. Interview with Ira Jackson.

7. Ibid.

8. Interview with Milton Friedman.

9. Interview with William Niskanen.

10. Interviews with Peter Drucker, Debora Spar, and Noam Chomsky.

11. Carol Gelderman, *Henry Ford: The Wayward Capitalist* (New York: Dial Press, 1981), 83. Gelderman says that E. G. Pipp, editor in chief of *The Detroit News,* quoted Ford as saying this in his testimony at the trial in *Dodge v. Ford*; as cited in D. Gordon Smith, "The Shareholder Primacy Norm," *The Journal of Corporation Law* 23 (1998): 277.

12. Gelderman, *Henry Ford,* 84, as cited in Smith, "The Shareholder Primacy Norm," 277 ("bonanza" and "incidentally"). *Dodge v. Ford Motor Co.,* 684 ("organized" and "benefiting").

13. In an interview, corporate law scholar Dr. Janis Sarra accurately described the relationship between the best-interests principle and corporate social responsibility as follows: "In North America, the best interests of the corporation have been defined as best interests of the shareholders. Courts usually only consider shareholder wealth maximization as the benchmark of whether the directors and officers are acting in the best interests of the corporation. Directors and officers are therefore restricted by what has been a very powerful

set of court decisions. As long as the best-interest-of-the-corporation principle is taken to mean shareholder wealth maximization, any real initiatives to shift the considerations and decision making to environmental concerns or other kinds of social equity concerns are going to be very, very limited. The way in which corporate law is currently constructed requires directors and officers to justify any socially responsible actions under the guise of, or the aim of, either short-term or long-term shareholder wealth maximization. Similarly, shareholders are frequently prohibited from expressing preferences for corporate social responsibility, human rights protection, or environmental sustainability, unless they can justify it under shareholder wealth maximization. Even where shareholders have the information and resources to bring forward such proposals or proxy resolutions and frame them in the language of maximizing wealth, the directors and officers are not obligated to act on their wishes. Corporations do give donations and other kinds of support for causes that do not appear to be directly related to the activities of the corporation, because philanthropy legislation in the United States has carved out this limited role for corporation. The corporation can be considered a form of institutionalized self-interest in the sense that the best-interest principle, as it is being interpreted by the courts and by corporate decision makers, is clearly one in which wealth of shareholders is paramount, ignoring all other constituencies."

14. Robert Hinkley, "How Corporate Law Inhibits Social Responsibility," *Business Ethics: Corporate Social Responsibility Report,* January–February 2002, available at www.commondreams.org/views02/0119-04.htm.

15. *Hutton v. West Cork Railway Company,* 23 Chancery Division 654 (1883) (C.A.), 672 ("instance"), 673 ("Draconian" and "cakes").

16. American Bar Association, Committee on Corporate Laws, "Other Constituencies Statutes: Potential for Confusion," *The Business Lawyer* 45 (1990): 2261, as cited in Smith, "The Shareholder Primacy Norm."

17. Interview with Chris Komisarjevsky. Corporate philanthropy is often described as "strategic philanthropy" to capture the idea that philanthropy is a strategy for serving corporations' own interests. See Nicole Harris, "Things Go Better with Coke's Money," *Business Week,* September 15, 1997, 36.

18. Marjorie Kelly, *The Divine Right of Capital: Dethroning the Corporate Aristocracy* (San Francisco: Berrett-Koehler, 2001).

19. As reported in Danielle Knight (IPS), "Mixed Reaction to Oil Company's Earth Day Award," April 22, 1999, available at http://www.oneworld.org/ips2/april99/21_05_076.html.

20. Sir John Browne, "International Relations: The New Agenda for Business," The 1998 Elliott Lecture, St Antony's College, Oxford, June 4, 1998.

21. Sir John Browne, speech at the Earth Day Awards Ceremony at UN Headquarters, New York, on the occasion of his being presented with the Award for Individual Environmental Leadership by the UN Environmental Programme and Earth Day, New York, April 22, 1999, available at www.bp.com.

22. Interview with Jim Gray.

23. Interview with Milton Friedman.

24. Interview with Norma Kassi.

25. The Bush administration is seeking to open up the Arctic National Wildlife Refuge to drilling. In March 2003, the Senate rejected the administration's plan in a budget vote. But on April 11, 2003, the House endorsed drilling in the ANWR. The debate continues.

26. Interview with Norma Kassi. Also see Robert Matas, "Survival Tactic: Can the Hunters Save the Caribou?" The Globe and Mail (Toronto), August 19, 2000, A10–A11.

27. John Gore, group vice president, government and public affairs, BP, letter to Rebecca O'Malley of Ecopledge, January 16, 2001.

28. Found at www.bpamoco/alaska/qanda/qanda.htm (print copy on file with the author).

29. Letters to Presidents Clinton, December 11, 2000, and Bush, March 20, 2001, from groups of scientists; Kenneth Whitten, retired research biologist, Alaska Department of Fish and Game, gave written testimony at a hearing on the Republican energy bill on July 11, 2001: U.S., Energy Security Act of 2001: Hearing on H.R. 2436 Before the House Committee on Resources: 107th Cong. (Washington, D.C.: U.S. Government Printing Office, 2002).

30. Sir John Browne, "The Case for Social Responsibility," presentation to the Annual Conference of Business for Social Responsibility, Boston, November 10, 1998.

31. The company's stated position has been that it cannot create a plan to drill unless and until the ANWR is opened to drilling. At the same time, it consistently has refused to commit to not drilling. See, e.g., www.bpamoco.com/alaskaqanda/qanda.htm (print version on file with author).

32. From the following speeches by Sir John Browne: "International Relations ("guilt," "self-interest"); "Public Pressure and Strategic Choice," World Economic Forum, Davos, Switzerland, February 2, 1998 ("good busi-

ness"); "The Case for Social Responsibility" ("reality," "hard-headed," "direct"); "Mobility and Choice," Detroit Economic Club, January 25, 1999 ("coldly," "imperative").

33. BP Press Release, "BP Beats Greenhouse Gas Target by Eight Years and Aims to Stabilise Net Future Emissions," March 11, 2002, available at www.bp.com (under Press Center Archives).

34. Sir John Browne, "International Relations."

35. Sir John Browne, "Mobility and Choice" ("explore," "drive"); "International Relations" ("captive").

36. Interview with Hank McKinnell.

37. Ibid.

38. Interview with Rachel Cohen.

39. Interview with Hank McKinnell.

40. Interview with Rachel Cohen. Cohen also points out that there are many hidden costs associated with the "free" drug programs. She says, "Giving drugs away to developing countries has many hidden costs. One of them is that the public health system, that has to find a way to absorb the donation program, has to set aside resources to manage the program. . . . They might actually second public health staff to manage that program. And we're talking about countries with very, very limited health budgets. So there are enormous costs to the public health systems in countries that are recipients of drug donations that we don't often hear about."

41. Statistics in this paragraph are from interview with Rachel Cohen.

42. Interview with Tom Kline.

43. Interview with Danny Schecter.

44. Alisdair MacIntyre, "Utilitarianism and Cost-Benefit Analysis: An Essay on the Relevance of Moral Philosophy to Bureaucratic Theory," in *Values in the Electric Power Industry,* ed. Kenneth Sayre (Notre Dame, Ind.: University of Notre Dame Press, 1977), 217–37. Interview with Sam Gibara.

45. Interview with Anita Roddick.

46. Ibid.

47. As quoted on www.thebodyshop.com.

48. Interview with Anita Roddick.

49. Ibid.

50. Julia Finch, "Body Shop Buyers Line Up," *The Guardian,* October 3, 2001 ("aware"); Finch, "Body Shop Gains a New Head," *The Guardian,* February 13, 2002; Sarah Ryle, "Body Shop Seeks New Life with Major

Surgery," *The Observer,* February 17, 2002.

51. Interview with Marc Barry.
52. Ibid.
53. Ibid.
54. Interview with Anita Roddick.
55. Interview with Dr. Robert Hare.
56. Ibid.
57. Ibid.
58. Enron, Corporate Responsibility Annual Report, Houston, 2000.
59. Interview with Hank McKinnell.

Chapter 3: The Externalizing Machine

1. The creation of externalities by corporations relates directly to the legal rule that corporations must always act in ways that serve their own best interests, i.e., that maximize their shareholders' wealth. As corporate law scholar Janis Sarra stated in an interview: "Corporate law, as it is currently constructed in the Anglo-American paradigm, requires that corporate officers take account of short-term costs and long-term costs *to the corporation,* but not to anyone else. Anything that is not considered such a cost is called an externality and includes the costs of corporate harms that are borne by workers, small creditors, consumers, or community members. If a corporation makes a decision that will harm the land or have some sort of long-term effect on fishing waters of First Nations people or results in environmental contamination of communities, those kinds of costs are external to the corporation and do not need to be accounted for in the corporation's decision. These externalities also do not need to be costed on the corporate balance sheet because only the profit is recorded, but not the costs to others. That is how corporate law is currently constructed."

2. Interview with Milton Friedman.
3. Ibid.
4. "Record $4.9 Billion Award Against GM for Dangerous Fuel Tanks," www.cnn.com, July 9, 1999; Milo Geyelen, "How a Memo Written 26 Years Ago Is Costing General Motors Dearly," *The Wall Street Journal,* September 29, 1999, 1.
5. Geyelen, "How a Memo Written 26 Years Ago Is Costing General Motors Dearly."

6. Ibid.

7. The $8.19 figure comes from other GM documents, not the Ivey Report. For a description, see, "GM Fuel Tanks," www.safetyforum.com; Public Citizen, "Profits over Lives—Long-Hidden Documents Reveal GM Cost-Benefit Analyses Led to Severe Burn Injuries; Disregard for Safety Spurred Large Verdict," July 19, 1999, available www.citizen.org/congress/civjus/tort/.

8. The case is currently embroiled in procedural wrangling and has not yet been heard by the California Court of Appeal.

9. *Patricia Anderson v. General Motors*, Brief of Chamber of Commerce of the United States as *amicus curiae* in support of the Appellant, California Court of Appeal for the Second Appellate District—Division Four, 3 ("illegitimate"), 1 ("troubling" and "manufacturing"), 3 ("despicable"), 8 ("hallmark"), 10 ("unimpeachable").

10. Meiring de Villiers, "Technological Risk and Issue Preclusion: A Legal and Policy Critique," *Cornell Journal of Law and Public Policy* 9 (2000): 523, as cited in the Chamber of Commerce Brief, p. 9.

11. MacIntyre, "Utilitarianism and Cost-Benefit Analysis," 218.

12. Ivey Report (print version on file with the author).

13. Chamber of Commerce Brief, 10. ("Skillful" and "sanctity," citing Gary T. Schwartz, Deterrence and Punishment in the Common Law of Punitive Damages: A Comment (1982) 56 5.Cal L. Rev. 133, p. 152.)

14. See Chapter 1 for a more detailed discussion of economic globalization.

15. Interview with Charles Kernaghan.

16. Ibid.

17. Ibid.

18. Ibid.

19. Ibid.

20. Ibid.

21. Dexter Roberts and Aaron Bernstein, "Inside a Chinese Sweatshop: 'A Life of Fines and Beating,' " *BusinessWeek Online*, October 2, 2000. According to the report, "Since 1992, Wal-Mart has required its suppliers to sign a code of basic labor standards. After exposés in the mid-1990s of abuses in factories making Kathie Lee products, which the chain carries, Wal-Mart and Kathie Lee both began hiring outside auditing firms to inspect supplier factories to ensure their compliance with the code. Many other

companies that produce or sell goods made in low-wage countries do similar self-policing, from Toys 'R' Us to Nike and Gap. While no company suggests that its auditing systems are perfect, most say they catch major abuses and either force suppliers to fix them or yank production.

"What happened at Chun Si [the factory making Kathie Lee handbags] suggests that these auditing systems can miss serious problems—and that self-policing allows companies to avoid painful public revelations about them." See also the National Labor Committee's Web site, www.nlcnet.org, for complete and up-to-date information on major U.S. companies' use of sweatshops throughout the developing world. Examples of successful resistance to sweatshops can also be found at the site.

22. Roberts and Bernstein, "Inside a Chinese Sweatshop."

23. Interview with Noam Chomsky.

24. Interviews with Charles Kernaghan and Robert Monks.

25. Interview with Robert Monks. See also Robert Monks, *The Emperor's Nightingale: Restoring the Integrity of the Corporation in the Age of Shareholder Activism* (Reading, Mass.: Addison-Wesley, 1998); Hilary Rosenberg, *A Traitor to His Class: Robert A. G. Monks and the Battle to Change Corporate America* (New York: John Wiley and Sons, 1999).

26. Interview with Robert Monks.

27. Ibid.

28. Interview with Ray Anderson.

29. Ibid.

30. Ibid. The book was Paul Hawkens, *The Ecology of Commerce* (New York: HarperCollins, 1993), in which the author quotes E. O. Wilson's phrase "the death of birth."

31. For some further examples of externalities, see Russell Mokhiber and Robert Weissman, *Corporate Predators: The Hunt for Mega-Profits and the Attack on Democracy* (Monroe, Maine: Common Courage Press, 1999); M. F. Hawkins, *Unshielded: The Human Cost of the Dalkon Shield* (Toronto: University of Toronto Press, 1997).

32. The events occurred on January 31, 2000. An account of them can be found in Bob Port, "Fear and Fire a Deadly Mix," *Daily News* (New York), July 9, 2001, available at www.sweatshopwatch.org/swatch/headlines/2001/fearfire_jul01.html.

33. See, e.g., Bob Port, "Sweat and Tears Still in Fashion in City: Clothing Factories Skirt Laws, Exploit Immigrants," *Daily News* (New York),

July 8, 2001, available at www.sweatshopwatch.org/swatch/headlines/2001/sweattears_jul01.html. Developing-world sweatshop factories are also notorious for horrific fires in which many people die due to locked and blocked fire exits. See, e.g., Associated Press, "Fire in Bangladesh Garment Plant Kills at Least 45, Injures over 100," *The Wall Street Journal*, Interactive Edition, November 27, 2000, available at www.sweatshopwatch.org/headlines/2000/bangfire_nov00.

34. A U.S. Department of Labor (DOL) survey similarly found that only 35 percent of ninety-three garment shops in New York City followed applicable labor laws. See www.dol.gov/opa/media/press/opa/opa99300.

35. U.S. Department of Labor, "Only One-third of Southern California Garment Shops in Compliance with Federal Labor Laws," News Release, USDL-112, August 25, 2000, available at www.dol.gov/esa/media/press/whd/sfwh112.htm (last accessed June 11, 2003). See also Andrew Gumbel, "Fashion Victims: Inside the Sweatshops of Los Angeles," *The Independent* (London), available at www.sweatshopwatch.org/swatch/headlines/2001/fashionvictims_aug01.html.

36. For discussions of corporate crime, see Harry Glasbeek, *Wealth by Stealth: Corporate Crime, Corporate Law, and the Perversion of Democracy* (Toronto: Between the Lines, 2002); E. Colvin, "Corporate Personality and Criminal Liability," *Criminal Law Forum* 6 (1995): 1; D. Stuart, "Punishing Corporate Criminals with Restraint," *Criminal Law Forum* 6 (1995): 219; S. M. Rosoff, H. N. Pontell, and R. Tillman, *Profit Without Honor: White-Collar Crime and the Looting of America* (New Jersey: Prentice Hall, 1998); D. O. Friedrichs, *Trusted Criminals: White Collar Crime in Contemporary Society* (California: Wadsworth, 1996), 80; R. Mokhiber, and R. Weissman. "No Mind, No Crime?," *Multinational Monitor,* December 2, 1998; F. Pearce and L. Snider, eds., *Corporate Crime: Contemporary Debates* (Toronto: University of Toronto Press, 1995); R. Paehlke, "Environmental Harm and Corporate Crime," in *Corporate Crime: Contemporary Debates,* ed. F. Pearce and L. Snider, 305. Empirical analyses have demonstrated that, as stated in one of them, Richard Brown and Murray Rankin, "Persuasion, Penalties, and Prosecution: Administrative v. Criminal Sanctions," in M. L. Friedland, ed., *Securing Compliance: Seven Case Studies* (Toronto: University of Toronto Press, 1990), 347–348, "A substantial number of firms habitually violate regulatory requirements."

37. "GE: Decades of Misdeeds and Wrongdoing," *Multinational*

Monitor, 22, nos. 7 and 8, July–August 2001.

38. Frank H. Easterbrook and Daniel R. Fischel, "Antitrust Suits by Targets of Tender Offers," *Michigan Law Review* 80 (1982): 1177.

39. Interview with Robert Monks.

40. Bruce Welling, *Corporate Law in Canada* (Toronto: Butterworths, 1991), 165.

41. This account of Shugak's ordeal is based upon Wesley Loy, "Survivor: Don Shugak Recalls the Wellhead Explosion That Nearly Killed Him," *Anchorage Daily News*, November 3, 2002.

42. Loy, "Survivor."

43. Quoted in letter from Charles Hamel, on behalf of Concerned BP Operators at Prudhoe Bay, to Officer Mary Frances Barnes, United States Probation Officer, July 16, 2001, available at www.anwrnews.com.

44. Quoted in Jim Carlton, "BP Amoco Technicians Question Safety of Drilling Systems Bush Touts for Refuge," *The Wall Street Journal*, April 13, 2001, 1.

45. Ibid.

46. Ibid.

47. *United States of America v. BP Exploration (Alaska) Inc.*, Plea Agreement, U.S. Dist. Ct. (Alaska), No. A99–0141C 12 (JKS), September 23, 1999.

48. Statement of William B. Burkett, Production Operator for BP Exploration (Alaska), to Chairman Joseph Lieberman and Chairman Bob Graham. See also Carlton, "BP Amoco Technicians."

49. Jim Carlton, "Are Alaska's Many Oil Fields Safe?," *The Wall Street Journal*, July 10, 2001, 1. After this article was published, Alaska governor Tony Knowles vowed to increase funding for oversight of the oil fields. Critics said his plan would have little impact. See Jim Carlton, "Alaska Will Increase State Funding for Oversight of Local Oil Industry," *The Wall Street Journal*, December 13, 2001.

Chapter 4: Democracy Ltd.

1. Samuel Rosenman, ed., *The Public Papers and Addresses of Franklin D. Roosevelt, Volume Two: The Year of Crisis, 1933* (New York: Random House, 1938), as cited in Cass Sunstein, *The Partial Constitution* (Cambridge, Mass.: Harvard University Press, 1993), 57–58.

2. The following account of this story is based primarily on Jules Archer, *The Plot to Seize the White House* (New York: Hawthorn Books, 1973).

3. Archer, *The Plot,* 21.

4. National Archives, "U.S. Strategic Bombing Surveys" 243/190/62—Box 696, August 14, 1944; Box 697, August 23, 1945; Box 946. Ford Werke, the Ford Motor Company's German subsidiary, also contributed to the Nazi war effort, providing nearly a third of the German Army's trucks. For discussions of GM and Ford's alleged involvement with the Nazis, see Bradford C. Snell, "American Ground Transport: A Proposal for Restructuring the Automobile, Truck, Bus and Rail Industries," report presented to the Committee of the Judiciary, Subcommittee on Antitrust and Monopoly, United States Senate, February 26, 1974 (Washington, D.C.: U.S. Government Printing Office, 1974), 16–24; Michael Dobbs, "Ford and GM Scrutinized for Alleged Nazi Collaboration," *The Washington Post,* November 30, 1998.

5. Interview with Edwin Black. Also see Edwin Black, *IBM and the Holocaust: The Strategic Alliance Between Nazi Germany and America's Most Powerful Corporation* (New York: Crown Publishers, 2001).

6. Interviews with Edwin Black and Peter Drucker. Quotes from Dobbs, "Ford and GM Scrutinized," who reports as follows: "Less than three weeks after the Nazi occupation of Czechoslovakia in March 1939, GM Chairman Alfred P. Sloan defended this strategy [GM not divesting its German assets] as sound business practice, given the fact that the company's German operations were 'highly profitable.'

"The internal politics of Nazi Germany 'should not be considered the business of the management of General Motors,' Sloan explained in a letter to a concerned shareholder dated April 6, 1939. 'We must conduct ourselves [in Germany] as a German organization. . . . We have no right to shut down the plant.'"

7. According to David Jessup, executive director of New Economy Information Service, an organization whose survey data found a disturbing trend by U.S. corporations to invest in authoritarian countries, "I doubt that the issue of democracy-or-no-democracy is on businessmen's minds when they make an investment decision. But maybe it's an unconscious preference [for authoritarian countries]." Quoted in R. C. Longworth, "Globalization Survey Reveals U.S. Corporations Prefer Dictatorships" November 19, 1999,

available at www.globalexchange.org. *The Wall Street Journal* recently reported that eighty-six companies, among them IKEA, Goodyear, First Union Bank, and CAN Financial, had been fined under the Trading with the Enemy Act between 1998 and the date of its article. The act makes it an offense to trade with a list of countries that includes Iran, Iraq, Cuba, North Korea, and Taliban-controlled Afghanistan. When Vice President Dick Cheney was CEO of Halliburton in 2000, the company opened an office in Tehran, though it was not among the group of companies fined under the act. See Stephanie M. Horvath, "U.S. Slaps 86 Firms with Fines for Deals Made with 'Enemies,'" *The Wall Street Journal,* July 3, 2002. On July 23, 2001, ABC News reported that most of Iraq's UN-approved oil exports were being bought by U.S. oil companies from Russian middlemen and refined in Louisiana and Texas. John K. Cooley, "Trading with the Enemy: U.S. Refiners Reportedly Buying Most of Iraq's Oil," June 20, 2002, available at http://abcnews.go.com. For further examples, see Guy Dinmore and Najmeh Bozorgmehr, "US Companies Skirt Ban on Trade with Iran," *Financial Times,* February 27, 2002.

8. Archer, *The Plot,* 146.

9. Butler's testimony to the House Un-American Activities Committee, as quoted in Archer, *The Plot,* 153.

10. Archer, *The Plot,* 156.

11. Ibid., 30 ("combat").

12. Ibid., 198.

13. Ibid., 118–119.

14. Ibid., 192–193.

15. Ibid., 213 ("doubt," "plotters," "fellows"), 214 ("patriot").

16. Quoted in Hendrik Hertzberg, "Comment: Mine Shaft," *The New Yorker,* August 19 and 26, 2002, 58.

17. History from U.S. Department of Labor, Mine Safety and Health Administration, History of Mine Safety and Health Legislation, available at www.msha.gov/mshainfo/mshainf2.htm.

18. Interview with Main; also see AFL-CIO, "The Bush Administration's FY 2004 Budget," available at www.aflcio.org/issuespolitics/bush-watch, which explains the $6.3 million cut this way: "For coal enforcement activities, an increase of $1.1 million over the president's FY 2003 proposal is requested. However, this request—$113.4 million—is less than the $117.8 million currently authorized and less than the $119.7 million approved by the

Senate for the FY 2003. The FY 2004 proposal requests 10 additional coal enforcement positions over the FY 2003 request. However, the proposed staffing levels for coal enforcement (1,086 positions) is still less than the number of positions currently authorized (1,141 positions)."

19. WTAE-TV's Paul Van Osdol Reports, "Team 4: Senate Has Mining Safety Concerns," July 26, 2002, available at www.thepittsburghchannel.com/news. Main recently confirmed this observation to us in an interview.

20. Don Hopey, "Lawmakers Urge Fisher to Convene a Grand Jury Probe of Quecreek Mine Accident," *Pittsburgh Post-Gazette,* August 3, 2002, available at www.post-gazette.com/localnews.

21. According to the Natural Resources Defense Council, "There He Goes Again: Bush Budget Bashes the Environment," available at www.nrdc.org/legislation/abudget04.asp: "One of the principal losers in the president's budget is the Environmental Protection Agency. In general, funding for the agency would be slashed by half a billion dollars between FY 2002 and FY 2004—dropping from $8.1 billion to $7.6 billion. . . . EPA continues to seek major cutbacks in enforcement personnel from the levels in place at the start of the administration—reducing the total workforce by nearly 100 positions (more than 6 percent)." See also Katharine Q. Seelye, "Bush Slashing Aid for E.P.A. Cleanup at 33 Toxic Sites," *The New York Times,* July 1, 2002.

22. The cuts to OSHA over the years have been further compounded by Bush's 2004 budget proposal, which would reduce the OSHA budget from $462 million to $450 million and slash 77 positions (from 2,313 to 2,236). The 2004 budget also proposes cutting $30 million from the National Institute for Occupational Safety and Health budget.

23. Paul Krugman, "Business as Usual," *The New York Times,* October 22, 2002.

24. He stated this to CNN, as reported on January 19, 2001. See editions.cnn.com/2001/US/01/19/power.woes.01/index.htm/#1.

25. As cited in Public Citizen, "Blind Faith: How Deregulation and Enron's Influence over Government Looted Billions from Americans," Washington, D.C.: December 2001, available at www.citizen.org/documents/Blind_Faith.pdf.

26. The following account is based primarily on Public Citizen, "Blind Faith," including quoted passages, 12 (Blair and English), 19 ("light of day"). See also Kenneth Bredemeier, "Memo Warned of Enron's Calif. Strategy: West Coast Senators Complain About Market Manipulation During Power

Crisis," *The Washington Post,* May 16, 2002, A4; Ellen Nakashima, "Army Secretary Defends Support from Enron," *The Washington Post,* April 5, 2002, A2; Mike Allen and Dan Morgan, "White House–Enron Ties Detailed," *The Washington Post,* May 24, 2002; Bethany McLean, "Monster Mess," *Fortune,* February 4, 2002, and "Why Enron Went Bust," *Fortune,* December 24, 2001; Andrew Wheat, "System Failure: Deregulation, Political Corruption, Corporate Fraud and the Enron Debacle," *Multinational Monitor,* 23, nos. 1 and 2 (January–February, 2002), available at multinationalmonitor.org/mm2002/02jan-feb02economics.html.

27. Public Citizen, "Blind Faith," 12 ("dangerous" and "irresponsible").

28. Ibid., 19 ("survive").

29. Interviews with Anne Wexler and William Niskanen.

30. Interview with Anne Wexler ("awareness"). Business Round Table, "History of the Business Round Table," available at www.brt.org ("pluralistic," "intrusion").

31. At the same time, corporate influence over government was endemic in American politics throughout the post–World War II era and even before. See Elizabeth A. Fones-Wolf, *The Selling of Free Enterprise: The Business Assault on Labor and Liberalism 1945–1960* (Urbana: University of Illinois Press, 1994). My point is not that corporate influence was absent before the 1970s, only that it has deepened profoundly since then. See, e.g., Morton Mintz and Jerry Cohen, *America, Inc.: Who Runs and Operates the United States* (New York: Dial Press, 1971).

32. In addition to lobbying, corporations enjoy direct representation in government and the bureaucracy, certainly to a much greater degree than any other group in society, by virtue of the disproportionate number of high-ranking government officials who were formerly top executives—White House Chief of Staff Andy Card, to take just one example, was previously a lobbyist for the auto industry and a General Motors executive. Conversely, many lobbyists for corporations formerly held high positions in government, such as Anne Wexler, who ran the Office of Public Liaison in Bill Clinton's White House. Then there are the links between regulatory agencies and those whom they regulate. According to Robert Monks in an interview: "There is a terminology that people use to describe the relationship between regulatory agencies and the people they regulate. It's called the revolving door. . . . One of the persistent characteristics of regulation is that people

who start to work in the government, as young ambitious executives, serve time there. And then come out into the private sector and work for the companies who are being regulated by that agency. The difficulty with this is that it creates a culture where the general public doesn't have much of a chance of dealing with that agency well."

33. *Bellotti v. First National Bank of Boston,* 435 U.S. 765.

34. Aristotle, *Politics,* Book 2 (Oxford: Oxford World Classics, 1998).

35. Interview with Anne Wexler.

36. The Center for Responsive Politics, "Top Contributors: Coal Mining," available at www.opensecrets.org/industries/contrib.asp?Ind = E1210.

37. Cat Lazaroff, "USA: Energy Task Force Documents Show Industry Influence," May 22, 2002, available at www.corpwatch.org/news/PND.jsp? articleid = 2613.

38. Richard Oppel, Jr., "Documents Show Parties Often Mix Fund-Raising and Policy," *The New York Times,* December 7, 2002.

39. See, Dan Morgan, "Homeland Bill Rider Aids Drugmakers: Measure Would Block Suits over Vaccines; FBI Powers Also Would Grow," *The Washington Post,* November 15, 2002, A07; Jonathan Weisman, "A Homeland Security Whodunit: In Massive Bill, Someone Buried a Clause to Benefit Drug Maker Eli Lilly," *The Washington Post,* November 28, 2002, A45.

40. Interview with William Niskanen.

41. Interviews with Joe Badaracco and Robert Monks. See also Stanley Deetz, *Democracy in an Age of Corporate Colonization* (Albany: State University of New York Press, 1992); D. Vogel, *Kindred Strangers: The Uneasy Relationship Between Politics and Business in America* (Princeton, N.J.: Princeton University Press, 1996); William Greider, *Who Will Tell the People: The Betrayal of American Democracy* (New York: Simon & Schuster, 1993).

42. Interviews with Anne Wexler and Chris Komisarjevsky. Cato Institute Chairman Niskanen believes that corporate donations to politicians actually benefit democracy. "I want corporations as well as other wealthy people to be able to participate in the political system with their money as well as their time and their vote," he said in an interview, "and I think our political system would be healthier for that."

43. Interview with Hank McKinnell. In the 2002 election cycle, Pfizer contributed $1.2 million to federal parties and candidates, with most of that, more than two thirds, going to Republicans. Only one other pharmaceutical

company contributed more than Pfizer during that cycle.

44. Interview with Anne Wexler.

45. Interview with Hank McKinnell.

46. The rhetoric and practices of partnership between corporations and governments are especially prominent in the domain of international trade and investment. To take an example, the Asia Pacific Economic Cooperation organization, whose members are the heads of state of various Asian and Pacific Rim countries, including the United States and Canada, celebrates its "commitment to business facilitation and the regular involvement of the private sector in a wide range of APEC activities. Business expertise and resources can help APEC to achieve its objectives, and business is a key constituency for APEC both regionally and in individual member economies. Business already participates in many of APEC's working groups and helps shape the policy dialogue in partnership with member economy officials. APEC Economic Leaders receive advice from the APEC Business Advisory Council (ABAC). . . . Such involvement is important to ensure that APEC's work is relevant to real problems. However, a major APEC goal is to continue to expand business participation in the APEC process" (from an APEC brochure, as cited in Joel Bakan, "The Significance of the APEC Affair," in Wes Pue, ed., *Pepper in Our Eyes: The APEC Affair* (Vancouver: University of British Columbia Press, 2000), 77, 81).

At the World Trade Organization, too, business and government work in close cooperation. TRIPs (Trade-Related Aspects of Intellectual Property Rights), a set of standards enforced by the WTO that strengthens intellectual property rights, mainly to the benefit of the pharmaceutical and biotechnology industries, was a result of initiatives taken by industry, in particular a coalition of U.S., EU, and Japanese companies known as the Intellectual Property Committee (which included among its members Bristol-Myers Squibb, DuPont, Monsanto, and General Motors). As James Enyart of Monsanto stated of the committee's work on TRIPs, "Industry has identified a major problem in international trade. It crafted a solution, reduced it to a concrete proposal and sold it to our own and other governments. . . . The industries and traders of world commerce have simultaneously played the role of patients, the diagnosticians and the physicians." Former Pfizer head Edmund Pratt, an official adviser to the U.S. Trade Representative at GATT negotiations, stated that "our [industries'] combined strength enabled us to establish a global private sector–government network which laid the groundwork for what became TRIPs." (The quotes from Enyard and Pratt are cited in Belén Balanyá, Ann Doherty, Olivier Hoedeman, Adam Ma'anit, and Erik Wesselius, *Europe Inc.: Regional and Global Restructuring and the Rise of Corporate Power* (London: Pluto Press, 2000), 129).

The relationship between business and government in creating the General Agreement on Trade in Services (GATS), which is developing a regime for WTO oversight of the accounting industry (as discussed in Chapter 1), among other things, provides further evidence of the partnership theme. Like TRIPs, this agreement likely would not have emerged were it not for sustained lobbying from industry, in this case through the U.S. Coalition of Service Industries (CSI). Recently, Bob Vastine, chairman of the CSI, called the relationship between service industries and U.S. administrations an "extraordinary example of government/industry cooperation that should serve as a benchmark for the rest of the world." Indeed, the rest of the world seems to have been watching, as a European organization, the European Services Network, modeled upon the CSI, was launched on January 26, 1999 (and renamed the European Services Forum in October 1999). Upon its launch, Sir Leon Brittan, who, as vice president of the European Commission, had suggested that the network be created, said, "I am in your hands to listen to what are your objectives, your priorities for liberalization. . . . I count on your support and input, at the company, CEO and Chairman as well as at the European or National Federation levels, so that we can refine our strategy and set out clear, priority negotiation objectives which will make a difference in the international expansion of service businesses." (Vastine and Brittan cited in Erik Wesselius, "Behind GATS 2000: Corporate Power at Work," TNI Briefing Series, No. 2002/6 (Amsterdam: Transnational Institute, 2002), 7, 9.)

47. Interviews with Hank McKinnel, Doug Pinkham, and Jim Gray. Speech by John Browne, "The Century of Choice," Institute of Petroleum, London, February 16, 1999.

Chapter 5: Corporations Unlimited

1. Interview with Carlton Brown.

2. Indeed, like Carlton Brown and his clients, corporations have exploited September 11, 2001, for profit. See, e.g., Jim Lobe, "Post–September 11, the Rich Get Richer in the US," *Asia Times Online,* November 8, 2001;

Michael Moran, "Cashing In on September 11," MSNBC News, July 9, 2002.

3. Adolf A. Berle and Gardiner C. Means, *The Modern Corporation and Private Property* (New York: Harcourt, Brace & World, 1968), 14–17.

4. For discussions of the general scope of privatization and some examples, see David Bollier, *Public Assets, Private Profits: Reclaiming the American Commons in an Age of Market Enclosure* (Washington, D.C.: New America Foundation, 2001); Reason Public Policy Institute, *Privatization 2002: Putting the Pieces Together, 16th Annual Report on Privatization* (Los Angeles: Reason Public Policy Institute, 2002); Pamela Winston, Andrew Burwick, Sheena McConnell, and Richard Roper, "Privatization of Welfare Services: A Review of the Literature," Washington D.C., Mathematica Policy Research Inc., 2002; Alex Tysbine, *Water Privatization: A Broken Promise* (Washington, D.C.: Public Citizen, 2001); *Government for Sale: An Examination of the Contracting Out of State and Local Government Services* (Washington, D.C.: American Federation of State, County and Municipal Employees, AFL-CIO, 2002); Mark Cassell, *How Governments Privatize: The Politics of Divestment in the United States and Germany* (Washington, D.C.: Georgetown University Press, 2002); Maude Barlow and Tony Clarke, *Blue Gold: The Fight to Stop the Corporate Theft of the World's Water* (New York: New Press, 2003); Vandana Shiva, *Water Wars: Privatization, Pollution, and Profit* (Boston: South End Press, 2002); R. Mokhiber and R. Weissman, "Smithsonian for Sale?," *Multinational Monitor,* November 19, 1997; Robert Kuttner, *Everything for Sale: The Virtues and Limits of Markets* (New York: Alfred A. Knopf, 1997); Allison Campbell, Andrew Coyle, and Rodney Neufeld, eds., *Capitalist Punishment: Prison Privatization and Human Rights* (Atlanta: Clarity Press, 2003); Brian Forst and Peter K. Manning, *The Privatization of Policing: Two Views* (Washington, D.C.: Georgetown University Press, 1999).

5. Interviews with Milton Friedman, William Niskanen, and Michael Walker.

6. Interview with Michael T. Moe. See also, Maude Barlow and Heather Jane-Robertson, *Class Warfare: The Assault on Canada's Schools* (Toronto: Key Porter Books, 1994).

7. Interviews with Michael T. Moe and Milton Friedman. Expansion will likely continue beyond 10 percent after the next decade to as high as 30 percent, according to another Edison financier, Jeffrey Fromm, in an interview.

8. Interviews with Benno Schmidt and Michael T. Moe.

9. Michael Scherer, "Schools: Some of Bush's Largest Donors Stand to Profit from Privatizing Public Education," March 5, 2001, available at www.motherjones.com/web_exclusives/special_reports/mojo_400/schools.html (under Web Exclusives).

10. Gary Miron and Brooks Applegate, *An Evaluation of Student Achievement in Edison Schools Opened in 1995 and 1996* (Kalamazoo, Mich.: Evaluation Center, Western Michigan University, December 2001), as cited in Gerald Bracey, "The Market in Theory Meets the Market in Practice: The Case of Edison Schools," Education Policy Research Unit, College of Education, Arizona State University, February 2002.

11. Wyatt Edward, "Challenges and the Possibility of Profit for Edison," *The New York Times,* January 1, 2001, cited in Bracey, "The Market in Theory."

12. Doug Sanders, "For-Profit US Schools Sell Off Their Textbooks," *The Globe and Mail* (Toronto), October 30, 2002, A1.

13. Interview with Jeffrey Fromm.

14. Interview with Milton Friedman. For an excellent account of why skilled, professional, and public-minded civil servants are not only possible but also essential for a functioning democracy, see Ezra N. Suleiman, *Dismantling Democratic States* (Princeton, N.J.: Princeton University Press, 2003).

15. For further examples, see Karen Bakker, David Cameron, and Adele Hurley, "Don't Tap into the Private Sector," *The Globe and Mail* (Toronto), February 6, 2003, A17; Linda McQuaig, *All You Can Eat: Greed, Lust and the New Capitalism* (Toronto: Penguin Books, 2001); Elliott D. Sclar, *You Don't Always Get What You Pay For: The Economics of Privatization* (Ithaca, N.Y.: Cornell University Press, 2001); P. W. Singer, *Corporate Warriors: The Rise of the Privatized Military Industry* (Ithaca, N.Y.: Cornell University Press, 2003); Gerald W. Bracey, *The War Against America's Public Schools: Privatizing Schools, Commercializing Education* (Boston: Pearson Allyn & Bacon, 2001), and *What You Should Know About the War Against America's Public Schools* (Boston: Allyn & Bacon, 2002); Brenda Cossman and Judy Fudge, eds. *Privatization, Law, and the Challenge to Feminism* (Toronto: University of Toronto Press, 2002); Martha Minow, *Partners, Not Rivals: Privatization and the Public Good* (Boston: Beacon Press, 2002).

16. Interview with Raffi.

17. Interview with Lucy Hughes.

18. Ibid.

19. Ibid.

20. Ibid.

21. Kia News Release, "Kia Partners with The Lord of the Rings: New Line Entertainment Taps Kia as Exclusive Automotive Partner," June 4, 2002, available at www.kia.com/060402.shtml.

22. T. L. Stanley, "Kiddie Cars," *Brandweek* 36 (October 23, 1995).

23. "Profile—Kid You Not: Discussion with Julie Halpin," available at www.reveries.com/reverb/kids_marketing/halpin.

24. Interview with Lucy Hughes.

25. Official Policy Statement from the American Academy of Pediatrics, February 1995, available at www.aap.org/policy/00656.html.

26. The former chair and CEO of Prism Communications, Elliot Ettenberg, quoted in Ontario Secondary School Teachers' Federation, "Commercialization in Our Schools," (2001), available at www.osstf.on.ca.

27. Interviews with Lucy Hughes and Raffi.

28. As cited in John P. Murray Kansas, "Children and Television Violence," *Journal of Law & Public Policy* 4 (1995): 7–14.

29. Interview with Dr. Susan Linn. Television advertisement for Frito-Lay chips.

30. Interview with Dr. Susan Linn.

31. As quoted in Nic Rowan, "TV Junk Food Ads Spur Kids' Obesity—Group," *Reuters Health,* August 6, 2002, available at www.reutershealth.com.

32. Editorial, "Selling to—and Selling Out—Children," *The Lancet* 360, September 28, 2002, 959.

33. Sonya Schroeder of the Geppetto Group, "Discussions—What Makes a Brand 'Cool' for Kids?," available at www.reveries.com/reverb/revolver/geppetto/.

34. Statement to my research assistant, Dawn Brett, May 2003.

35. Quoted in John Heinzl, "Health Group Aims to Fry Kids' Junk Food Ads," *Globe and Mail* (Toronto), January 24, 2003, B7.

36. The industry's claims can be criticized for the way they downplay the role of advertising in creating a demand for unhealthy food. At the same time, there is a grain of truth to their insistence that other factors create demand too. Social and economic pressures on parents are one of these. Worn-out parents, often single, poor, working overtime or even two jobs, have little time to shop for and prepare a full meal at the end of the day. Cheap, fast, and easily accessible food—albeit not necessarily healthy food—may be their only option.

37. Interview with Chris Hooper.

38. Interview with Steve Kline.

39. Ibid.

40. LEGO has a program called Serious Play; see www.seriousplay.com. A recent advertisement for a workshop using Serious Play states, "This innovative workshop introduces Leaders and Senior Managers to the concept of creating and implementing business strategies using the Lego Serious Play, Real Time Strategy process. Get your hands on the Lego bricks and experience first-hand how the Real Time Strategy application transforms strategic planning into strategic thinking.

"Real Time Strategy is the most effective way to embed strategic thinking into your organization. Using 3 dimensional models, metaphors and story telling, participants learn to articulate complex ideas and successfully bring them to action." *The Globe and Mail* (Toronto), September 12, 2002, A10.

41. Interviews with Steve Kline and Dr. Susan Linn.

42. For an overview, see: Alex Molnar and Joseph A. Reaves, *Buy Me! Buy Me!: The Fourth Annual Report on Trends in Schoolhouse Commercialism: Year 2000–2001,* Education Policy Studies Laboratory, Arizona State University, 2002; Maude Barlow and Jane-Robertson, *Class Warfare;* Consumers Union, *Captive Kids: A Report on Commercial Pressures on Kids at School* (Yonkers, N.Y.: Consumer Education Services, 1995).

43. Cited in Barlow and Jane-Robertson, *Class Warfare,* 84.

44. Cited in David Shenk, "Tomorrow's Classroom Today," *Spy Magazine,* July–August, 1994, 22. I cite these examples in Joel Bakan, "Beyond Censorship: An Essay on Free Speech and Law," in *Interpreting Censorship in Canada,* ed. Klaus Petersen and Allan C. Hutchinson (Toronto: University of Toronto Press, 1999), 86.

45. This is a modified version of a paragraph from Joel Bakan, "Beyond Censorship." The study mentioned is Bradley S. Greenberg and Jeffrey E. Brend, "Television News and Advertising in Schools: The 'Channel One' Controversy," *Journal of Communications,* 43 (1993): 143–151.

46. This is a modified version of a paragraph from Joel Bakan, "Beyond Censorship." Both quotes were originally cited in David Shrek, "Tomorrow's Classroom Today," 22.

47. A picture of the sign appears on the cover of Herbert Schiller, *Culture Inc.: The Corporate Takeover of Public Expression* (New York: Oxford University Press, 1989). I also refer to it in Joel Bakan, *Just Words: Constitutional Rights and Social Wrongs* (Toronto: University of Toronto

Press, 1997), 68, where I argue that the encroaching privatization of public space erodes free speech rights. See also Jerold S. Kayden, New York City Department of City Planning, and the Municipal Art Society of New York, *Privately Owned Public Space: The New York City Experience* (New York: John Wiley and Sons, 2000).

48. This paragraph is a modified version of one that appears in Joel Bakan, "Beyond Censorship."

49. Jeffrey Hopkins, "Excavating Toronto's Underground Streets: In Search of Equitable Rights, Rules and Revenue," in *City Lives and City Forms,* ed. John Caulfield and Linda Peake (Toronto: University of Toronto Press, 1996), 63.

50. This paragraph is a modified version of one that appears in Joel Bakan, "Beyond Censorship."

51. Hopkins, "Excavating Toronto's Underground Streets."

52. See citylitesusa.com.

53. Hopkins, "Excavating Toronto's Underground Streets," 70–71.

54. See Joel Bakan, "Beyond Censorship," and Joel Bakan, *Just Words.* As Schiller states in *Culture Inc.,* p. 100: "To the extent that private-property owners legally can decide what kind of activity is permissible in their malls, a vast and expanding terrain is withdrawn from serving as a site of public expression."

55. This paragraph is a modified version of one that appears in Joel Bakan, "Beyond Censorship." See also Margaret Crawford, "The World in a Shopping Mall," in *Variations on a Theme Park,* ed. Michael Sorkin (New York: Noonday Press, 1992), 27, and Mike Davis, "Fortress Los Angeles: The Militarization of Urban Space," in *Variations on a Theme Park,* 169.

56. This paragraph is a modified version of one that appears in Joel Bakan, "Beyond Censorship." The quote is originally from Mary Massaron Ross, Larry Smith, and Robert Pritt, "The Zoning Process: Private Land-Use Controls and Gated Communities: The Impact of Private Property Rights Legislation, and Other Recent Developments in the Law, *Urban Lawyer,* vol. 28, 1996, 801–17, pp. 802–803.

57. Interview with Jonathon Ressler.

58. Ibid.

59. Ibid.

60. Interview with Michael Moe.

61. Interview with Noam Chomsky

62. Ibid.

63. Interview with Mark Kingwell.

64. Interview with Chris Barrett and Luke McCabe.

65. Ibid.

66. Ibid.

67. Ibid.

68. Ibid.

69. Ibid.

70. Molnar and Reaves, *Buy Me! Buy Me!*

Chapter 6: Reckoning

1. Special Report: "Global Capitalism—Can It Be Made to Work Better?," *Business Week*, November 6, 2000, 74–75. To similar effect, Robert Monks warned in an interview that "the issues that are raised [by the antiglobalization protesters] are legitimate and we ignore them to our peril."

2. Even Milton Friedman worries, as he expressed in an interview, that in our society of two classes, haves and have-nots, "you cannot maintain a real democracy" because of the risk of the have-nots "blowing up the system."

3. Interview with Ira Jackson.

4. Interview with Joe Badaracco.

5. Kunal Basu, Henry Mintzberg, and Robert Simons, "Memo to: CEOs," reprinted in *Fast Company* 59 (June 2002): 117.

6. Interview with Ira Jackson.

7. Interviews with Chris Komisarjevsky and Hank McKinnell. Speeches by Sir John Browne, "The Case for Social Responsibility" ("monster"); "Century of Choice" ("win back"), available at www.bp.com.

8. Robert Monks, *The Emperor's Nightingale: Restoring the Integrity of the Corporation in the Age of Shareholder Activism* (New York: Perseus Publishing, 1998), 183–184. Corporations became irresponsible, Monks said in an interview, when "the atom of ownership" was broken and "owners became one group of people and managers became another, suddenly nobody became responsible to society."

9. Monks, *The Emperor's Nightingale*, 163 ("same"), 171 ("safe").

10. Interview with Robert Monks ("effective").

11. Interview with Elaine Bernard.

12. Interviews with Ira Jackson, Charles Kernaghan, and Debora Spar.

13. Interview with Robert Monks.

14. Interview with Debora Spar. In lieu of sharing the hard facts about what they actually do, corporations often formulate inspiring codes of conduct that they happily share with the public. The codes speak of how workers are treated with great respect and the environment looked after. Kernaghan believes that corporations' voluntary codes of conduct are the ultimate privatization of human rights, a "dead end."

15. Interview with Charles Kernaghan.

16. Interview with Simon Billenness.

17. *Louis K. Liggett Co. et al. v. Lee, Comptroller et al.*, 288 US 517 (1933) 567, 548 ("evils").

18. Interview with Milton Friedman. As Harvard's Elaine Bernard pointed out in an interview, deregulation simply shifts costs from corporations onto individuals and society, "If a factory is polluting, it's saving money. Why? Because it's using worse technology. It's using up resources that it's not paying for, and it's putting the cost of that waste onto the community as a whole. So in the company's books it looks very good. In society's books it's running a big deficit. . . . And today I think that corporations are externalizing a lot of costs onto the community, whether it's the cost of burning up employees by increasing the work time, by working them for a few years and then throwing them out, by not paying the full cost of the labor that employees give to a firm, by coming into a community, getting all sorts of grants, and then turning around and leaving it in worse shape than they entered. All of those things externalize the cost onto the community of the corporation."

19. Quoted in Editorial, *The Sunday Herald* (Scotland), August 26, 2001.

20. Interview with Naomi Klein.

21. Interview with Noam Chomsky.

22. Indeed, from the perspective of its supposed beneficiaries, the regulatory system was imperfect from the beginning. Historically, regulation was a compromise, supported by many among the business elite, between business's desire for freedom from controls and calls for more radical change. As Harvard's Elaine Bernard points out, "It wasn't the labor movement and the reformers who proposed regulation. [They] proposed expropriation. [They] proposed breaking up these tremendous concentrations of wealth and power. And in response the corporations came back with regulation. We will accept regulation [they said]. So regulation was, if you like, the corporate response to a tremendous groundswell over their unaccounted, unacceptable power."

23. Interview with Noam Chomsky.

24. Daniel Yergin and Joseph Stanislaw. *The Commanding Heights: The Battle for the World Economy* (Touchstone/Simon & Schuster, 1998), 417.

25. Morton J. Horwitz, "Santa Clara Revisited: The Development of Corporate Theory," in *Corporations and Society: Power and Responsibility,* ed. Warren Samuels and Arthur Miller (New York: Greenwood Press, 1987), 51.

26. Note, *Columbia Law Review* 35 (1935): 1090, 1091–1092, as cited in Sunstein, *The Partial Constitution,* 52–53.

27. Robert Hale, *American Bar Association Journal* 8 (1922): 638, as cited in Sunstein, *The Partial Constitution,* 51.

28. As cited in Sunstein, *The Partial Constitution,* 58.

29. Interviews with Smith Windsor and Richard Geisenberger.

30. Spitzer made the statement in November 1999 as part of his election campaign platform. See Geov Parrish, "Killing Corporations," *Seattle Weekly,* July 15–21, 1999.

31. As quoted in Russell Mokhiber, "The Death Penalty for Corporations Comes of Age," *Business Ethics* 12, November–December 1998, available at www.corpwatch.org/issues/PID.jsp?articleid = 1810.

32. Charlie Cray, "Chartering a New Course: Revoking Corporations' Right to Exist," *Multinational Monitor* 23, October–November 2002, available at multinationalmonitor.org.

33. Interview with Richard Geisenberger.

34. Cray, "Chartering a New Course."

35. Interviews with Vandana Shiva and Joe Badaracco.

36. Title 39, U.S. Code, as adopted in the Postal Reorganization Act. The post office is a target for privatization advocates, however. See Edward L. Hudgins, ed., *The Last Monopoly: Privatizing The Postal Service for the Information Age* (Washington, D.C.: Cato Institute, 1996), and Edward Hudgins, ed., *Mail at the Millennium: Will the Postal Service Go Private?* (Washington, D.C.: Cato Institute, 2001).

37. Canada recently effectively banned electoral financing by corporations and trade unions and committed to public financing of elections.

38. Interview with Oscar Olivera.

39. Ibid.

40. Ibid.

41. Interview with Mark Kingwell.

42. Interviews with Mae-Wan Ho and Vandana Shiva.

21. Daniel Yergin and Joseph Stanislaw, *The Commanding Heights: The Battle for the World Economy* (New York: Simon & Schuster, 1998), 41.

25. Morton J. Horwitz, "Santa Clara Revisited: The Development of Corporate Theory," in *Corporations and Society: Power and Responsibility*, ed. Warren Samuel and Arthur Miller (New York: Greenwood Press, 1987), 31.

26. *First National ... Law Review* 54 (1977) 1090-1092, as cited in Sciulli, *The Critical Corporation*, 53.

27. Robert Hale, *American Bar Association Journal* 5 (1922) 638, as cited in Sciulli, *The Ruskin Constitution*, 51.

28. As cited in Sciulli, *The Ruskin Constitution*, 51.

29. Interviews with Scott Vincent and Richard Grünenberg.

30. Spitzer made the statement in November 1997 as part of his election campaign platform. See Gary Parrish, *Killing Corporations*, Seattle (Wesley Press, FAIR, 1998).

31. As quoted in Russell, Mahathir, "The Death Penalty and Opposition Chatter of Stage," *Business Ethics*, 12, November–December 1995, available at www.corpwatch.org/issues/PID.jsp?articleid=13101.

32. Michelle Gray, "Gathering a New Course: Resolving Corporate Kinds to host," *International Workforce 7*, October–November 2002, available at amnthanterlonalyouth.com.

33. Interview with Richard Cartwright.

34. Gary, "Gathering a New Course."

35. Interviews with Vincent Shive and Joe Ballantine.

36. Title 39 U.S. Code-l, adopted in the Postal Reorganization Act. The post office is a magnet for privatization advocates, however. See Edward L. Hudgins, ed., *The Last Monopoly: Privatizing The Postal Service for the Information Age* (Washington, D.C.: Cato Institute, 1996), and Edward L. Hudgins, ed., *Mail at the Millennium: Will the Postal Service Go Private?* (Washington, D.C.: Cato Institute, 2001).

37. Companies regularly effectively hand held electoral financing by corporations and trade unions and committed to public financing of elections.

38. Interview with David Olesen.

39. Ibid.

40. Ibid.

41. Interview with Saul Sanjour.

42. Interviews with Mae Ho and Vandana Shiva.

Selected Bibliography

Aharoni, Yair. *The Evolution and Management of State Owned Enterprises.* Melrose, Mass: Ballinger Publishing Company, 1986.

Archer, Jules. *The Plot to Seize the White House.* New York: Hawthorn Books, 1973.

Bagdikian, Ben H. *The Media Monopoly,* 6th ed. Boston: Beacon Press, 2000.

Bakan, Joel. "Beyond Censorship: An Essay on Free Speech and Law." In *Interpreting Censorship in Canada,* eds. Klaus Petersen and Allan C. Hutchinson. Toronto: University of Toronto Press, 1999.

Bakan, Joel. *Just Words: Constitutional Rights and Social Wrongs.* Toronto: University of Toronto Press, 1997.

Bakan, Joel. "The Significance of the APEC Affair." In *Pepper in Our Eyes: the APEC Affair,* ed. Wes Pue. Vancouver: University of British Columbia Press, 2000.

Balanyá, Belén, Ann Doherty, Olivier Hoedeman, Adam Ma'anit, and Erik Wesselius. *Europe Inc.: Regional and Global Restructuring and the Rise of Corporate Power.* London: Pluto Press, 2000.

Barlow, Maude, Tony Clarke. *Blue Gold: The Fight to Stop the Corporate Theft of the World's Water.* New York: New Press, 2003.

Barlow, Maude, and Heather Jane-Robertson. *Class Warfare: The Assault on Canada's Schools.* Toronto: Key Porter Books, 1994.

Basu, Kunal, Henry Mintzberg, and Robert Simons. "Memo to: CEOs." Reprinted in *Fast Company* 59, April 2002, 117.

Beatty, Jack, ed. *Colossus: How the Corporation Changed America.* New York: Broadway Books, 2002.

Berle, Adolf A., and Means, Gardiner C. *The Modern Corporation and*

Private Property. New York: Harcourt, Brace & World, 1968.

Black, Edwin. *IBM and the Holocaust: The Strategic Alliance Between Nazi Germany and America's Most Powerful Corporation.* New York: Crown Publishers, 2001.

Blair, Margaret. *Ownership and Control: Rethinking Corporate Governance for the Twenty-first Century.* Washington, D.C.: Brookings Institution Press, 1995.

Blair, Margaret M., and Lyan A. Stout. "Trust, Trustworthiness, and the Behavioral Foundations of Corporate Law." *University of Pennsylvania Law Review* 149 (2001), 1735–1810.

Blumberg, Phillip. *The Multinational Challenge to Corporation Law: The Search for a New Corporate Personality.* New York: Oxford University Press, 1993.

Bollier, David. *Public Assets, Private Profits: Reclaiming the American Commons in an Age of Market Enclosure.* Washington, D.C.: New America Foundation, 2001.

Bonsignore, J. *Law and Multinationals: An Introduction to Law and Political Economy.* Englewood Cliffs, N.J.: Prentice Hall, 1994.

Bowman, Scott. *The Modern Corporation and American Political Thought: Law, Power and Ideology.* University Park, Pa.: Pennsylvania State University Press, 1996.

Bracey, Gerald. "The Market in Theory Meets the Market in Practice: The Case of Edison Schools." Education Policy Research Unit, College of Education, Arizona State University, February 2002.

Bracey, Gerald W. *The War Against America's Public Schools: Privatizing Schools, Commercializing Education.* Boston: Allyn & Bacon, 2001.

Bracey, Gerald W. *What You Should Know About the War Against America's Public Schools.* Boston: Allyn & Bacon, 2002.

Brummer, James J. *Corporate Responsibility and Legitimacy: An Interdisciplinary Analysis.* New York: Greenwood Press, 1991.

Cadman, John W. *The Corporation in New Jersey.* Cambridge, Mass.: Harvard University Press, 1949.

Carswell, John. *The South Sea Bubble.* London: Cresset Press, 1960.

Cassels, Jamie. *The Uncertain Promise of Law: Lessons from Bhopal.* Toronto and London: University of Toronto Press, 1993.

Chandler, Afred D., Jr., ed. *The Railroads: The Nation's First Big Business.*

New York: Harcourt, Brace & World, 1965.

Chappell, Tom. *The Soul of a Business: Managing for Profit and the Common Good.* New York: Bantam Books, 1993.

Clarkson, M. B., ed. *The Corporation and Its Stakeholders: Classic and Contemporary Readings.* Toronto: University of Toronto Press, 1998.

Clawson, Marion. *New Deal Planning: The National Resources Planning Board.* Baltimore: Johns Hopkins University Press, 1981.

Colclough, Christopher, and James Manor, eds. *States or Markets?: Neoliberalism and the Development Policy Debate.* Oxford: Oxford University Press, 1995.

Colvin, E. "Corporate Personality and Criminal Liability," *Criminal Law Forum* 6 (1995), 1–44.

Cossman, Brenda, and Judy Fudge, eds. *Privatization, Law, and the Challenge to Feminism.* Toronto: University of Toronto Press, 2002.

Court, Jamie. *Corporateering: How Corporate Power Steals Your Personal Freedom . . . And What You Can Do About It.* New York: Tarcher/Putnam, 2003.

Crawford, Margaret. "The World in a Shopping Mall." In *Variations on a Theme Park,* ed. Michael Sorkin. New York: Noonday Press, 1992.

Cray, Charlie. "Chartering a New Course: Revoking Corporation's Right to Exist," *Multinational Monitor* 23, nos. 10 and 11, October–November 2002.

Crespi, Gregory Scott. "Rethinking Corporate Fiduciary Duties: The Inefficiency of the Shareholder Primacy Norm." *Southern Methodist Law Review* 55 (2002), 141–155.

Crooks, H. *Giants of Garbage: The Rise of the Global Waste Industry and the Politics of Pollution Control.* Toronto: Lorimer, 1993.

Curlo, E., and Strudler, A. "Cognitive Pathology and Moral Judgement in Managers." *Business Ethics Quarterly* 7 (October 1997), 4.

Damm, Kenneth W. *The GATT: Law and International Economic Organization.* Chicago: University of Chicago Press, 1970.

Davis, Mike. "Fortress Los Angeles: The Militarization of Urban Space." In *Variations on a Theme Park,* ed. Michael Sorkin. New York: Noonday Press, 1992.

Deetz, Stanley. *Democracy in an Age of Corporate Colonization: Developments in Communications and the Politics of Everyday Life.* Albany:

State University of New York Press, 1992.

Derber, Charles. *Corporation Nation: How Corporations Are Taking over Our Lives and What We Can Do About It.* New York: Griffin Trade, 2000.

Derber, Charles. *People Before Profit: The New Globalization in an Age of Terror, Big Money and Economic Crisis.* New York: St. Martin's Press, 2002.

Dobbin, Murray. *The Myth of the Good Corporate Citizen: Democracy Under the Rule of Big Business.* Toronto: Stoddart, 1998.

Dodd, Edwin Merrick. *American Business Corporations Until 1860.* Cambridge, Mass.: Harvard University Press, 1954.

Dodd, Edwin Merrick. "For Whom Are Corporate Managers Trustees?" *Harvard Law Review* 45 (1932).

Downs, Alan. *Beyond the Looking Glass: Overcoming the Seductive Culture of Corporate Narcissism.* New York: Amacom, 1997.

Drucker, Peter F. *Concept of the Corporation.* New York: John Day, 1946.

Drucker, Peter F. *The New Society: The Anatomy of the Industrial Order.* New York: Harper & Brothers, 1950.

Easterbrook, F., and D. Fischel. "Limited Liability and the Corporation." *University of Chicago Law Review* 52 (1985).

Easterbrook, Frank H., and Daniel R. Fischel. "Antitrust Suits by Targets of Tender Offers." *Michigan Law Review* 80 (1982), 1177.

Enron, "Corporate Responsibility Annual Report," Houston, 2000.

Estes, Ralph. *Tyranny of the Bottom Line: Why Corporations Make Good People Do Bad Things.* San Francisco: Berrett-Koehler, 1996.

Everling, Clark. *Social Economy: The Logic of Capitalist Development.* London: Routledge, 1997.

Feigenbaum, Harvey. *Shrinking the State: The Political Underpinnings of Privatization.* Cambridge, England: Cambridge University Press, November, 1998.

Fones-Wolf, Elizabeth A. *The Selling of Free Enterprise: The Business Assault on Labor and Liberalism 1945–1960.* Urbana: University of Illinois Press, 1994.

Fort, T. L. "Corporate Constituency Statutes: A Dialectical Interpretation." fifteen *Journal of Law and Commerce* 257 (1995).

Fox, D. R. "The Law Says Corporations Are Persons, But Psychology Knows Better." *Behavioural Sciences and the Law* 14 (Summer 1996), 339.

Frank, Thomas. *One Market Under God: Extreme Capitalism, Market*

Populism, and the End of Economic Democracy. New York: Anchor Books, 2001.

Friedman, Milton. *Capitalism and Freedom.* Chicago: University of Chicago Press, 1982.

Friedman, Milton. "The Social Responsibility of Business Is to Increase Its Profits." *The New York Times Magazine,* September 13, 1979.

Friedman, Thomas L. *The Lexus and the Olive Tree.* New York: Farrar, Straus and Giroux, 2000.

Friedrichs, David. *Trusted Criminals: White Collar Crime in Contemporary Society.* Belmont, Calif.: Wadsworth Publishing Company, 1996.

Fudge, J., and H. J. Glasbeek. "A Challenge to the Inevitability of Globalization: Repositioning the State as the Terrain of Contest." In *Global Justice, Global Democracy,* ed. Jay Drydyk and Peter Penz. Winnipeg: Society for Socialist Studies/Fernwood, 1997.

Galambos, Louis. *The Public Image of Big Business in America, 1880–1940.* Baltimore: Johns Hopkins University Press, 1975.

Galbraith, John Kenneth. *The Affluent Society.* Boston: Houghton Mifflin, 1958.

Galbraith, John Kenneth. *American Capitalism: The Concept of Countervailing Power.* Boston: Houghton Mifflin, 1952.

Galbraith, J. K. *The Socially Concerned Today.* Toronto: University of Toronto Press, 1998.

Giddens, Anthony. *Runaway World: How Globalisation Is Reshaping Our Lives.* London: Profile Books, 1999.

Giddens, Anthony, and Will Hutton, eds. *On the Edge: Living with Global Capitalism.* London: Jonathan Cape, 2000.

Glasbeek, H. J. "The Corporate Social Responsibility Movement: The Latest in Maginot Lines to Save Capitalism." *Dalhousie Law Journal* 11 (1988).

Glasbeek, Harry. *Wealth by Stealth: Corporate Crime, Corporate Law, and the Perversion of Democracy.* Toronto: Between the Lines, 2002.

Glasbeek, H. J. "Why Corporate Deviance Is Not Treated as Corporate Crime: The Need to Make 'Profits' a Dirty Word." *Osgoode Hall Law Journal* 22 (1984).

Goldman, Robert, and Stephen Papson. *Sign Wars: The Cluttered Landscape of Advertising.* New York: Guilford Press, 1996.

Gray, John. *False Dawn: The Delusions of Global Capitalism.* London: Granta Books, 1998.

Gray, Rob. *Accounting for the Environment.* Princeton, N.J.: Markus Wiener Publishing, 1993.

Greenwood, D. "Fictional Shareholders: For Whom Are Corporate Managers Trustees?" *Southern California Law Review* 69 (1996).

Greider, William. *One World, Ready or Not: The Manic Logic of Global Capitalism.* New York: Simon & Schuster, 1997.

Greider, William. *Who Will Tell the People: The Betrayal of American Democracy.* New York: Simon & Schuster, 1992.

Hadden, Tom. *Company Law and Capitalism.* London: Weidenfeld and Nicolson, 1977.

Hardt, Michael, and Antonio Negri. *Empire.* Cambridge, Mass.: Harvard University Press, 2000.

Hawkins, Mary F. *Unshielded: The Human Cost of the Dalkon Shield.* Toronto: University of Toronto Press, 1997.

Hawkens, Paul. *The Ecology of Commerce.* New York: HarperCollins, 1993.

Heilbroner, Robert. *Twenty-first Century Capitalism.* New York: Norton, 1992.

Herman, Edward. *Corporate Control, Corporate Power.* Cambridge, England: Cambridge University Press, 1981.

Herman, Edward S., and Noam Chomsky. *Manufacturing Consent: The Political Economy of the Mass Media.* New York and Toronto: Pantheon Books/Random House, 1988.

Hertz, Noreena. *Silent Takeover: Global Capitalism and the Death of Democracy.* New York: Free Press, 2002.

Hicks, A. "Corporate Form: Questioning the Unsung Hero." *Journal of Business Law* (1997), 306.

Hinkley, Robert. "How Corporate Law Inhibits Social Responsibility." *Business Ethics,* January–February 2002.

Hirst, P., and G. Thompson. *Globalization in Question: The International Economy and the Possibilities of Governance.* Cambridge, Mass.: Blackwell, 1996.

Horwitz, Morton J. "Santa Clara Revisited: The Development of Corporate Theory." In *Corporations and Society: Power and Responsibility,* eds. Warren Samuels and Arthur Miller. New York: Greenwood Press, 1987.

Horwitz, Morton J. *The Transformation of American Law, 1780–1860.* Cambridge, Mass.: Harvard University Press, 1977.

Hunt, B. C. *The Development of the Business Corporation in England, 1800–1867*. Cambridge, Mass.: Harvard University Press, 1936.

Hurst, J. W. *The Legitimacy of the Business Corporation in the Law of the United States, 1780–1970*. Charlottesville: University of Virginia, 1970.

Ireland, Paddy. "Capitalism Without the Capitalist: the Joint Stock Company Share and the Emergence of the Modern Doctrine of Separate Corporate Personality." *Journal of Legal History* 17 (1996), 63.

Ireland, P. "Corporate Governance, Stakeholding and the Company: Toward a Less Degenerate Capitalism?" *Journal of Law and Society* 23 (1996).

Ireland, P., I. Grigg-Spall, and D. Kelly. "The Conceptual Foundations of Modern Company Law." *Journal of Law and Society* 14 (1987), 149.

Irwin, Douglas A. *Against the Tide: An Intellectual History of Free Trade*. Princeton, N.J.: Princeton University Press, 1996.

Jones, Barry J. *The World Turned Upside Down?: Globalization and the Future of the State*. Manchester, England.: Manchester University Press, 2000.

Karliner, Joshua. *The Corporate Planet: Ecology and Politics in the Age of Globalization*. San Francisco: Sierra Club Books, 1997.

Kayden, Jerold S., New York City Department of City Planning, Municipal Art Society of New York. *Privately Owned Public Space: The New York City Experience*. New York: John Wiley & Sons, 2000.

Kelly, Marjorie. *The Divine Right of Capital: Dethroning the Corporate Aristocracy*. San Francisco: Berrett-Koehler, 2001.

Keynes, John Maynard. "The End of Laissez-Faire." In *The Collected Writings of John Maynard Keynes*, vol. 9: *Essays in Persuasion*. London: Macmillan, 1972.

Keynes, John Maynard. *The General Theory of Employment, Interest and Money*. London: Macmillan, 1936.

Kingwell, Mark. *The World We Want: Virtue, Vice, and the Good Citizen*. Toronto: Viking, 2000.

Klein, Naomi. *No Logo: Taking Aim at the Brand Bullies*. Toronto: Knopf Canada, 2000.

Korten, David C. *The Post-Corporate World: Life After Capitalism*. San Francisco: Berrett-Koehler, 2000.

Korten, David C. *When Corporations Rule the World*, 2nd ed. San Francisco: Berrett-Koehler, 2001.

Krugman, Paul. *The Accidental Theorist and Other Dispatches from the Dismal Science.* New York: Norton, 1998.

Kuttner, Robert. *Everything for Sale: The Virtues and Limits of Markets.* New York: Alfred A. Knopf, 1997.

MacIntyre, Alisdair. "Utilitarianism and Cost-Benefit Analysis: An Essay on the Relevance of Moral Philosophy to Bureaucratic Theory." In *Values in the Electric Power Industry,* ed. Kenneth Sayre. Notre Dame, Ind.: University of Notre Dame Press, 1977.

Maitra, Priyatash. *The Globalization of Capitalism in Third World Countries.* Westport, Conn.: Praeger, 1996.

Mander, J. "The Myth of the Corporate Conscience." *Business and Society Review* 81 (Spring 1992), 56.

Mander, Jerry, and Edward Goldsmith, eds. *The Case Against the Global Economy.* San Francisco: Sierra Club Books, 1996.

Manning, Peter K., and Brian Forst. *The Privatization of Policing: Two Views.* Washington, D.C.: Georgetown University Press, 1999.

Marchand, Roland. *Creating the Corporate Soul: The Rise of Public Relations and Corporate Imagery in American Big Business.* Berkeley: University of California Press, 1998.

Mark, Gregory A. "The Personification of the Business Corporation in American Law." *University of Chicago Law Review* 54 (1987), 1441–1483.

McQuaid, Kim, "Young, Swope and General Electric's 'New Capitalism': A Study in Corporate Liberalism, 1920–33." *American Journal of Economics and Sociology* 36 (1977), 323.

McQuaig, Linda. *The Cult of Impotence: Selling the Myth of Powerlessness in the Global Economy.* Toronto: Viking, 1998.

Meiksins Wood, Ellen. *Empire of Capital.* New York: Verso, 2003.

Minda, G. "Democratic Pluralism in the Era of Downsizing." *California Western Law Review* 33 (Spring 1997), 179.

Minow, Martha. *Partners, Not Rivals: Privatization and the Public Good.* Boston: Beacon Press, 2002.

Mintz, Morton, and Jerry Cohen. *America, Inc.: Who Owns and Operates the United States?* New York: Dial Press, 1971.

Mitchell, Lawrence E. "Cooperation and Constraint in the Modern Corporation: An Inquiry into the Causes of Corporate Morality." *Texas Law Review* 73, (1995), 477–537.

Mitchell, Lawrence E. *Corporate Irresponsibility: America's Newest Export*. New Haven, Conn.: Yale University Press, 2002.

Mitchell, Neil J. *The Conspicuous Corporation: Business, Public Policy, and Representative Democracy*. Ann Arbor: University of Michigan Press, 1997.

Mokhiber, Russell. "The Death Penalty for Corporations Comes of Age." *Business Ethics*, November 1, 1998.

Mokhiber, Russell, and Robert Weissman. *Corporate Predators: The Hunt for Mega-Profits and the Attack on Democracy*. Monroe, Maine: Common Courage Press, 1999.

Molnar, Alex, and Joseph A. Reaves. "Buy Me! Buy Me!: The Fourth Annual Report on Trends in Schoolhouse Commercialism: Year 2000–2001." Education Policy Studies Laboratory, Arizona State University.

Monks, Robert. *The Emperor's Nightingale: Restoring the Integrity of the Corporation in the Age of Shareholder Activism*. Reading, Mass.: Addison-Wesley, 1998.

Moore, Michael. *Downsize This! Random Threats from an Unarmed American*. New York: Crown Publishers, 1996.

Moore, Michael. *Stupid White Men . . . and Other Sorry Excuses for the State of the Nation!* New York: ReganBooks, 2002.

Muller, Jerry Z. *Adam Smith in His Time and Ours: Designing the Decent Society*. New York: Free Press, 1993.

Murray, Andrew. *Off the Rails: Britain's Great Railway Crisis*. London: Verso Books, 2001.

Nader, Ralph. *Cutting Corporate Welfare*. New York: Seven Stories Press, 2000.

Nader, Ralph. *Crashing the Party: How to Tell the Truth and Still Run for President*. New York: St. Martin's Press, 2002.

Neufeld, Rodney, Allison Campbell, and Andrew Coyle, eds. *Capitalist Punishment: Prison Privatization and Human Rights*. Atlanta: Clarity Press, 2003.

Ohmae, Kenichi. *The End of the Nation State: The Rise of Regional Economies*. New York: Free Press, 1995.

Palast, Greg. *The Best Democracy Money Can Buy: An Investigative Reporter Exposes the Truth About Globalization, Corporate Cons, and High Finance Fraudsters*. London: Pluto Press, 2002.

Palmer, Bryan D. *Capitalism Comes to the Backcountry: The Goodyear Invasion of Napanee*. Toronto: Between the Lines, 1994.

Pearce, Frank, and Laureen Snider. "Regulating Capitalism." In *Corporate Crime: Contemporary Debates,* ed. F. Pearce and L. Snider. Toronto: University of Toronto Press, 1995.

Pearce, Frank, and S. Tombs. *Toxic Capitalism: Corporate Crime and the Chemical Industry.* Toronto: Canadian Scholars' Press, 1999.

Pickering, Murray A. "Company as a Separate Legal Entity." *Modern Law Review* 31 (1968).

Public Citizen. "Blind Faith: How Deregulation and Enron's Influence over Government Looted Billions from Americans." Washington, D.C., December 2001.

Ramanadam, V. V., ed. *Privatization and Equity.* London: Routledge, 1995.

Reason Public Policy Institute. *Privatization 2002: Putting the Pieces Together, 16th Annual Report on Privatization.* Los Angeles: Reason Public Policy Institute, 2002.

Rebick, Judy. *Imagine Democracy.* Toronto: Stoddart, 2000.

Rifkin, Jeremy. *The Age of Access: The New Culture of Hypercapitalism Where All of Life Is a Paid-for Experience.* New York: Tarcher/Putnam, 2000.

Rodengen, Jeffrey L. *The Legend of Goodyear: The First 100 Years.* Fort Lauderdale, Fla.: Write Stuff Syndicate, 1997.

Rodrik, Dani. *Has Globalization Gone Too Far?* Washington, D.C.: Institute of International Economics, 1997.

Romano, Roberta, ed., *Foundations of Corporate Law.* New York: Oxford University Press, 1993.

Rosenberg, Hilary. *A Traitor to His Class: Robert A. G. Monks and the Battle to Change Corporate America.* New York: John Wiley and Sons, 1999.

Rosoff, S. M., H. N. Pontell, and R. Tillman. *Profit Without Honor: White-Collar Crime and the Looting of America.* New Jersey: Prentice Hall, 1998.

Ross, Andrew, ed. *No Sweat: Fashion, Free Trade and the Rights of Garment Workers.* New York: Verso, 1997.

Roy, William G. *Socializing Capital: The Rise of the Large Industrial Corporations in America.* Princeton, N.J.: Princeton University Press, 1997.

Sassen, Saskia. *Globalization and Its Discontents: Essays on the New Mobility of People and Money.* New York: New Press, 1998.

Sassen, Saskia. *Losing Control?: Sovereignty in an Age of Globalization.* New York: Columbia University Press, 1996.

Savan, Leslie. *The Sponsored Life: Ads, TV, and American Culture.* Philadelphia: Temple University Press, 1994.

Schiller, Herbert. *Culture Inc.: The Corporate Takeover of Public Expression.* New York: Oxford University Press, 1989.

Schlesinger, Arthur M., Jr. *The Coming of the New Deal.* Boston: Houghton Mifflin, 1958.

Schlosser, Eric. *Fast Food Nation.* Boston: Houghton Mifflin, 2001.

Sclar, Elliott D. *You Don't Always Get What You Pay For: The Economics of Privatization.* Ithaca, N.Y.: Cornell University Press, 2001.

Scott, Walter. *The Waverley Novels: The Bethrothed, vol. 19.* Philadelphia: John Morris & Co, 1892.

Seavoy, Ronald E. *The Origins of the American Business Corporation, 1784–1855: Broadening the Concept of Public Service During Industrialization.* Westport, Conn.: Greenwood Press, 1982.

Sennett, Richard. *The Corrosion of Character: The Personal Consequences of Work in the New Capitalism.* New York: Norton, 1998.

Shiva, Vandana. *Water Wars: Privatization, Pollution, and Profit.* Boston: South End Press, 2002.

Shorris, Earl, ed. *A Nation of Salesmen: The Tyranny of the Market and the Subversion of Culture.* New York: Avon Books, 1994.

Simon, David R. *Elite Deviance,* 7th ed. Boston: Allyn & Bacon, 2001.

Simpson, Sally S. *Corporate Crime, Law, and Social Control.* Cambridge, England: Cambridge University Press, 2002.

Singer, P. W. *Corporate Warriors: The Rise of the Privatized Military Industry.* Ithaca, N.Y.: Cornell University Press, 2003.

Smith, Adam. *The Wealth of Nations.* New York: Modern Library, 1994.

Smith, D. Gordon. "The Shareholder Primacy Norm." *The Journal of Corporation Law* 23 (1998), 277.

Smith, Toby M. *The Myth of Green Marketing: Tending Our Goats at the Edge of Apocalypse.* Toronto: University of Toronto Press, 1998.

Smith, Thomas A. "The Efficient Norm for Corporate Law: A Neo-traditional Interpretation of Fiduciary Duty." *Michigan Law Review* 98 (1999–2000), 214–268.

Snell, Bradford C. "American Ground Transport: A Proposal for Restructuring the Automobile, Truck, Bus and Rail Industries." Report presented to the Committee of the Judiciary, Subcommittee on Antitrust and Monopoly, United States Senate, February 26, 1974. Washington, D.C.: U.S. Government Printing Office, 1974.

Soros, George. *George Soros on Globalization*. New York: Public Affairs Books, 2002.

Stiglitz, Joseph. *Globalization and Its Discontents*. New York: W. W. Norton, 2002.

Stuart, D., "Punishing Corporate Criminals with Restraint." *Criminal Law Forum* 6 (1995), 219.

Suleiman, Ezra N. *Dismantling Democratic States*. Princeton, N.J.: Princeton University Press, 2003.

Sunstein, Cass. *The Partial Constitution*. Cambridge, Mass.: Harvard University Press, 1993.

Swope, Gerard. *The Swope Plan: Details, Criticisms, Analysis*. New York: Business Bourse, 1931.

Symposium, "Is the Good Corporation Dead?" *Business and Society Review* 87 (Fall 1993), 9.

Tabb, William K. *The Amoral Elephant: Globalization and the Struggle for Social Justice in the Twenty-first Century*. New York: Monthly Review Press, 2001.

Tedlow, Richard S. *Giants of Enterprise: Seven Business Innovators and the Empires They Built*. New York: HarperCollins, 2001.

Teeple, Gary. *Globalization and the Decline of Social Reform: Into the Twenty-first Century*. Aurora, Ont.: Garamond Press, 2000.

Testy, Kellye Y. "Linking Progressive Corporate Law with Progressive Social Movements." *Tulane Law Review* 76 (2002), 1227–1252.

Tonelson, Alan. *The Race to the Bottom: Why a Worldwide Worker Surplus and Uncontrolled Free Trade Are Sinking American Living Standards*. Boulder, Colo.: Westview Press, 2000.

Tysbine, Alex. *Water Privatization: A Broken Promise*. Washington, D.C.: Public Citizen, 2001.

Useem, Michael. *The Inner Circle: Large Corporations and the Rise of Business Political Activity in the US and UK*. New York: Oxford University Press, 1984.

Vogel, David. *Kindred Strangers: The Uneasy Relationship Between Politics and Business in America*. Princeton, N.J.: Princeton University Press, 1996.

Wallach, Lori, and Michelle Sforza. *The WTO: Five Years of Reasons to Resist Corporate Globalization*. New York: Seven Stories Press, 2000.

Weaver, Paul H. *The Suicidal Corporation.* New York: Simon & Schuster, 1988.

Weiss, Barbara. *The Hell of the English: Bankruptcy and the Victorian Novel.* Lewisburg, Pa.: Bucknell University Press, 1986.

Welling, Bruce. *Corporate Law in Canada,* 2nd. ed. Toronto: Butterworths, 1991.

Wells, Celia. *Corporations and Criminal Responsibility,* 2nd. ed. Oxford: Oxford University Press, 1993.

Wolff, M. "On the Nature of Legal Persons." *Law Quarterly Review* 54 (1938).

Yergin, Daniel, and Joseph Stanislaw. *The Commanding Heights: The Battle for the World Economy.* New York: Simon & Schuster, 1998.

Zunz, Olivier. *Making America Corporate, 1870–1920.* Chicago: University of Chicago Press, 1990.

1986.

1991.

Acknowledgments

Mark Achbar had a special impact on this book. I first met him at the buffet table of a reception, where we were drawn to the same spot by a shared appetite for egg salad. We introduced ourselves and began to chat. I told him about a book I was planning to write. He told me he wanted to make a documentary film about globalization. That was the beginning of our friendship and of our collaboration in the creation of a film and television miniseries based upon the ideas from this book. I benefited greatly in writing the book from the many conversations I had with Achbar over the years and from the support he and his company, Big Picture Media, provided, especially in relation to interviews. I also thank Jennifer Abbott, who codirected the film and miniseries with Achbar, for her ideas and insights, and am grateful to others who worked on the production, particularly Bart Simpson, Dawn Brett, and Tom Shandel. As well, I thank the people who generously agreed to be interviewed for the project, none of whom are responsible for how their words have been interpreted and judged.

I am indebted to the following people who read earlier drafts of *The Corporation* and offered suggestions on how it could be improved: Ruth Buchanan, Clayton Burns, Jon Festinger, Harry Glasbeek, Bruce MacDougall, Andrew Petter, Murray Rankin, Janis Sarra, and Steve Wexler. I also thank my various research assistants, particularly Justine Wiltshire and Gil Yaron, my colleagues and students, and the Faculty of Law at the University of British Columbia.

I am indebted to Cynthia Good for committing to this project when it was little more than an idea, and for her friendship and continuing encouragement. I thank my agent, Ellen Geiger, for believing in the project, and for her unflagging patience and enthusiasm.

I am very lucky to have Fred Hills as my editor. He has a brilliantly intuitive sense of what needs to be said in a book (and what does not) and is always a pleasure to work with—respectful, humorous, and without a hint of pretense. His suggestions, often demanding, improved the book considerably.

I thank members of my family for their love and for their tangible and emotional support, in particular, Rita and Paul Bakan (my parents), Laura Bakan, Michael and Megan Bakan, Carol and Terry Kline, Ronnie Kline and Ruth Buckwold, and Sandy Kline. To my parents, I am grateful for the gifts of intellect, idealism, and compassion, and for teaching me to challenge convention, think critically, and care about the deeper things in life.

Many friends, in various ways, provided support and inspiration. I thank them all, and in particular Didi Herman, Sadie Jenkins-Wade, Mark Ostry, Lisa and Fonda Papaphanasiou, Bruce Ryder, and Margot Young. Very special thanks to Anita Santos.

There are several people without whom this book would not have been written. Myim Bakan Kline, my son, inspired me with his relentless optimism and his innate sense of fairness. He kept my life in balance with bike rides, hockey games, and, most of all, his love. He was always gently patient with, even compassionate toward, a busy and distracted father. I only hope this book makes some small contribution to building a better world for him and generations to come.

Rita Bakan read draft after draft of the manuscript and reworked key passages with the eye of a great editor and the care and concern of a loving mother. She improved the manuscript substantially and, along with my father, Paul Bakan, provided necessary and continuous encouragement.

Rebecca Jenkins, my constant companion and best friend, kept me focused, calm, and confident with her love. She greatly improved the flow and clarity of the prose with her remarkable ear for good writing and strengthened the book's arguments with her probing insights.

Marlee Kline, to whom this book is dedicated, inspired and challenged me, encouraged and believed in me—loved me deeply and I her—during our twenty-five years together. Where she ends and I begin, as a thinker, as a person, is a boundary I cannot easily identify. During the formative stages of this project, Marlee, though gravely ill, applied her brilliant mind to help me understand what I wanted to say and how I should say it. She had a profound influence on the book in so many ways. I only wish she were here to see it.

Index

ABOUT THE AUTHOR

Born in East Lansing, Michigan in 1959, Joel Bakan is professor of law at the University of British Columbia and an internationally renowned legal scholar. A former Rhodes Scholar and law clerk to Chief Justice Brian Dickson of the Supreme Court of Canada, he has law degrees from Oxford, Dalhousie, and Harvard. His academic work examines the social, economic, and political dimensions of law, and he has published in leading legal and social science journals, as well as in the popular press. His most recent book, *Just Words: Constitutional Rights and Social Wrongs,* was widely and favorably reviewed. Bakan is also writer and cocreator of *The Corporation,* a documentary film and television miniseries based on this book. He has won numerous awards for his scholarship and teaching, worked on landmark legal cases and government policy, and served frequently as a media commentator. He lives in Vancouver, Canada, with his son, Myim, his partner, Rebecca Jenkins, and her daughter Sadie.

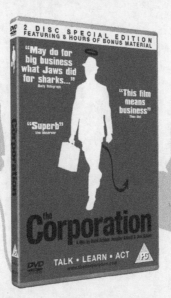